ENTREPRENEURS IN HISTORY—
SUCCESS VS. FAILURE

Entrepreneurial Role Models

Emerson Klees

Emerson Klees

Cameo Press, Rochester, New York

THE ROLE MODELS OF HUMAN VALUES SERIES

"Example teaches better than precept. It is the best modeler of the character of men and women. To set a lofty example is the richest bequest a man [or woman] can leave behind.... "

S. Smiles

The Role Models of Human Values Series provides examples of role models and of lives worthy of emulation. The human values depicted in this series include teamwork, entrepreneurship, perseverance, and determination. Role models are presented to the reader in biographical sketches that describe the environment within which these individuals strived and delineate their personal characteristics.

These profiles illustrate how specific human values helped achievers reach their goals in life. Readers can learn from these examples in strengthening the human values that are so important to our success and happiness.

The Introduction in each book highlights the factors that contributed to these achievers' success. Since we are all different and we operate in varied environments, all readers won't take away the same messages from these books. The objective of the series is to present material that is useful to everyone.

The Role Models of Human Values Series:

*One Plus One Equals Three—Pairing Man / Woman
      Strengths: Role Models of Teamwork* (1998)
*Entrepreneurs in History—Success vs. Failure:
      Entrepreneurial Role Models* (1999)
Staying With It: Role Models of Perseverance (1999)
The Will to Stay with It: Role Models of Determination (2000)

LIST OF ILLUSTRATIONS

Cover design by Dunn and Rice Design, Inc., Rochester, NY

The images used herein, except for Dover Publications line art of Ford, Bell, and the Wright brothers, were obtained from IMSI's MasterClips Collection, 1895 Francisco Blvd. East, San Rafael, CA 94901-5506, USA.

PREFACE

This book highlights the factors that contributed to the success of entrepreneurs in history. Why did some fail and others succeed? The environment within which they strived was a key factor in their success or failure. Their personal characteristics were important in overcoming the obstacles in their paths and contributed heavily to their achievements.

Entrepreneurs in History—Success vs. Failure provides examples of entrepreneurship in nine sets of three chapters. The first chapter in each set is a profile of an unsuccessful or a less successful entrepreneur, the second chapter is a biographical sketch of an entrepreneur who succeeded, and the third chapter in the set provides a summary and analysis of the factors that caused one entrepreneur to fail and allowed another to succeed.

Profiles of four entrepreneurs provide examples of early failure / late success and cases of converting failure into success. Evaluation of the factors contributing to the ultimate success of these entrepreneurs helps to understand their achievements.

The following topics are covered in the book:

Economies of Scale—Production of the Automobile
Nautical Entrepreneurs—Invention of the Steamboat
Telephone Pioneers—Invention of the Telephone
Revolutionary Development—The Mainframe Computer
Engineering Entrepreneurs—Introduction of the Minicomputer
Personal Computing—Introduction of the Personal Computer
Rubber Made Practical—Development of Vulcanization
Evolutionary Development—Invention of the Airplane
New Uses of Old Inventions—Sewing Machine Invention
    Early Failure / Late Success
Evaporated Milk Development—Gail Borden
Urban Department Store Evolution—R. H. Macy
    Converting Failure into Success
Rescuing a Failing Company—Lee Iacocca
Saving a Failing Project—Al Neuharth

TABLE OF CONTENTS

PROLOGUE

"Entrepreneurship is the process of creating something with value by devoting the necessary time and effort, assuming the accompanying financial, psychic, and social risks, and receiving the resulting rewards of monetary and personal satisfaction."

Robert D. Hisrich and Candida Bush[1]

The derivation of the word entrepreneur is from French *entre,* between; *prendre,* to take. In the Middle Ages in Europe, an entrepreneur was the person in charge of a large construction project, such as an abbey or a church. The entrepreneur, usually a cleric, managed the project using the resources provided; he wasn't a risk-taker.

In 1725, Richard Cantillon, author and economist, distinguished between the roles of two types of people: the person bearing the risks and the individual supplying the capital. Cantillon viewed the entrepreneur as the individual bearing the risks. He considered sole proprietors, such as craftsmen, farmers, and tradesmen, to be risk-takers, because they "buy at a certain price and sell at an uncertain price, therefore operating at a risk."[2]

In 1803, the French economist Jean Baptiste Say distinguished the profits of the entrepreneur (the person needing capital) from the profits of the person with the capital (the capital-provider). In Say's opinion, the role of the entrepreneur was to shift economic resources out of an area of low productivity into an area of higher productivity with an accompanying greater yield. Say's capital-providers were the nineteenth century equivalent of today's venture capitalists—professional money managers who make risk investments from an equity pool anticipating a high rate of return.

Eventually, the definition of entrepreneur evolved to include a reference to innovation:

To an economist, an entrepreneur is one who brings resources, labor, materials, and other assets into combinations that make their value greater than before, and also one who introduces changes, innovations, and a new order. To a psychologist, such a person is typically driven by certain forces—need to obtain something, to experiment, to accomplish, or perhaps to escape the authority of others.... To one businessman, an entrepreneur appears as a threat, an aggressive competitor, whereas to another businessman the same entrepreneur may be an ally, a source of supply, a customer, or someone good to invest in.... The same person is seen by a capitalist philosopher as one who creates wealth for others as well, who finds better ways to utilize resources, and reduce waste, and who produces jobs.... [3]

Starting new ventures and managing small businesses had an increasing impact on the United States economy in the last third of the twentieth century. Growth in small and medium-sized businesses more than compensated for the reduction of jobs in large corporations due to layoffs and early retirements.

In the introduction to his 1985 book, *Innovation and Entrepreneurship: Practice and Principles*, Peter Drucker provides an enlightening summary of the shift from large organizations to small and medium-sized businesses in creating new jobs between 1965 and 1985, two decades of significant change during which the number of paying jobs in the U.S. increased by over forty million:

> • In the twenty-five years after World War II ...
> America's economic dynamics centered in
> institutions that were already big and getting
> bigger: the *Fortune* 500, that is, the country's

largest businesses; governments, whether federal, state, or local; the large and super-large
universities; the large consolidated high
school with its six thousand or more students;
and the large and growing hospital.

- These institutions created practically all of the
  new jobs provided in the American economy in
  the quarter century after World War II....
- But since the late 1960s, job creation and job
  growth in the United States have shifted to a
  new sector. The old job creators have actually
  lost jobs in these last twenty years ... By 1984,
  the *Fortune* 500 had lost permanently at least
  four to six million jobs....
- In other words, we have not created thirty-five
  million new jobs; we have created forty million
  or more, since we had to offset a permanent
  shrinkage of at least five million jobs in the tra-
  ditional employing institutions.
- All of these new jobs were created by small
  and medium-sized institutions, most of them
  small and medium-sized businesses, and a great
  many of them, if not the majority, new businesses that did not exist even twenty years ago.
- According to *The Economist*, 600,000 new
  businesses are being started in the United
  States every year now—about seven times as
  many as were started in each of the boom years
  of the fifties and sixties.[4]

Many of the new jobs accommodated the "baby-boomers,"
who began to enter the work force in the 1970s and early 1980s.
The creation of new jobs by small and medium-sized businesses also provided openings for married women, who entered the
job market in large numbers beginning in the mid-1970s.

By the 1990s, the two-income family had become a way of

life. The trend of small and medium-sized companies creating new jobs compensating for the loss of jobs in large organizations continued into the twenty-first century.

INTRODUCTION

"An intelligent plan is the first step to success. The man who plans knows where he is going, knows what progress he is making, and has a pretty good idea when he will arrive. Planning is the open road to your destination. If you don't know where you are going, how can you expect to get there?"

Basil S. Walsh

Entrepreneurs / Inventors in History might be a more appropriate title for this book. Of the twenty-two biographical sketches, five consider pure entrepreneurs—William Durant, Lee Iacocca, R. H. Macy, Al Neuharth, and Thomas J. Watson. Another five are about virtually pure inventors: John Fitch, Charles Goodyear, Philipp Reis, Alexander Graham Bell, and Samuel Langley. However, most of these inventors personally solicited the necessary financing for their early experiments. Each of them begrudged the time spent obtaining funds, and none of them was very successful at it.

Entrepreneur / inventor is an appropriate label for the remaining twelve individuals or teams: Gail Borden, Edson de Castro, Henry Ford, Robert Fulton, Thomas Hancock, Elias Howe, Steve Jobs and Steve Wozniak, John Mauchly and Presper Eckert, Ken Olsen, Isaac Singer, the Wright brothers, and the developers at PARC-Xerox. Most of these twelve were inventors or teams who were also involved with the entrepreneurial tasks of obtaining financing, marketing and promoting a product, and organizing and managing a business.

An inventor is an individual who creates or develops a product or process for the first time. Inventors are highly motivated, imaginative individuals driven by their own ideas. They are creative, usually well-educated, and willing to take risks. They have high self-esteem and self-assurance, an elevated tolerance for ambiguity and uncertainty, and the ability to reduce complex issues to straightforward ones.

Achievement is a high priority for inventors, but their measure of achievement is the number of inventions and developments and the number of patents granted, not the accumulation of wealth. Frequently, inventors become so closely associated with a particular design that they refuse to make changes, or they make changes reluctantly, even if the changes will make the product more marketable.

The entrepreneur's personal feeling for the organization is analogous to the inventor's close association with the product. Entrepreneurs will sell their cars, mortgage their homes and property and, generally, go to great lengths to promote their ventures. Both the entrepreneur's strengths and the inventor's strengths are needed by a business. Working together, as a team, is the optimal arrangement.

Most individuals decide to become entrepreneurs because of a desire to be independent, which frequently leads to a decision to leave their present employer. They may be concerned about limited chances for advancement in their current position, or they may have become jaded by doing the same job over and over with little opportunity for growth. Their suggestions may have gone unheeded. Ultimately, they reach the point at which they want to be their own boss.

This desire for independence is the principal reason that both men and women entrepreneurs decide to start a venture. The second most frequent reason for men is to earn more money. For women, the reasons, in order, following the desire to be independent are job satisfaction, achievement, opportunity, and money. Beginning in the late 1980s, the number of self-employed women has been increasing at six times the rate of self-employed men.

The motivation to start a venture may have been created by disruption: one person in a two-career family is transferred, an individual retires early and decides to start a business, or an employee is laid off by his or her employer. Another frequently stated motivation is the knowledge that a customer's wants and needs are not being filled, coupled with the desire to start a new enterprise to fill those wants and needs.

Frequently, an entrepreneur is the oldest child in the family or an only child. The first-born or only child usually receives considerable attention from parents and relatives; this contributes to building self-confidence and self-esteem. Many entrepreneurs are influenced by parents or close relatives who are entrepreneurs or who are self-employed.

Most entrepreneurs begin their first significant business venture between the ages of twenty-two and fifty-five. Entrepreneurs in their thirties are the age group most frequently involved with business start-ups. One of the most evident traits of a successful entrepreneur is the appearance of being a winner. They consider themselves winners and are characterized as winners by their friends, which is virtually a prerequisite for being an entrepreneur.

Entrepreneurs are risk-takers, but they usually don't undertake high-risk ventures. They are considered moderate risk-takers. An exception is the entrepreneur faced with the need for high capital investment to begin his or her venture, such as a manufacturing start-up. A high risk may have to be taken in borrowing money to get the venture underway.

Luck is a key factor of success for the entrepreneur. Being "in the right place at the right time" might be critical. The entrepreneur's definition of luck is "to have prepared oneself to take advantage of an opportunity." The old line "whatever will be, will be" doesn't fit the attitude of an entrepreneur. He or she must be actively engaged in making it happen.

Success doesn't seek entrepreneurs; they must go after it. They must have the vision to see the need for a new product or service and then be the doers who create it or develop it. If they just design a new mousetrap, the world will *not* beat a path to their door. They also have to promote and market their product and themselves.

Determination, drive, motivation, and perseverance are critical qualities for an entrepreneur. They must be willing to take the individual responsibility to set goals, to solve problems, and to reach goals by their own striving. In attempting to meet their goals, entrepreneurs demand feedback on how the venture is doing. They need to know the results of completed tasks.

Determination, drive, motivation, and perseverance were displayed by all of these twenty-two individuals / teams. Many of us would have given up long before these individuals did. However, their human values led to accomplishment. We can learn from them; they enlighten us by their example.

ECONOMIES OF SCALE

Production of the Automobile

CHAPTER 1

WILLIAM DURANT

Founder of General Motors Corporation

"Business is always a struggle. There are always obstacles and competitors. There is never an open road, except the wide road that leads to failure. Every great success has always been achieved by a fight. Every winner has scars.... The men who succeeded are the efficient few. They are the few who have the ambition and the will power to develop themselves."

Herbert N. Casson

William Crapo Durant, born in Boston on December 8, 1861, was the second child and first son of William Clark Durant, a bank clerk, and Rebecca Crapo Durant. Durant's parents separated in 1872; Rebecca Durant returned home to Flint, Michigan, with her two children to be with her mother and other relatives. Although young Durant did well in algebra, French, Latin, physiology, and rhetoric at Flint High School, he dropped out halfway through his senior year.

Durant's first job was piling lumber in his uncle's lumber yard. At night he worked in a drugstore whose owner mixed and sold patent medicine. Durant, a born salesmen, went on the road selling patent medicine. Subsequently, he became a traveling salesman for a Flint cigar manufacturer; he sold 22,000 cigars in his first two days on the job.

Next, Durant worked part-time collecting overdue bills for the privately-owned Flint Water Works. Service was poor and many customers wouldn't pay their bills. He interviewed all of the customers, listened to their complaints, corrected the problems, and made the waterworks profitable within eight months.

Durant consolidated several regional fire insurance companies and within two years created one of the largest insurance agencies in central Michigan before going into construction and real estate. In 1884, he was part-owner of a roller skating rink and a year later was sufficiently well established to marry Clara Pitt, the daughter of a railway ticket agent, and to buy a home in Flint.

In September 1886, Durant began his lifetime career in the automobile business. He was hurrying to a meeting of the board of directors of the Flint Gas Company when he saw his friend, Dallas Dort, in a two-wheeled cart. Dort offered him a ride to the meeting in the cart, which had a novel suspension system. Durant was impressed with the comfort of the ride of the cart built by the Coldwater Road Cart Company.

The next morning Durant traveled 120 miles to Coldwater, Michigan, to visit the cart manufacturer. He asked the owner of the small, out-of-date carriage shop if he might buy a part interest in the shop. The owner asked, "Why not buy it all? It wouldn't take much." The purchase price of $1,500 included the dies, patterns, and all materials. The owner asked for a royalty on the patent for the suspension system. When Durant hesitated, the owner offered to assign the patent to Durant as part of the purchase price.

Durant didn't have the money to buy the company, so he told the owner that he would return to Flint to obtain it if the owner would execute the bill of sale, transfer the patent, and deposit the necessary papers with his bank. The deal was off if Durant couldn't obtain the money within five days. He had followed one of the principles expressed in his autobiographical notes: "Decide quickly, make your pitch, nail down the details, and don't worry about the money."

Durant visited a Flint bank, where he outlined details of the purchase and his plans for the cart company, including moving it to Flint. He was immediately given a $2,000 renewable loan by a banker he knew only slightly.

Durant described the venture to Dort, whose hardware business wasn't prospering. Dort offered to buy half of the business for $1,000. Durant readily agreed and immediately went on the road selling the cart. His first stop was a fair in Madison, Wisconsin, where the cart won the blue-ribbon prize. He sold 100 carts to a Madison company and visited companies in Milwaukee and Chicago prior to returning to Flint. He returned to Flint with orders for 600 carts; the Flint Road Cart Company hadn't yet made its first one. William Patterson, owner of a carriage factory in Flint, built the first 600 carts for them. Patterson manufactured the carts for $12.50; Durant and Dort sold them for $25.00.

Durant and Dort manufactured 4,000 road carts in their first full year of operation as the Flint Road Cart Company. Dort, a good administrator and the company's president, admitted that Durant was "the firm's leading force and genius." Rejecting the title of president, Durant said, "Elect me janitor or office boy." Instead, he was elected treasurer.

Flint Road Cart's second product was an attractive, sturdy four-wheel buggy that was competitively priced. An early employee was automobile pioneer Charles Nash, a leader who was good at solving manufacturing problems; he moved up quickly into a position of authority. The initial team had strengths that fit well together. Durant was the positive thinker and visionary who excelled at promoting and selling their products.

Durant's theory of selling was: "Assume that the man you are talking to knows as much or more than you do. Do not talk too much. Give the customer time to think. In other words, let the customer sell himself." The success of this theory requires that you have a good product. Durant said, "Look for a self-seller. If you cannot find one, make one."[5]

On September 9, 1893, the Flint Road Cart Company was incorporated with $150,000 capitalization generated from profits. Durant and Dort backed a bicycle company that failed, causing investors to lose their money. Since Durant and Dort had encouraged people to invest, they made up the investors' losses because they felt responsible for them.

During the 1890s, Durant and Dort added four vehicle subsidiaries, manufactured their own supplies to remain competitive in a crowded industry, and became the largest carriage company in the United States. A key company manager became ill from overwork and traveled to Europe to recuperate. He observed the burgeoning automobile industry in Europe and returned with the advice, "Get out of the carriage business before the automobile ruins you."

Durant and Dort didn't hear the message. In Flint, they were surrounded by poor roads and were isolated from major cities. Initially, Durant considered "horseless carriages" to be "noisy, dangerous, smelly contraptions that disturbed tranquility and frightened horses."

Durant, a millionaire by age forty, became restless with the carriage business and needed new challenges. He invested heavily in the stock market and spent most of his time in New York City. In 1901, he was away from Flint so much that he asked to be removed from the company's payroll. The directors refused in a unanimous vote.

In April 1901, David Buick built the first Buick automobile. The early Buicks had a valve-in-head engine, a much more efficient engine than the L-head design then in use. The Buick engine, with the valves mounted directly over the pistons, was more powerful than other engines its size. However, Buick argued with his partners and got into financial trouble. He was more interested in advancing engine design than in running an automobile company.

In 1904, the Buick Motor Car Company was reorganized and began to produce cars with two-cylinder, twelve-horsepower engines in Flint. When the initial capitalization was gone, investors asked Durant if he would invest in and manage the company, which was in financial difficulty.

In November 1904, Durant was elected to the board of directors. Again, he declined the title of president. He immediately talked creditors into waiting for payments of their claims and went to an automobile show in New York City where he sold 1,108 cars. Up to that point, Buick had produced only forty cars. The powerful Buick engine, which had won many races and hill-climbs, lured many buyers.

Durant purchased a 220-acre site on the north side of Flint and built the largest automobile factory in the country. Buick production climbed from 725 in 1905 to 1,400 in 1906, 4,641 in 1907, 8,820 in 1908, 14,606 in 1909, and 30,525 in 1910. Louis Chevrolet, a driver on Buick's car racing team, won 500 trophies in two years.

In 1908, Benjamin Briscoe of the Maxwell-Briscoe Company, manufacturer of the Maxwell automobile, asked Durant to merge Buick with his company. The proposed consolidation included their companies plus the Ford Motor Company and the Reo Motor Car Company, formed by Ransom E. Olds after he left the Olds Motor Works.

Durant suggested that, for the purposes of consolidation, the Ford Motor Company should be evaluated at $10 million and Reo at $6 million. Henry Ford agreed to join the consolidation if he received $3 million in cash. Olds said that if Ford received $3 million, he should receive $3 million for Reo also. That killed the proposed consolidation; Durant didn't have access to $6 million in cash.

Durant and Briscoe agreed to merge their companies and the Olds Motor Works. On September 15, 1908, the articles of incorporation for the General Motors Company were filed with the New Jersey secretary of state's office. Durant again declined the title of president.

General Motors bought Buick for $3.75 million and Olds for $3 million. Most of the Olds payment was for goodwill. Although production had been small, the Olds car had an excellent reputation, and the public was familiar with the popular song, "In My Merry Oldsmobile." Durant directed the Olds Motor Works to lengthen and widen the Model 10 Buick and change its appearance to create a new Olds model, making the Oldsmobile Division of General Motors profitable in a minimum of time.

In 1909, Durant created the Pontiac Division by adding the Oakland Motor Car Company of Pontiac, Michigan, to General Motors. Later that year, Durant bought the Cadillac Automobile Company for $4.75 million. Within fourteen months, Cadillac earnings had returned the entire purchase price to General Motors. Durant also purchased many suppliers, including AC Spark Plug.

Durant was ready for another attempt to bring the Ford Motor Company into General Motors. In 1909, he approached Henry Ford with another offer to buy his company. Ford was willing to sell the Ford Motor Company for $8 million: $2 million cash, $2 million in stock for James Couzens (Ford's business manager), and the remaining $4 million at five percent interest payable within three years. Durant asked his bank, the National City Bank of New York, for a loan of $2 million. The bank denied him the loan.

A few years later, when Durant met Couzens on a train, earnings of the Ford Motor Company were $35 million a year. Durant had no regrets about his bankers turning him down. He admitted, "I would never have built up that business the way Ford did. The Ford business would never have been what it is without Henry Ford, who has done more for America than any other man—more for the world."[6]

General Motors, in contrast, was heading for trouble. No consistent bookkeeping procedures were in place, and inventory control was almost nonexistent. Durant didn't believe in a large central staff organization, but it was very difficult to manage a company the size of General Motors without one. He relied on his boundless optimism and his selling ability. The divisions, to a large extent, operated autonomously.

Durant made a poor decision in purchasing the Heany Lamp companies for over $7 million, more than he paid for Buick and Olds combined. Heany had patent problems; the eventual loss to General Motors was $12 million. Net earnings of General Motors wasn't increasing fast enough to pay for expansion and for suppliers' bills. Durant borrowed large sums from commercial banks and from his suppliers.

At Durant's suggestion, Charles Nash was appointed president of Buick in 1910 and two years later became president of General Motors. Nash was a capable car man; he was assisted by his choice of an extremely competent works manager, Walter Chrysler.

Early in 1910, General Motors' creditors met in New York City and agreed to "effect a reorganization of management and a restriction of enthusiasm." On May 1, all of General Motors' bank loans were called, reducing working capital to zero and shutting down the factories. On September 26, 1910, a contract was signed with the banks. The banks' requirements were traumatic:

- The loan to GM was for $15 million, but GM only received $12.75 million.

- The bankers received a blanket mortgage on all of GM's Michigan properties.
- The bankers received a commission of $4.1 million in preferred stock and $2 million in common stock.
- The bankers received control of the company through a voting trust for five years, the duration of the loan.
- Durant had to resign as chief executive officer, but he could remain as a vice president and a member of the finance committee.

Durant had no choice but to sign the agreement. He disagreed with many of the decisions of the new managers, many of whom weren't familiar with the automobile business. Durant had a vice president's title but no significant role in the operation of the company. He turned to Louis Chevrolet and said, "I need a car." Chevrolet had retired as a Buick racing driver and wanted to design and manufacture a car.

Early in 1911, Durant bought the Flint Wagon Works, the low-volume manufacturer of the Whiting car. On July 31, 1911, the Mason Motor Company was formed to manufacture engines, and, on October 30, 1911, the Little Motor Car Company was incorporated to produce a small, reasonably priced car using Mason engines.

On November 3, 1911, the Chevrolet Motor Company was incorporated. Durant again declined the title of president. Louis Chevrolet wasn't an officer; he concentrated on the development of his Classic Six, a large, expensive luxury vehicle. It wasn't Durant's type of car, and it didn't sell well.

The Chevrolet automobile grew out of the inexpensive Little automobile, not the expensive car that Louis Chevrolet designed. The Little name was discontinued in 1913; from 1914 on, it was called a Chevrolet. Durant and Louis Chevrolet parted company in late 1913 over some petty disagreements, including Chevrolet's smoking habits. Louis Chevrolet went back to designing and producing racing cars. He drove the winning cars in the Indianapolis 500 in 1920 and 1921.

In 1914, over 5,000 Chevrolets were produced. In 1915, Chevrolet introduced the popular "490" model, which sold for $550 initially and for $490 within a year. Chevrolet's sales went from 13,292 cars in 1915 to 70,701 one year later.

In early 1915, Durant purchased large blocks of General Motors stock. He was backed by Louis Kaufman of the Chatham & Phenix Bank and by Pierre du Pont, president of the E. I. du Pont de Nemours Company. John J. Raskob, treasurer of the Du Pont Company, convinced Pierre du Pont to invest in Chevrolet. Many of Durant's friends supported him, permitting him to offer GM stock to Du Pont at a bargain price. By September 16, Durant could say, "I'm in control of General Motors." Charles Nash was reelected president, Pierre du Pont was elected chairman of the board, and Durant continued as a vice president even though he controlled over fifty percent of the stock.

On December 23, Durant purchased the controlling interest in General Motors. Nash, who had been president of General Motors for the bankers, resigned on June 1, 1916, to form the Nash Motor Company in Kenosha, Wisconsin. Durant wanted to retain Nash but was told that if he could hold onto Walter Chrysler, Buick's general manager, he could afford to lose Nash. Durant offered Chrysler a lucrative contract and promised not to interfere between him and his subordinates, a Durant habit that Chrysler disliked.

In 1916, Durant formed a holding company for General Motors' wholly-owned parts suppliers, including Dayton Engineering Laboratories (Delco), Hyatt and New Departure roller bearing companies, and Remy Electric. Alfred Sloan of Hyatt Roller Bearing was named president of the holding company and later became a driving force in General Motors.

In late 1917, when the United States entered the first World War, the price of General Motors stock dropped to about a third of its recent value. Durant, who owned many shares purchased on margin, attempted to prop up the stock and found himself in financial trouble. Du Pont had enormous profits from its sale of smokeless powder to France, Great Britain, and Russia. In January 1920, Du Pont invested $25.1 million for an additional 23.8 percent ownership in GM-Chevrolet. Durant was no longer in control; however, he was chairman of the executive committee. Raskob chaired the finance committee.

Raskob was at least as much an optimist as Durant. No one was strong enough to curtail the excesses of Durant and Raskob as the company began a substantial expansion program. GM manufactured tractors but, after three years, withdrew from the tractor business with losses of $33 million. In 1919, Du Pont doubled its investment in GM to finance the anticipated postwar expansion. That year, over the objections of Durant, Raskob authorized the funds to build the General Motors Building. The fifteen-story building with thirty acres of floor space cost $20 million.

Durant still had no central staff group to help run the company, and little bidding was done on contracts with suppliers. He involved himself in too much detail and ignored Sloan's suggestions to implement improved management methods. In 1919, Walter Chrysler resigned because he disagreed with the oversized expansion program and was unhappy with Durant's continuing interference between him and his subordinates. Chrysler formed the Chrysler Corporation and became a competitor of General Motors.

Sloan captured Durant's method of operation in his *Adventures of a White-Collar Man*:

> I was constantly amazed by his daring ways of making a decision. Mr. Durant would proceed on a course of action guided solely, as far as I could tell, by some intuitive flash of brilliance. He never felt obliged to make an engineering hunt for facts. Yet at times he was astoundingly correct in his judgments.... Durant's integrity? Unblemished. Work? He was a prodigious

worker. Devotion to General Motors? Why it
was his baby! He would have made any sacrifice for it....[7]

In 1920, the postwar boom ended, and the country went
into a recession. From November 1919 to November 1920,
sales of GM cars dropped by two thirds and the stock price
dropped accordingly. However, Raskob's finance committee
continued to authorize large expenditures for expansion.
Durant wrote Raskob to express his alarm, but spending was-
n't curtailed.

Durant continued his attempts to prevent the decline of the
price of GM stock. He refused to sell short and lost over $90
million. An assistant said of Durant, "He didn't think it was
right for someone to sell something he didn't have." Sloan
commented in *My Years with General Motors*, "I think Mr.
Durant's personal stock market operations were motivated
essentially by his great pride in General Motors and everything relating to it, and by his unbounded confidence in the
future.... " Personally, Sloan thought that Durant's buying in
a falling market to support the market price "had about as
much chance of success as if he had tried to stand at the top
of Niagara Falls and stop it with his hat."

Parts inventories were out of control and the Chevrolet,
Pontiac, and Oldsmobile Divisions were in trouble due to
engineering problems and inadequate testing. Morgan Bank
had lent money to General Motors to help pay for the expansion. Representatives of Morgan Bank, du Pont, and Raskob
met to discuss Durant's financial problems. Morgan Bank and
the du Ponts made a cash offer of $20 million to cover
Durant's debt, contingent upon his resignation as president of
General Motors.

Durant told his wife that the manipulation of stock by the
GM-controlled syndicate was a "well-conceived plan to take
over his holdings." The du Ponts purchased Durant's 2.5 million shares of GM stock for the undervalued price of $9.50 a

share; they regained their value within a short time. Durant received a settlement of $1.1 million: $328,325 in cash and 55,159 shares of GM stock. Durant assured Pierre du Pont that "I shall make no attempt to obtain control of General Motors, through exchange of securities or otherwise." In addition to being chairman of the board, du Pont assumed the office of president of General Motors. Alfred Sloan became the executive vice-president. On May 10, 1923, Sloan was named president of GM.

Six weeks after leaving GM, Durant established Durant Motors, Inc., to design and build "just a real good car." Durant Motors was incorporated at Albany on January 12, 1921. Durant hired Alfred Sturt of Chevrolet to design the Durant Four to sell for $890. Another car, the Star, was introduced to compete directly with Ford.

Durant bought a large factory in New Jersey to produce these two cars and a plant in Indiana to manufacture the Durant Six while acquiring or building factories in California, Michigan, and the Province of Ontario. He remained loyal to Flint by establishing the Flint Motor Company to produce the Flint Six. Durant also purchased the Locomobile Company of Connecticut and announced another new car, the Princeton.

However, Durant Motors was fueled by an overwhelming public interest in the company stock, not by earnings from operations. The Star couldn't be produced at a low enough cost to compete with Ford, and the Locomobile Company was too far gone to salvage; it immediately lost $4 million. The Princeton never went into production. In 1926, the new factory at Flint was sold to GM for $4 million, and many of the sales offices were closed. Durant had expanded too fast. Loyal subordinates, such as Dallas Dort and Charles Nash who had helped check Durant's boundless optimism in the early days of GM, were no longer with him.

Durant traveled extensively and turned over the administration of Durant Motors to others. By 1927, he was back on the job full time. In January 1929, he again relinquished the management of Durant Motors, this time to four retired Dodge executives. Durant set aside $5 million, later increased to $10 million, to reimburse investors who had lost money in Durant Motors. He planned to run an ad in the *Saturday Evening Post* to inform investors of this plan until he was told that $10 million wouldn't cover all of the losses.

In 1929, Durant realized that the country's economic problems were worsening. Financial advisors counseled him to sell short, but, as before, he couldn't bring himself to do it. Not only did Durant lose what remained of his fortune in the stock market crash of 1929, but he lost his wife's trust fund as well. He had borrowed 75,000 shares of her GM stock in 1927 and the remainder, 187,000 shares, in 1930. During the Depression, Durant Motors' plants were closed; many were purchased by General Motors.

On February 8, 1936, Durant filed for bankruptcy with debts of $914,231 and assets of $250. He opened a food market and lunchroom in Asbury Park, New Jersey. In 1940, he operated North Flint Recreation, an 18-lane bowling alley in Flint, Michigan. On January 11, 1940, GM celebrated the production of its twenty-millionth car, and Durant was introduced by Alfred Sloan, who said, "Too often we fail to recognize the creative spirit so essential to start the enterprises that characterize American business and that have made our system the envy of the world."

On October 2, 1942, Durant suffered a stroke; his left side was partially paralyzed. Old friends, including Walter Chrysler and Alfred Sloan, provided financial assistance to the Durants, but, by 1947, the family had nothing left. Mrs. Durant sold her jewelry to pay medical bills. On March 18, 1947, Durant died in New York City.

Durant's friends honored him in Flint with a memorial, a long rectangular block of marble that serves as a base for flagpoles at the cultural center. Durant once observed to his wife, "Well, they took it away from me, but they cannot take away the credit for having done it."[8]

Henry Ford

CHAPTER 2

HENRY FORD

Father of the Automobile Assembly Line

"The miracle, or the power, that elevates the few is to be found in their industry, application, and perseverance under the promptings of a brave, determined spirit."

Mark Twain

Henry Ford, the second child and first son of William and Mary Litogot Ford, was born on Springwells Township Farm near Dearborn, Michigan, on July 30, 1863. He attended the Scotch Settlement School where he excelled in mathematics and reading but did poorly in penmanship and spelling. He helped with the milking, planting, and plowing on the farm, but he disliked farm work and considered it drudgery. He preferred maintaining the mowers and plows and keeping the tools sharpened.

In his youth, Ford built waterwheels, steam engines, and a forge. Instead of having a hobby, he fixed clocks and watches. He was a born mechanic. His mother, a strong influence on him during his formative years, counseled him to always do his best at whatever he did. In 1875, the family was devastated when Mary Ford died in childbirth.

At the age of seventeen, Ford left the farm to become an apprentice in Detroit at the Flower Machine Shop, manufacturers of fire hydrants and valves. In his spare time, he repaired watches to augment his income. Next, he became an apprentice at the Detroit Drydock Company, builders of schooners and steamboats. The company also built engines for their boats, and Ford was assigned to the engine shop. Most of Detroit Drydock's experience was with steam engines; however, they investigated the expanded use of internal combustion engines.

In 1882, Ford completed his apprenticeship and was hired by the Westinghouse Company to set up and operate steam engines for Michigan farmers. During the winters, he lived on his parents' farm, where he built a small machine shop. He enjoyed going to dances; he met Clara Bryant at one of the parties in the area. They went to cornhusking parties, church socials, and sleigh rides together for four years and were married in 1888. Clara was a strong supporter of Ford's plans; he called her "the great believer." At times, she believed in the potential success of his plans more strongly than he did.

William Ford gave his son and daughter-in-law a forty-acre farm for their wedding present. Young Henry cut and sold maple and oak trees for a living while spending all of his spare time designing a lightweight steam engine. He considered boilers required by steam engines too dangerous to use on a tractor or a carriage; he planned to mount an internal combustion engine on a carriage. However, he realized that he needed to know more about electricity before he built his first "horseless carriage," so he accepted a job as an engineer with the Edison Illuminating Company in Detroit to learn this new field.

In 1893, Ford designed and built his first gasoline engine in the garage behind his home. By the spring of 1896, he had completed his first gasoline-engine-powered carriage, which he called a quadricycle. Power was supplied from the engine to the rear wheels by a belt; the carriage had no reverse gear. Early in the morning of June 4, he knocked out the wall of his garage with an ax. His first automobile was too large to fit through the garage door.

Ford steered his vehicle down Grand River Avenue until the engine quit. An actuating spring, a component of the ignition system, had broken. He fixed it quickly and was underway again in his one-person vehicle. He strengthened the frame and widened the seat so he could take Clara for a ride. His two-cylinder engine used Nikolaus Otto's four-cycle design: intake, compression, ignition, and exhaust. Charles and Frank Duryea, builders of the first car in America in 1892, also had used the Otto engine design.

Ford built two more cars in 1899 and, with a Detroit lumberman as a partner, formed the Detroit Automobile Company. Their cars didn't sell. Ford's partner rejected his design improvements, and the company went out of business. Ford wanted to build an economical car; his partner wanted to build expensive cars.

In early 1901, Ford built a light racing car with a twenty-six-horsepower engine. On October 10, 1901, he won his first race at the Grosse Pointe racetrack. The following year he built two eighty-horsepower racing cars, the *999* and the *Arrow*. On October 25, 1902, Barney Oldfield set a new American speed record and won his first race, the Manufacturers' Challenge Cup, driving the *999* in a five-mile race at the Grosse Pointe racetrack.

With his name in front of the public, Ford was ready to go back into business designing and manufacturing cars. Alexander Malcomson, a Detroit coal merchant, was his main financial backer. Malcomson convinced a friend to let them use an old wagon shop on Mack Avenue as an assembly plant. Ford and Malcomson made a great team. James Couzens was the office manager, and a mechanical designer was hired to assist Ford in designing low-priced, everyday cars.

Ford, the inventor and inveterate tinkerer, always wanted to improve the design. Couzens was the ideal controller for Ford. He told Ford that his enhancements were great, but if they didn't freeze the design and sell a few cars, they would be out of business. John and Harold Dodge, owners of a Detroit machine shop, built the Ford-designed chassis. The Dodge brothers paid for their own tooling and material expenses for the chassis, which included the axles, engine, and gear box. Ford and Malcomson repaid the Dodges' $15,000 investment in three installments.

On June 15, 1903, paperwork creating the Ford Motor Company was filed in Lansing. Two of the twelve shareholders, Ford and Malcomson, owned over half of the shares. The first car, the original Model A, had an eight-horsepower engine that generated speeds up to thirty miles per hour. The Model A had two forward speeds and a reverse gear; spark for the ignition was provided by dry-cell batteries. The Model A sold for $750. Ford built a ramp and struggled to improve the car's ability to climb hills. From the beginning, Ford emphasized service. A team of mechanics traveled to customers to fix early problems.

The company was confronted with a challenge just as it geared up for production. In 1877, George Selden, an inventor and lawyer from Rochester, New York, built a gasoline engine. Then he designed a carriage for the engine and obtained a patent for a gasoline-powered carriage; however, Selden didn't build a car based on the design. Others had already built this type of vehicle, but they hadn't applied for a patent. In 1899, the Selden patents were purchased by the Electric Vehicle Company. The Association of Licensed Automobile Manufacturers (ALAM) was formed to prevent the Electric Vehicle Company from charging a royalty for every car sold. ALAM gained control of most of Selden's patent rights.

Ford refused to pay royalties. Couzens published a notice in Detroit newspapers: "To dealers, importers, agents, and users of our gasoline automobiles. We will protect you against any prosecution for alleged infringement of patents. The Selden patent ... does not cover any practicable machines. No practicable machines can be made from it and never was.... "[9] On October 22, 1903, ALAM sued the Ford Motor Company and attempted to prevent Ford from exhibiting cars in the New York City automobile show, an important sales forum.

Ford received unexpected support from John Wanamaker, the Philadelphia department store merchant. Wanamaker, who knew the manager of Madison Square Garden, wrangled Ford's presence at the auto show to help "fight the automobile trust." However, Ford's allocated display space was in the basement.

To promote his new model, the Model B, Ford mounted a Model B engine in the racer *Arrow*. On a cold January day, he drove the *Arrow* over the ice on Lake St. Clair. He set a new speed record of 91.37 miles per hour while his mechanic, Spider Huff, blew into the gas tank to keep the fuel feeding. In becoming the first to drive over ninety miles per hour, Ford made national headlines that generated many orders for the Model B at the New York show.

In May 1909, Ford and his lawyer appeared in court to address the Selden patent suit. They pointed out that others had built gasoline engines before Selden, and that Selden's engine wasn't the same as the engine used in Ford cars. The Selden patent was determined to be valid; Ford appealed the court's decision. On January 9, 1911, Ford won the appeal. He wasn't to be restricted by the Selden patent because he didn't use the Selden engine. Ford used the Otto four-cycle engine, a completely different design from Selden's. Ford was hailed in the press as "a magnificent individualist" and "a giant-killer."

Ford expounded his goals clearly: "The way to make automobiles is to make one automobile like another automobile, to make them all alike ... just as one pin is like another when it comes from a pin factory. If you freeze the design and concentrate on production, as the volume goes up, the cars are certain to become cheaper. I mean to turn out a car that workingmen can buy."[10] That car was the Model T; it changed the automobile business irrevocably.

Models C, F, K, and N preceded the Model T. Ford's partner, Malcomson, wanted to concentrate on the Model K, a luxury model. Malcomson started his own car company, the Aerocar Company, to produce an expensive car. In retaliation, Ford formed the Ford Manufacturing Company to sell parts to the Ford Motor Company. As a competitor, Malcomson wasn't invited to join the Ford Manufacturing Company. Ford Manufacturing increased the cost of parts sold to Ford Motor until the original company's profits and dividends decreased considerably. Malcomson and four other original investors sold their stock in the Ford Motor Company. In effect, Ford forced Malcomson out of the company he had helped to establish.

On March 1, 1908, advance information about the Model T was mailed to dealers. The Model T's four-cylinder engine, which averaged twenty miles per gallon, produced twenty horsepower and could attain speeds of up to forty-five miles per hour. In its new magneto ignition system, magnets supplied sparks to the cylinders. Demand soon outstripped manufacturing capacity. Ford purchased the sixty-acre racetrack at Highland Park, north of Detroit, as a site for a larger factory.

Eli Whitney had introduced the concept of interchangeable parts in making rifles for the U.S. Government. The idea had been in use for years in the manufacture of many products, including Colt firearms and Singer sewing machines. Ford decided to use the concept on the first assembly line for automobiles in his new factory. Two principles guided the design of the new plant layout: the work must be brought to the man—not the man to the work, and the work must be brought to the man waist high. In other words, a worker shouldn't have to bend to attach a part to the chassis moving past him.

In Ford's words: "The man who places a part does not fasten it. The man who puts in a bolt does not put on a nut; the man who puts on the nut does not tighten it.... "[11] Assembly time dropped from twelve and a half hours for the first Model Ts to one hour, thirty-three minutes in January 1914.

The car was called the Tin Lizzie after the Model T, *Old Liz*, that won a race up Pike's Peak. To produce the increased demand, Ford expanded the work force from 5,700 in 1912 to 13,200 in 1913. However, the work was so repetitive that turnover of trained assembly line workers was high. Sales doubled from over $42 million in 1913 to $90 million in 1914. Ford shared profits with his workers and increased their wages to $5.00 a day while decreasing the workday from nine hours to eight. He doubled their daily wage.

He explained:

> Their homes are crowded and unsanitary. Wives are going out to work because their husbands are unable to earn enough to support the family. They fill up their home with roomers and boarders in order to help swell the income. Its all wrong—all wrong. It's especially bad for the children....[12]

Within two days, 10,000 job-seekers surrounded the Ford factory at Highland Park. Some were hired, but thousands suffered in the January cold only to be turned away.

When Ford became a public figure, he decided to move his family from Detroit to a more secluded environment. In 1915, he built a home, Fair Lane, on a 2,000-acre property in Dearborn. He became interested in national causes and was active in the peace movement in early World War I.

Initially, he rejected the government's requests to build war material. By 1917, when the United States entered the war, he reversed his earlier stand and reassigned William Knudsen from introducing the assembly line in Ford plants around the country to building ships for the U.S. Navy. Ford produced a 200-foot subchaser called the Eagle Boat as well as ambulances, armor plate, helmets, Liberty airplane motors, shells, tanks, and trucks.

Ford thought he could produce the Model T for the long term. In 1912, when the Model T had been in production for three years, his designers surprised him with a new model upon his return from a vacation in Europe. He tore off the doors, broke the windshield, and dented the top of the car. His designers got the message—no new designs. He was willing to make small changes, so Ford dealers asked him to replace the flickering headlights, enlarge the radiator, and improve the front wheels. Also, he installed a new muffler and made improvements to the carburetor, engine, and wiring system.

After World War I, Ford's new factory on the Rouge River near Dearborn was almost completed. Ore was unloaded at the docks, steel was made on the site, and the steel was used to fabricate crankshafts, cylinder blocks, and other car components. The site included blast furnaces, coke ovens, a thirty-acre foundry, and railroad yards. Ford financed the building of the River Rouge plant by diverting stock dividends to pay for plant expansion. He told stockholders that they were nonproducers, and that their dividends were unearned.

The early investors strongly objected, particularly the

Dodge brothers. They were were building a more expensive car than Ford; cheaper Fords would hurt their sales. They sued Ford for "reasonable" dividends. In early 1919, the Supreme Court of Michigan supported a lower court decision forcing Ford to pay a late dividend of $19 million to his stockholders. The Dodge brothers offered to sell their stock to Ford, but he didn't want to buy any more stock.

In 1918, Ford made an unsuccessful bid for the U.S. Senate. Late that year, Ford turned the presidency of the company over to his oldest son, Edsel. After the court decision in favor of the stockholders, Ford went on vacation to California. From California, he announced that he was planning to produce a new car that would undersell the Model T, possibly for as little as $250. The news dramatically depressed the price of Ford Motor Company stock.

When the investors became nervous about the plunging price of Ford stock, a silent agent for Ford began to buy the stock. All of the original investors, including the Dodge brothers, sold their stock. Couzens, who had argued with Ford and left the company in 1915, was the only major investor who wasn't duped by Ford's machinations. Eventually, Couzens received $29 million for an original investment of $2,500.

Ford now had total control of his company. He also had a dilemma. How was he going to pay out $75 million to buy the stock without turning to bankers, whom he distrusted? With profits at $60 million per year, he turned to short-term notes from Old Colony Bank in Boston and Chase Bank in New York. He would have had the loans paid off promptly, but a recession in 1920 reduced his profits considerably. The postwar inflation prevented him from meeting his repayment date in April 1921.

Ford resolved the dilemma by producing 90,000 cars for which there was no market and shipping them to the dealers. He demanded cash for cars that dealers hadn't ordered. Furthermore, he charged the dealers transportation costs and threatened to pull the dealer's franchise if they didn't buy the cars. Some dealers were forced out of business. Many dealers took out bank loans to get through this period. In effect, Ford shifted his need for a large loan to dealers who had to take out smaller loans. However, the dealers, not Ford, were responsible for repayment of their loans.

In 1925, sales of Ford cars decreased and sales of other cars, including Chevrolets and Buicks, increased. Other cars were available in Ford's price range, but the big demand was for cars with more modern features that the public was willing to pay for. In the summer of 1925, Ford gave in to his designers and agreed with rounding the square corners of the Model T design. Also, Ford gave in on his principle of "They can have any color they want, as long as it's black." Model Ts were now available in gunmetal blue, phoenix brown, fawn gray, and highland green.

However, it was too little and too late. A Model T sold for $290 and a Chevrolet for $645; however, the Chevrolet had features that buyers wanted, such as dismountable tires and a self-starter. Finally, the Ford Motor Company announced a new automobile and halted production of the Model T the following day. The last Model T down the assembly line was the fifteen millionth made.

The new car, the Model A, with a four-cylinder engine that produced forty horsepower, could achieve a maximum speed of sixty-five miles per hour. The Model A, a lower, more modern design than the Model T that used no Model T parts, had hydraulic shock absorbers, a state-of-the-art ignition system, and safety glass windshields. Best of all, it was priced lower than the Chevrolet. By the end of 1928, Ford made 6,400 Model A cars per day; production was increased to two million cars the following year.

During the 1930s, Ford became less involved with running the huge River Rouge complex and turned increasingly to Harry Bennett to manage the company. Bennett, who had started as director of personnel, had his own police force within the Ford Motor Company and had become extremely powerful. He provided bodyguards for the Ford children and grandchildren.

In 1937, the United Auto Workers Union (UAW) called strikes at the General Motors Corporation and the Chrysler Corporation and targeted the Ford Motor Company for a future strike. Union representatives marched over the Miller Road bridge to Gate No. 4 of the River Rouge factory. Bennett's men met the union representatives on the bridge, beat the leaders, and turned the marchers back. Walter Reuther, a UAW leader, was one of those beaten. Bennett's ruffians attacked newspaper reporters and photographers and destroyed film and photographic plates.

Union problems at Ford continued until the UAW called a strike at River Rouge on April 1, 1941, that completely shut down the plant. Ford gave in to the strikers and accepted terms, including the closed shop, that other automobile companies had rejected. When asked later why he had given in to union demands, he admitted that his wife had threatened to leave him unless he signed a "peace agreement" with the union. Clara told him that she was tired of the bloodshed.

Late in 1941, Ford had a serious stroke that removed him one step further from the management of the Ford Motor Company. Increasingly, the company was run by Edsel Ford and Bennett. Edsel played a major role in converting the Company's car production to the manufacture of war material such as gliders, tanks, and trucks for World War II. Edsel's key contribution was the construction and operation of the huge Willow Run plant to make B-24 Liberator bombers. By 1945, three quarters of the B-24s were produced at Willow Run.

Edsel, who had lost many arguments with his father over the years, wasn't in robust health. In 1942, he developed a bleeding stomach ulcer and undulant fever. The heavy overtime and the strain of the war effort took an additional toll. On May 26, 1943, Edsel, Ford's heir apparent, died of stomach cancer. Henry Ford II, Edsel's son, was brought home from serving in the U.S. Navy to join the board of the Ford Motor Company upon the death of his father. One of Henry II's early actions upon becoming president of the company was to fire Bennett. He reorganized the company and installed modern financial controls designed by the "whiz kids," including Robert McNamara, who later became Secretary of Defense.

On April 7, 1947, Ford died of a stroke at Fair Lane. Will Rogers, the popular humorist, once told Ford: "It will take a hundred years to tell whether you have helped us or hurt us, but you certainly didn't leave us like you found us."[13] The introduction of "horseless carriages" to America's poor roads early in the 20th century was a significant adjustment for an agrarian society.

Ford was once told that he was creating a social problem with his automobiles. He responded, "No. You' re wrong. I'm not producing a social problem. When I'm through everybody will be able to afford a car and about everybody will have one." The introduction of affordable automobiles improved the quality of life. Although Ford wasn't the first to use inter-changeable parts in mass production, he increased the poten-tial of mass production by using the moving assembly line. Ford, the man who said "history is bunk," had made history.

CHAPTER 3

PRODUCTION OF THE AUTOMOBILE

SUCCESS VS. FAILURE—SUMMARY AND ANALYSIS

"Men who have attained the things worth having in this world have worked while others idled, have persevered when others gave up in despair, have practiced early in life the valuable habits of self-denial, industry, and singleness of purpose. As a result, they enjoy in later life the success so often erroneously attributed to good luck."

Granville Kleiser

But for quirks of history, the Ford Motor Company would have become a division of the General Motors Corporation on two occasions. The merger was prevented on the first occasion when Ransom Olds demanded as much cash for his company as Henry Ford was offered for the Ford Motor Company. On the second occasion, the National City Bank refused to provide a $2 million loan to William Durant to complete the deal. The automobile industry would have been a different business if the merger had been successful. However, Durant of General Motors admitted that he couldn't have done as much with the Ford Motor Company as Henry Ford did.

Durant failed three times in the automobile business—spectacularly. Twice he failed as chief executive officer (in fact, if not in name) of General Motors and once as CEO of Durant Motors. The same factors were at work in all three failures: his boundless optimism, his wheeling and dealing in the stock market, and the belief that he could personally counter a downward slide in the market.

Durant's principal strengths were marketing and promotion. He was an entrepreneur, not an inventor. He had a charismatic personality, and he was able to gain and retain customers' and investors' trust. Durant was extremely ethical, to the point of accepting financial responsibility when an investment that he recommended caused monetary losses to others. His loyalty to employees was unquestioned, but he sometimes went around key managers when he should have consulted them. He knew how to attract superior people; he didn't always know how to keep them.

Durant's demonstrations of loyalty to his home base of Flint, Michigan, were legion. Flint could always count on manufacturing plants for any Durant enterprise. Durant needed cool heads around him to tell him when his latest idea wasn't practical or economical. Early in his career, he had that kind of advisor around him; later in his life, he didn't.

Henry Ford was an inventor who literally lived the legend

of starting out in a garage. He recognized the need for business-oriented people to help him run his company. He was a focused individual who never lost sight of his goal: the design and manufacture of an economical car for Everyman. As his company became more successful, he became more autocratic. He adhered to major design decisions long after it was desirable for him to do so. Two examples are "They can have any color they want as long as it's black," and freezing the Model T design while other car companies were providing innovations.

Ford could be as tough as conditions required. He knew how to dump a partner and retain a controlling interest in any business organization—partnership or corporation. He took a truculent stance when the United Auto Workers threatened a strike.

He valued independence and refused to accept loans from bankers who had the potential of taking his company away from him, as they had with Durant of General Motors on two occasions. In fact, Ford was so successful in avoiding being beholden to bankers or stockholders that the Ford Motor Company didn't have an initial public offering of stock until 1956.

Ford was strongly focused in his early career, but he became distracted later in life. His active participation in the peace movement prior to World War I and his refusal to produce war materials weren't popular positions. However, when the United States entered the war in 1917, he reversed his position and produced goods for the war effort.

Durant also was distracted from the automobile business on numerous occasions during his life. His principal distraction was the stock market, particularly during the late 1920s. Wall Street historians considered him to have been a "bull of bulls." In 1928, he manipulated 11 million shares of stock valued at $1.2 billion.

In *Mystery Men of Wall Street*, Earl Sparling described Durant's method of operation: "Acting as a sort of market commissioner of police, he watched for weak spots in the market and, whenever he found one, plugged it with millions of dollars. He placed other millions behind key stocks which, in rising, would drag the whole market upward in sympathy; nothing like that had ever been tried before."[14] This experience gave him false confidence. To his dismay, he found that what worked in the stock market in 1928 didn't work in 1929 when the stock market crashed.

Durant had many strong, human qualities; resilience was certainly one of them. Unfortunately, his overwhelming optimism didn't serve him well at General Motors or in establishing Durant Motors late in his career. He expanded Durant Motors too fast with insufficient earnings to sustain the infant company. His optimism was ineffective in a declining economy and in a falling market. Unfortunately, he kept no financial reserves either for himself or for his wife. The fall from being chief executive officer of General Motors to proprietor of a bowling alley was dramatic. However, it didn't seem to bother him; if it did, he didn't display it outwardly.

Durant and Ford were visionaries who have places in the business history of the United States. In terms of his relationship to the company that he left behind, Ford was the more successful of the two. One wonders what Durant could have done if he had been left in place at General Motors with some responsible advisors to control him at critical times. For example, the growth of General Motors during the five years that conservative bankers ran the company was much slower than it would have been under Durant.

However, success cannot always be measured in monetary terms. Durant observed, "There's much more to life than money. Many people value money too highly. I'm trying to do good for as many people as possible. After all, money is only loaned to a man. He comes into the world with nothing and goes out with nothing."[15]

NAUTICAL ENTREPRENEURS

Invention of the Steamboat

CHAPTER 4

JOHN FITCH

Steamboat Inventor

"He did persevere. We cannot begin to relate the obstacles he encountered. A considerable volume would scarcely afford the requisite space. Poor, ragged and forlorn, jeered at, pitied as a madman, discouraged by the great, refused by the rich, he and his few friends kept on, until in 1790, they had a steamboat running on the Delaware, which was the first steamboat constructed that answered the purpose of one. It ran with the tide, eight miles an hour, and six miles an hour against it."

Cyclopedia of Biography

John Fitch, the youngest of five children of Joseph and Sarah Shaler Fitch, was born on January 21, 1743, in Windsor, Connecticut. Joseph Fitch struggled to support his family on his hardscrabble farm. Young John realized at an early age that farming wasn't the career for him. As a young man, he was a silversmith and then a surveyor in Ohio and Kentucky. When he returned to the East, he settled in Bucks County, Pennsylvania.

On a sunny April Sunday in 1785, Fitch had the idea that led to the development of the steamboat. While walking home from church, hobbled by rheumatism, he watched a neighbor from nearby Hatboro ride by in a horse-drawn carriage. He thought: "What a noble thing it would be if I could have such a carriage without the expense of keeping a horse."[16] His inspiration was to propel a carriage by steam power.

Fitch soon decided against building a steam-propelled wagon because of the poor quality of the roads. However, his experience as a surveyor along the Ohio River motivated him to think about a steam-powered boat. The atmospheric-type of steam engine, such as the engines designed by Newcomen, had been in use for years, but Fitch wasn't familiar with them. In 1785, only three steam engines were in use in the United States, two in New England and one near Passaic, New Jersey, used to pump water from a mine.

Fitch made a sketch of a steam-powered boat and showed it to the local pastor, who told him about descriptions of early steam engines in the *Philosophia Britannica*. Fitch was chagrined to find that his thoughts weren't original. He would have been surprised to learn that, in England, Watt and Bolt were secretly working on a new double-acting design in which power was generated on the upward stroke of the cylinder as well as the downward stroke.

Fitch built a model propelled by flat wooden paddles driven by a loop of chain on a sprocket. He also designed a circular paddle wheel similar to those used later on side-wheelers and stern-wheelers on the Mississippi River. His first technical challenge was to transfer the reciprocal motion of the steam engine to the rotary motion of the propeller.

Fitch's greatest challenge, however, was obtaining financing for his project in the agrarian economy of the United States. He hoped that the fledgling U.S. Congress would fund his development, so he solicited letters of recommendation to use in presenting his request to Congress. Dr. John Ewing, provost of the University of Pennsylvania, wrote that he had "no doubt of the success of the scheme if executed by a skillful workman." Congressmen Cadwallader of New Jersey and Dr. Samuel Smith, provost of the College of New Jersey, also provided Fitch with testimonials supporting his cause.

In 1785, Fitch petitioned Congress for financial support of his development effort. Congress referred his petition to a committee who set it aside and ignored it. Unfortunately, it wasn't entered into congressional records. Fitch was indignant; he stated his feelings in his autobiography: "Determining to avenge myself on the committee of Congress ... I determined to pursue my scheme as long as I could strain a single nerve to forward it ... to prove to the world by actual experiment that they were blockheads."

Fitch then presented his petition to Don Diego, the Spanish Minister to the United States. In 1782, flatboats began to carry cargo down the Mississippi from Fort Pitt to New Orleans. However, the flatboats couldn't travel upstream, so they were broken up in New Orleans and sold for building materials. Don Diego was intrigued with Fitch's model of the steam-powered boat; he hoped to use them to return flatboats to their point of origin. He agreed to finance the project if Fitch would grant the patent to Spain and the exclusive right to manufacture to his Most Christian Majesty, the King of Spain. This conflicted with Fitch's concept of patriotism and was unacceptable to him.

Fitch presented his design to Benjamin Franklin, who usually supported the inventions of others. He also presented his proposal, accompanied by his model, drawings, and a written description of the steamboat, to the American Philosophical Society, of which Franklin was the most prominent member. He received no response from either Franklin or the Society.

Later, Fitch learned that Franklin had his own design for powering a boat. Franklin's scheme was based on the principle of the Bernoulli tube, with water entering the bow, moving through a hand-cranked pump, and exiting the boat through a pipe below the waterline. It wasn't practical; nevertheless, it received widespread support because Franklin sponsored it.

James Rumsey of Virginia developed a design for a boat powered by a wheel driven by river current and assisted by men using a system of poles to generate forward motion. Fitch was relieved to hear that the boat wasn't powered by a steam engine. The boat was impractical because it could only travel with the current and because the weight of the men using the poles limited the amount of cargo it could carry.

Fitch also appealed to the state assemblies in Delaware, Maryland, New Jersey, New York, Pennsylvania, and Virginia for financial support for his venture. He was unable to obtain financial assistance from the states, but they were willing to grant him the exclusive right to operate a steamboat on their rivers; granting that right didn't cost them anything. In March 1786, the New Jersey Legislature granted him exclusive rights for a period of fourteen years. In early 1787, Delaware, New York, and Pennsylvania granted him similar rights to those he had obtained from New Jersey.

Unfortunately, venture capitalists didn't exist in the eighteenth century. Fitch organized a joint-stock company with fifteen middle-income backers, who included merchants, shopkeepers, and tavernkeepers. He sold twenty shares for $300 and kept twenty shares for himself.

Fitch chose Henry Voight, a Philadelphia clockmaker and watchmaker, to build a steam engine for his boat. Fitch considered Voight a mechanical genius and, furthermore, a friend at a time when Fitch had few friends. Their first design was a double-acting engine in which power was generated on both the upward and downward strokes. Unfortunately, the size of the cylinder, one inch in diameter, was too small to generate sufficient power to propel the boat. The first trial on a small skiff with flimsy paddles was unsuccessful. Many spectators on the wharf jeered at their efforts. The jeering bothered Voight more than Fitch.

Their next engine had a three-inch-diameter cylinder without a separate condenser. A pump injected water directly into the cylinder, which cooled the steam and produced condensation. This engine wasn't sufficiently powerful to propel the forty-five-foot skiff in which it was mounted. Fitch needed help securing the boat, but the jeering of the crowd drove Voight off. Fitch tied up the boat by himself.

The idea for applying power to the paddles came to Fitch in the middle of the night. His "cranks and paddles" idea was implemented by attaching paddles to arms that were moved by a crank. When the crank went downward, paddles were pulled through the water to the stern of the boat; when the crank moved upward, the paddles were lifted out of the water and returned to the bow. This design was used with a steam engine that had a twelve-inch-diameter piston.

Fitch and Voight continued to innovate and to improve their design, including the use of a narrower hull with less water resistance. They redesigned the condenser and placed the furnace directly under the boiler, which eliminated the need for bricks and mortar surrounding the furnace.

Voight lost patience with the project, particularly with the shortage of funds. He returned to his watchmaking business to support his family. Voight was replaced by Dr. William Thornton, a doctor who had been educated at medical schools in Scotland and France. Thornton's first design was a condenser used on an engine with an eighteen-inch-diameter cylinder. The new condenser worked no better than the old one. The steamboat caught fire one night while tied up at the pier. Fitch had to sink the boat to save it from burning up.

Fitch's stockholders, unhappy with his lack of progress, attempted to push him aside and replace him with Thornton. Fitch not only fought off this maneuver, but he designed a straight-tube condenser that worked better than any of Thornton's designs. Fitch and Thornton conducted a series of successful trials using the engine with the larger cylinder and the new condenser.

The Governor of Pennsylvania, Thomas Mifflin, and members of the Pennsylvania Assembly were impressed with the trial run. Fitch scheduled regular, round-trip passenger runs from Philadelphia along the Delaware River to Burlington, Bristol, Bordentown, and Trenton. Fares were kept low to compete with the stagecoach route along the river. In fact, fares were so low that money was lost on every run.

This steamboat's record was impressive. She carried passengers a total of just under 3,000 miles from mid-May until the end of September 1790 and traveled over ninety miles in twelve and a half hours, or over seven miles an hour, upstream. Fitch continued to improve his design. He began construction of a second boat that he named, appropriately, *Perseverance*. In mid-October, *Perseverance* broke loose from her moorings, drifted into the Delaware River, and went aground. By the time she was towed back to the wharf, the season was almost over.

Personally, Fitch was in dire circumstances. His clothes were in tatters, and, unable to pay his landlady for his room or his meals, he was totally dependent on her charity. Voight had fared much better since leaving the steamboat project; he had been appointed Chief Coiner of the United States Mint in Philadelphia.

In the spring of 1791, the Commissioners for the Promotion of Useful Arts (Thomas Jefferson, Henry Knox, and Edmund Randolph) settled the Fitch-Rumsey invention dispute by awarding patents to both of them. Fitch was enraged to hear that the design for which he was awarded the patent wasn't his own successful design, but the Bernoulli-Franklin design that Rumsey sponsored. By this stroke, the commissioners gave any possible commercial value of Fitch's invention to Rumsey. Fitch had no recourse because Congress had made no record of his petition to them; the Patent Office wasn't established until 1802.

Fitch lost the support of his financial backers. He wanted to make improvements to *Perseverance*, but he didn't have the money to make them. He tried, unsuccessfully, to obtain additional funding for steamboat development in England and France. On Fitch's last trial on *Perseverance*, Voight left his office at the U.S. Mint to taunt the inventor dressed in rags and struggling with a sluggish piston. Voight knew how to fix it; furthermore, he knew how to improve it with little expense, but he wasn't going to help his old friend. Fitch's last memory of his steamboat development was this cruel treatment by Voight.

In June 1796, Fitch moved to Bardstown, Kentucky, to reclaim land for which he had filed warrants in 1782. His 1,300 acres had been divided up into six plantations with 400 acres of cleared land. He promised the landlord of the tavern in which he stayed that he would pay his bill when he received payment for his property. He died in Bardstown in 1798 as penniless as he had lived.

Despite his many disappointments, Fitch said:

> If mankind had been as good as they ought to be, I do not know of one instance of my life but I have acted with the same degree of prudence as it would have been if I had to do it again, and yet I have fell in character much below the meanest citizens.... when I take a view of my past life, as singular as it is, I am sure that if Deity is just, which I have no reason to doubt, I stand in need of no mediator or of applying to His particular friends to inter-

cede for me. Only let me tell plain simple truths, and I am sure I shall have the softest cushion in heaven to sit upon.[17]

Fitch was technologically successful in his steamboat development, even if his efforts weren't economically successful. In spite of overwhelming setbacks, he proved that a boat could be propelled by steam power.

CHAPTER 5

ROBERT FULTON

Developer of Commercially Successful Steamboats

"As the component parts of all new machines may be said to be old ... the mechanic should sit down among levers, screws, wedges, wheels, etc. like a poet among the letters of the alphabet, considering them as the exhibition of his thought; in which a new arrangement transmits a new idea to the world."[18]

Robert Fulton

Robert Fulton was born on November 14, 1765, in Little Britain Township, Pennsylvania. He spent the early years of his life in Lancaster. His father, Robert Fulton, Sr., was a tailor who became a farmer. In 1780, young Fulton was apprenticed to a jeweler in Philadelphia, which at that time had a population of 43,000 and was the largest and most enlightened city in the colonies. His apprenticeship evolved from silversmithing and jewelry-making to painting miniature portraits.

Fulton lived at Walnut and Second Streets, one block from the Delaware River. Although he never mentioned it in his writing, Fulton must have been familiar with John Fitch's struggle to develop a steamboat on the Delaware River. In the summer of 1787, Fulton left Philadelphia to study painting with the American painter, Benjamin West, in London. It isn't known whether Fulton observed the first trial run of Fitch's steamboat on August 22, 1787. However, Fulton later copied twelve pages from Fitch's 1790 diary, in which the inventor described the evolution of his steamboat and engine over the previous three years.

Fulton borrowed money to pay for passage to London to continue his study of art. When he boarded ship in Philadelphia in 1787, he didn't realize that he would be abroad for almost twenty years. His mentor, Benjamin West, who had also studied art in London, had become an extremely successful painter.

Fulton earned enough from the sale of his paintings to support himself, but not enough to pay for work on his inventions. He had a talent for borrowing money to finance his development work. Because he projected an air of trustworthiness, he was able to obtain loans for risky ventures that weren't well-defined. He paid back few of these loans, and the payments he made were partial.

Canal-building was popular in England at this time, before the advent of railroads. Fulton met the Earl of Stanhope, who planned to build a canal joining the Bristol Canal and the

English Channel near his manor in Devonshire. The Earl was one of the first to loan Fulton money for his projects. Fulton's early canal projects were a canal-digging machine, which he called an excavator, and an inclined plane that accommodated differences in elevations in a canal, a function later handled by locks. His projects weren't successful.

Other unsuccessful Fulton inventions were a marble-cutting machine, a device for spinning flax, and a leather tanning process. He also developed a rope-making device similar to a design by Edmund Cartwright, inventor of the power loom. Robert Owen, the social reformer, was another of Fulton's financial sponsors. Owen was repaid only £60 on his loan of £170 to Fulton.

Fulton obtained French patents for his canal inventions. He planned a brief trip to France, but stayed for many years. Benjamin West provided Fulton with a letter of introduction to Joel Barlow in Paris. Barlow and his wife, Ruth, became social and financial sponsors of the young inventor. Joel and Ruth Barlow formed an extremely close and unusual friendship with Fulton. Ruth functioned as an aunt and a sister to him as well as a friend. When Fulton married in his forties, Ruth was jealous of his wife.

Joel Barlow made his fortune running the blockade to provide supplies to France during the French Revolution. Barlow held a dual American and French citizenship because of his support of the rebels during the Revolution; he opened many doors for Fulton. Barlow provided much of Fulton's early development funding.

The Barlows were lukewarm to their young friend's effort to develop a submarine. They encouraged him to direct his efforts to the design of a steamboat. Reluctantly, Barlow backed Fulton's development of the *Nautilus*, which was similar to but larger than the undersea craft, *American Turtle*, developed by David Bushnell.

Development of a submarine, with accompanying torpedoes, became the principal outlet for Fulton's drive. The torpedoes described by Fulton were really mines designed to be attached to the hull of an enemy ship by the submarine.

Fulton used his salesmanship to convince the French government to provide development funds. They strung him along because they didn't want to miss any opportunity to overcome their disadvantage with respect to the British navy. When Fulton's tests weren't successful, the French government lost interest.

Fulton then attempted to interest the British navy in his undersea craft. In 1800, he negotiated with a British agent, "Mr. Smith," to move his development work to England. Prime Minister William Pitt offered Fulton a salary of £200 a month, £7,000 for development expenses, and £40,000 if his design proved to be practical. The agreement would be honored even if the government suppressed the invention and didn't use it. Again, his trials weren't successful, but Prime Minister Pitt's government provided another £10,000 of development funds to keep him working for them. Subsequent trials also failed.

Although initially the Barlows supplied him with money for his projects, Chancellor Livingston became the principal backer for his steamboat development. Robert R. Livingston, a wealthy patrician of the Hudson River Valley who had been Chancellor of New York State from 1777 to 1801, arrived in France as the American Minister in 1801. As Chancellor of New York State, Livingston had administered the oath of office to President Washington on April 30, 1789.

Fulton was introduced to Livingston by the Barlows, who convinced the Chancellor to provide financial backing for their friend. Livingston wasn't interested in underwater craft, but he indicated a strong interest in steamboat development. In 1798, the Chancellor acquired John Fitch's New York State rights to steamboat navigation.

Livingston had been introduced to steam power by his brother-in-law, John Stevens, whose development effort he had funded. Stevens turned to Nicholas J. Roosevelt, the great grand-uncle of Franklin D. Roosevelt, for help with this development work. Roosevelt, owner of a foundry and machine shop in Belleville, New Jersey, offered to build a steam engine instead of buying one from Bolton & Watt. Roosevelt installed his engine, which had a twenty-inch cylinder and a two-foot stroke, in a sixty-foot-long boat. The engine, built with the help of two former employees of Bolton & Watt, ran well, but the steamboat was unsuccessful due to problems linking power with the paddles.

Livingston became impatient with his brother-in-law's efforts. A dilettante in the invention arena, Livingston couldn't understand why construction of a successful steamboat didn't immediately follow the concept. He didn't want to receive second billing to Stevens, and he was unable to participate directly in the development after he moved to France. While in France, Livingston decided to back Fulton and provided £500 ($18,000) to build a trial vessel. If the trial succeeded, Fulton was to proceed to New York to build a boat that could carry sixty passengers at eight miles per hour from Manhattan to Albany.

The trial was moderately successful, and Fulton returned to New York on December 13, 1806, almost twenty years after departing for Europe. He had moved to England as a young, unsophisticated painter to study painting with Benjamin West. He returned as a polished forty-one-year-old entrepreneur who "looked like a English nobleman." He had negotiated with senior government ministers in both England and France and was endowed with elegance and social graces gained from moving in fashionable society. He was intelligent, refined, and talented, but he wasn't arrogant. Most people who knew him well liked him. In later years, the few who didn't like him were competitors that he had beaten in the race to develop a successful steamboat.

Shortly after Fulton's return to the United States, the British frigate H.M.S. *Leopard* fired upon the American frigate U.S.S. *Chesapeake* when the U.S. captain refused to allow boarding of his ship to search for British deserters. Three Americans were killed and eighteen were wounded.

Fulton was motivated by the incident to offer his design for a submarine and torpedoes to the U.S. government. He arranged a trial of his torpedoes to be witnessed by Secretary of State James Madison and Secretary of the Navy Robert Smith. This trial was no more successful than his trials in England and France. Interest in the incident waned, and Fulton focused his energy on steamboats.

Livingston was granted an extension on his state monopoly until 1823. The monopoly, originally granted in 1803, was contingent on his having the first steamboat in operation by April 1807. Fulton installed a Bolton & Watt engine in a 150-foot-long boat with a thirteen-foot beam and used paddles instead of propeller propulsion.

The boat was called *The North River Steamboat of Clermont*. The lower Hudson was called the North River; Clermont was the name of Livingston's estate 110 miles upriver from New York. Initially, the boat was referred to as *The Steamboat*, but eventually she was called *Clermont*.

The boat experienced minor damage from vandalism by anti-steam interests. Captains of sailing vessels frequently steered their ships into the *Clermont's* path. After all, sailing vessels had the right of way.

People were suspicious of a boat that belched smoke, and area farmers were concerned about its potential effect on their crops. On August 9, 1807, a secret test run was made, four years after Fulton's test with his earlier boat on the Seine River in France. The boat achieved a speed of four miles per hour upstream, despite the fact that the paddles were still not completed. The first publicized run was on August 17, 1807.

Many of Livingston's family and friends were on board. The *Clermont* traveled from Manhattan to Livingston's estate in twenty-four hours at an average speed of just under five miles an hour; the same average speed was maintained in the last forty miles to Albany.

On September 4, the first commercial run was made with fourteen paying passengers. The *Clermont* accommodated twenty-four passengers, with twelve berths at the bow for the men and twelve berths at the stern for women. The first steamboat cost $20,000. Fulton and Livingston each provided $8,500; the balance was provided by a loan. The *Clermont* earned $1,000 during her three months of operation in 1807. During the winter of 1807-08, the *North River*, with fifty-four berths, was built with a wider hull to increase stability. She was followed by the *Car of Neptune*, of similar design but larger, and then by the *Paragon*.

In 1808, New York, with a population of 83,000, surpassed Philadelphia as the most populous city in the country. When the Erie Canal was completed in 1825, New York became the undisputed commercial center of the United States. Fulton built twenty-one steamboats to serve the early years of this market; each one incorporated improvements over the previous model.

Although Fulton is frequently called the inventor of the steamboat, he was really the technologist who built the first commercially successful steam-powered vessel. He built and tested models before proceeding with a full-scale project, and he kept detailed records. He didn't invent any of the components of the steamboat; they had all been invented previously. Rather, he combined components that had previously been determined to be successful and made them into a practical, working unit. He had no formal engineering training, but he brought to the task of building a steamboat years of development on submarines and other technical projects.

Fulton designed steamboats for operation on the Ohio and Mississippi Rivers, but he let others make the more powerful boats required for those waterways. He was more successful building ferryboats for use between New Jersey and New York. Increasing numbers of Fulton steamboats were built for the New York-to-Albany run in the second decade of the 1800s. It was a popular trip because the Hudson has high, rocky banks, and most of the north / south roads were distant from the population centers along the river, such as West Point, Beacon, Newburgh, Poughkeepsie, and Kingston. Providing direct access to these and other river towns was economically feasible.

Fulton used various methods of selling shares in his ventures: advertisements, articles in magazines, lectures, pamphlets, and the personal touch. According to the standards of the time, he was a successful marketer. He selected his employees carefully, trained them well, and gave them wage increases to keep them at work on his projects. His real strengths were in combining quality components into a quality system and in selling that system to the public. According to Fulton, "Invention in mechanics consists of a new combination in the mechanical powers, or a new combination of parts of known machines producing thereby a new machine for a new purpose and thus ... forming a machine which has in itself a new character or principle that is ... performing something new and useful."[19]

On February 26, 1813, Chancellor Livingston died at Clermont. Competitors frequently sued Fulton to settle claims, and Livingston's New York monopoly on steamboats was no longer a strong defense. Increasingly, Fulton had to rely on his patents, which weren't strong either.

The U.S. Superintendent of Patents from 1802, when the office was established, until 1828, was Dr. William Thornton—the same Thornton who had been John Fitch's associate in steamboat development. Thornton held a steamboat boiler patent and saw no conflict of interest in granting patents to himself as Superintendent of Patents. The law prevents this practice today. He made suggestions for the improvement of one patent application and then became a co-patentee. Thornton blatantly used his office to promote his personal interests.

Thornton was appointed to the office by his Georgetown next-door neighbor, James Madison, with whom he was joint owner of a racehorse. Thornton considered Fulton's patents worthless. Fulton complained to Secretary of State James Monroe, who was responsible for the Patent Office:

> The case of Dr. Thornton is very simple. If he is an inventor, a genius who can live by his talents, let him do so, but while he is a clerk in an office of the Secretary of State and paid by the public for his services, he should be forbidden to deal in patents, and thereby torment patenters, involving them in vexatious suits. He should have his choice to quit the office or his pernicious practices.[20]

Thornton's written response contained observations on the development of the steamboat:

> Finding that Robert Fulton, whose genius and talents I highly respect, has been considered by some to be the inventor of the steamboat, I think it is a duty to the memory of John Fitch to set forth ... the following of this opinion; and to show moreover, that if Mr. Fulton has any claim whatever to originality in his steamboat, it must be exceedingly limited.[21]

In January 1815, Fulton, who had a cold, accompanied his lawyer to a hearing in a poorly heated hall in New Jersey. His lawyer was working to repeal the New Jersey law that gave a steamboat monopoly to Fulton's competitor. Fulton was his lawyer's chief witness.

The ferry was delayed by bad weather, causing them to wait in the cold for three hours on the New Jersey side of the river. The lawyer fell through the ice into the river while hurrying to the ferry, and Fulton saved his life. However, the exposure and overexertion made Fulton ill. Three days later, he insisted on inspecting one of his boatbuilding projects. On February 24, 1815, Fulton died of pneumonia.

CHAPTER 6

INVENTION OF THE STEAMBOAT

SUCCESS VS. FAILURE—SUMMARY AND ANALYSIS

"If you wish success in life, make perseverance your bosom friend, experience your wise counselor, caution your elder brother, and hope your guardian genius."

Joseph Addison

A comparison of the personal characteristics of John Fitch and Robert Fulton reveals dramatic differences. Fitch, the pure inventor, was a driven introvert who was perseverance personified. He was willing to endure poverty and to depend on the charity of his landlady for meals and a roof over his head. He tolerated ridicule from spectators and criticism from partners who turned against him.

However, Fitch persevered; he even named one of his steamboats *Perseverance*. He was a highly motivated individual who didn't fit the mold of Abraham Maslow's hierarchy of needs. Self-actualization and achievement needs are usually addressed after lower-level needs are fulfilled. Fitch's development work on the steamboat falls into the category of self-actualization and / or achievement needs. He placed satisfying these needs ahead of fulfilling physiological needs such as the need for food, drink, clothing, and shelter. Fitch had no family to give him support and encouragement; he faced his obstacles alone.

By comparison, Robert Fulton was a polished, outgoing individual with important social contacts to help finance and promote his development effort. He was more entrepreneur than inventor; his strength was the modification and packaging of things invented by others. Fulton was well-liked, and he moved in influential circles. He placed success ahead of ethics. He repaid few of his early loans that he used to support his development work; the payments that he made were partial payments.

Fulton's principal goal in developing the submarine and the torpedo was to earn money from them. He didn't care who he sold them to. First, he attempted to sell them to France, who planned to use them against England—and possibly against his native country. Next, he tried to sell them to England for use against France—and, again, potentially against the United States. Finally, after returning to America, he attempted to sell them to the U.S. Government.

Fitch displayed his loyalty to his native country by refusing to sell his steamboat design to Spain. He thought that the United States should have the benefit of his invention. He admitted to having second thoughts on this decision when the "blockheads" in Congress turned him down; in fact, he considered himself a "blockhead," the most negative word in his vocabulary, for turning down the Minister of Spain.

Fulton was clearly a better fund raiser than Fitch. Fitch spent considerable time and effort obtaining letters of recommendation for use in acquiring financial grants from state governments and from the U.S. Government. Merchants, shopkeepers, and tavernkeepers were the shareholders in his joint-stock company. The total subscription of one fund raising effort was $300. Fitch conducted his development on a shoestring and attempted to support himself.

Fulton moved in higher circles than Fitch and had access to people who could afford to sponsor him. He was successful in his fundraising efforts, beginning with his early years in England. He was very willing to be supported by sponsors. After his early years as a painter, he didn't have to support himself. Initially, the Barlows supported him, and then his path was eased by the financial backing of Chancellor Livingston.

Fulton was considerably more effective than Fitch in the areas of marketing and promotion. Fitch spent all of his time looking inward toward the invention, which is typical for an inventor. Fulton spent time and effort on design and construction tasks, but he continued to promote the steamboat. His work was on a larger scale than Fitch's, and he couldn't tolerate gaps in the flow of financing for his effort.

Fulton is also the winner in a comparison of organizational ability. Fitch had difficulty keeping the services of one key assistant. However, much of this difficulty was due to his financial troubles. At one point, his joint-stock company almost removed him from directing the development effort to replace him with Dr. Thornton, his assistant. Fulton was a strong organizer who managed a much larger and more complex organization than Fitch. Fulton had no difficulty in firing a captain when it was required.

Fitch failed and Fulton succeeded, in part, due to factors such as financial acumen, marketing / promotion skills, and organizational ability. However, Fitch failed, and Fulton succeeded, primarily due to strategic factors. Fitch's steamboat couldn't compete with the stagecoach lines running along the Delaware River, particularly on the New Jersey side of the river. He lowered his fares to undercut his land-based competition until he eliminated any profit.

By choosing the Hudson River, with its high cliffs and lack of good roads between the towns along the river, Fulton filled a transportation need. Good roads were located inland from the river, but not along the river. A market existed for transporting people and goods along the route from New York to Albany. Fitch failed because he picked the wrong river; Fulton succeeded because he picked the right one.

If John Fitch's *Perseverance* had raced Robert Fulton's *Clermont* on the Hudson River in 1807, the *Perseverance* would have arrived at Albany about twelve hours before the *Clermont*. However, Fitch carried passengers for only one season with no profits, and Fulton was economically successful in operating multiple passenger boats for a number of years.

TELEPHONE PIONEERS

Invention of the Telephone

CHAPTER 7

PHILIPP REIS

Inventor of the Telephone I

"Did you ever hear of a man who had striven all his life faithfully and singly toward an object and in no measure obtained it? If a man constantly aspires, is he not elevated?"

Henry David Thoreau

Johann Philipp Reis was born on January 7, 1834, in Gelnhausen, Germany. Reis's father was a master baker. His mother died young, and he was raised by his maternal grandmother. He described the influence of his father and his grandmother on his upbringing: "While my father strove constantly to cultivate my mental powers by instruction concerning the things which surrounded me ... my grandmother turned her activity to the development of the religious sentiments to which she was eminently fitted by the experiences of a long life, by being well-read, and especially by her gift of narration."[22]

When Reis entered the Gelnhausen common school, his teachers recognized his intelligence and his academic potential and convinced his father to send him to an institution of higher learning. His father agreed with this plan when Reis passed the middle class of the common school. Unfortunately, Reis's father died before Reis was ten years old. However, his guardian and his grandmother sent him to Garnier's Institute at Friedrichsdorf when he was eleven.

When Reis graduated at the age of fifteen, he enrolled in Hassel's Institute at Frankfort-am-Main, where he developed a serious interest in mathematics and the natural sciences. His strong record at Hassel's Institute confirmed his academic potential. However, Reis's teachers were unable to convince his guardian, who was his uncle, to allow him to continue with his schooling at the Polytechnic School at Karlsruhe. His uncle chose a mercantile career for him. Reis was obedient to his uncle but told him that he would continue his studies later.

In March 1850, Reis began his apprenticeship with the color dye firm of J. F. Beyerbach in Frankfort. He also attended lectures in mechanics at the local trade school and took private lessons in mathematics and physics. When he completed his apprenticeship, he enrolled in Dr. Poppe's Institute in Frankfort.

In 1851, Reis joined the Physical Society of Frankfort and attended their lectures in chemistry and physics as well as their weekly presentations on new discoveries and inventions in astronomy, physical science, and other scientific subjects. Professor Faraday and Sir Charles Wheatstone of Britain and many German scientists were corresponding members and honorary members of the Society.

Reis chose a teaching career and spent the academic year of 1854-55 preparing to become a teacher. The following year, he completed his mandatory military service in Cassel and returned to Frankfort to take education courses, to work in a laboratory, and to attend lectures in mathematics and science. He planned to complete his training as a teacher at the University of Heidelberg. However, in the spring of 1858, his old master, Hofrath Garnier, offered him a position at the Garnier Institute. He accepted the offer because of an "ardent desire to make myself right quickly useful" and began teaching in the fall of 1858. He settled in Friedrichsdorf and was married in September 1859.

In 1858-59, Reis began his first scientific experiments without the guidance of a mentor. He used an electrical source, an electroscope, and a concave mirror in an attempt to prove that electricity could be propagated in air similarly to the propagation of light. Reis submitted a paper, "On the Radiation of Electricity," to Professor Poggendorff for inclusion in his *Annalen der Physik*, but it was rejected.

Other experiments led to his invention of the telephone in 1860. In his words:

> Incited thereto by my lessons in physics in the year 1860, I attacked a work begun much earlier concerning the organs of hearing, and soon had the joy to see my pains awarded with success, since I succeeded in inventing an apparatus, by which it is possible to make clear and evident the functions of the organs of hearing, but with which also one can reproduce tones of all kinds at any desired distance by means of

the galvanic current. I named the instrument "Telephon." The recognition of me on many sides, which as taken place in consequence of this invention, especially the Naturalists' Association ... at Giessen, has continually helped me to quicken my ardor for study, that I may show myself worthy of the luck that has befallen me.[23]

Reis made his first telephones in a small workshop behind his home. He ran wires for his experiments from the workshop to an upstairs room in his house and from the main building of the Garnier Institute to a classroom located across the playground from the main building. His experiments were the first to reproduce sounds at a distance using electromagnetism.

Reis invented "a" telephone; the question is whether or not he invented "the" telephone. The word "telephone" is derived from the Greek words for "far" and "voice." A German writer, Huth, first used the word in 1796 to refer to a megaphone. Sir Charles Wheatstone, the English physicist and telegraph pioneer, used the word in 1840 with its present meaning.

Reis's work was preceded by that of a Frenchman, Charles Bourseul, in 1854. Although Bourseul did some experimentation, he didn't do enough to demonstrate a workable device. His main contribution to the telephone was to advance the theory:

I have asked myself whether speech itself may not be transmitted by electricity—in a word, if what is spoken in Vienna may not be heard in Paris. The thing is practical in this way ... Suppose that a man speaks near a moveable disc sufficiently flexible to lose none of the vibrations of his voice; that the disc alternately makes and breaks the current from a battery;

you may have at a distance another disc which will simultaneously execute the same vibrations ... it is certain that in a more or less distant future, speech that will be transmitted by electricity. I have made some experiments in this direction; they are delicate, and demand time and patience but the approximations obtained promise a favorable result.

A principal difference between the Reis design and the later design of Alexander Graham Bell is that Reis used an intermittent, direct current provided by a battery, and Bell used an uninterrupted, "undulating" current. In Reis's device, the interrupted current didn't vary in strength with the volume of the sound activating the transmitter as the undulating current did in Bell's design.

Reis's design couldn't reproduce the degrees of loudness and the variations in amplitude and frequency that are the components of sound, both of music and of speech. In effect, his equipment could only transmit the pitch and rhythm of the original sound. It was a more limited device than Bell's, but it worked. Reis demonstrated it on many occasions.

Reis's transmitter contained a six-inch-long cone to speak into, which tapered from a diameter of four inches to a diameter of one and a half inches. A collodion membrane was mounted in the smaller diameter end of the cone to move in sympathy with the sound entering the cone. A lightweight lever attached to the membrane made and broke contact with a flat spring that caused an intermittent current to flow through a conducting wire in electrical connection with the lever. The spring's support was connected to one pole of a battery whose other pole was attached to the return wire from the receiver at the distant location.

The receiver was constructed of a resonator that formed a base for an electromagnet connected to the circuit coming from the transmitter. An armature attached to a broad lightweight plate in the field of the electromagnet vibrated as the intermittent current was received from the transmitter. The resulting vibrations of the lightweight plate in the receiver, initially triggered by vibrations in the membrane in the transmitter, were transmitted to the surrounding air and conveyed to the ear of the listener. Vowels were difficult to understand, however, because the device couldn't transmit the amplitude and intensity of the sound—just the pitch and rhythm.

In October 1861, Reis presented his paper "On Telephony by the Galvanic Current" to the Physical Society of Frankfort-am-Main. In addition to describing the design and operation of his telephone, he displayed detailed knowledge of the anatomy and function of the human ear:

> Apart from our ear, every tone is nothing more than the condensation and rarefaction of a body repeated several times in a second (at least seven or eight times). If this occurs in the same medium (the air) as that with which we are surrounded, then the membranes of our ear will be compressed toward the drum-cavity by every condensation, so that in the succeeding rarefaction it moves back in the opposite direction.

> These vibrations occasion a lifting-up and a falling down of the "hammer" upon the "anvil" with the same velocity, or, according to others, occasion an approach and a recession of the atoms of the auditory ossicles, and give rise, therefore, to exactly the same number of concussions in the fluid of the cochlea, in which the auditory nerve and its terminals are spread out. The greater the condensation of the sound-conducting medium at any given moment, the greater will be the amplitude of

the vibration of the membrane and the "hammer," and the more powerful, therefore, the blow on the "anvil" and the concussion of the nerves through the intermediary action of the fluid.

The function of the organs of hearing, therefore, is to impart faithfully to the auditory nerve, every condensation and rarefaction occurring in the surrounding medium. The function of the auditory nerve is to bring our consciousness the vibrations of matter resulting at the given time, both according to their number and magnitude. Here, first, certain combinations acquire a distinct name; here, first, the vibrations become musical tones or discords.

That which is perceived by the auditory nerve is, therefore, merely the action of a force affecting our consciousness, and as such may be represented graphically, according to its duration and magnitude, by a curve [a sine wave].[24]

In November 1861, Reis presented another paper to the Society: "Explanation of a New Theory Concerning the Perception of Chords and of Timbre as a Continuation and Supplement of the Report on the Telephone." In the following month, his paper "On Telephony by the Galvanic Current" was published in the *Jahresbericht*. On May 8, 1862, notice of his invention appeared in *Didaskalia*. Three days later, Reis lectured and demonstrated his telephone to the Free German Institute at Frankfort.

In 1862, Reis forwarded his paper "On Telephony by the Galvanic Current" to Professor Poggendorff, accompanied by letters of testimonial from Professor Bottger of Frankfort and Professor Mueller of Freiburg. The result was the same as before; Professor Poggendorff rejected his paper. Reis thought it was because he was "only a poor schoolmaster." However, his paper was forwarded by Inspector von Legat of the Royal Prussian Telegraphs to the Austro-German Telegraph Society and published in their journal.

In July 1863, Reis demonstrated his telephone to the Physical Society of Frankfort-am-Main. It was also shown to the Emperor of Austria and the King of Bavaria when they visited Frankfort. In February 1864, he exhibited the telephone at a meeting of the Oberhessische Gesellschaft fur Natur und Heilkunde at Giessen. In September 1864, he demonstrated the operation of his telephone to Germany's most distinguished scientists at Giessen at a meeting of the Deutscher Naturforscher and explained its development.

Reis's telephones were sent to laboratories in Germany, as well as in Dublin, London, Manchester, Tiflis, and other locations. Other scientists, such as Dr. P. H. Van der Weyd, lectured on the subject of telephony using Reis's equipment in their demonstrations. Van der Weyd made several improvements to Reis's design.

The Physical Society lost interest in his invention, and Reis resigned his membership in the society in 1867. The Free German Institute in Frankfort elected him an honorary member and then dismissed his invention as a philosophic toy. His welcome by the scientists at Giessen came too late; he was already ill with tuberculosis that would take his life. By 1872, hemorrhaging of the lungs and an almost total loss of voice prevented him from either teaching or experimenting. In 1873, he gave all of his instruments and tools to the Garnier Institute.

Reis's invention didn't receive the promotion and marketing that usually accompany successful products. He considered himself ahead of his time, so he didn't apply for a patent on his invention. Reis confided to Garnier that he "showed the world the way to a great invention, which must now be left for others to develop." Reis died on January 14, 1874. In 1878, the Physical Society of Frankfort erected a monument to him in the Friedrichsdorf Cemetery. The words "Inventor of the Telephone" are inscribed on the monument.

In 1867, Elisha Gray, an American inventor who made significant contributions to the development of the telephone, began experiments in the reproduction and electrical transmission of musical sounds. Gray was familiar with the work of Reis. One of Gray's early designs used a sounding-box receiver with a single Reis-type electromagnet. G. B. Prescott commented on Gray's work in his article, "The Speaking Telephone," in the June 4, 1878, issue of *Scribner's Magazine*:

> In the spring of 1874, Gray, now of Chicago, invented a method of electrical transmission by means of which the intensity of the tones, as well as their pitch, was perfectly reproduced at the receiving station.... Subsequently, he conceived the idea of controlling the formation of what he termed electric waves ... by means of the vibrations of a diaphragm, capable of responding to the sounds of every kind traversing the atmosphere, so arranged as to reproduce these waves at a distance. When this was accomplished, the problem of the transmission and reproduction of articulate speech over an electrical conductor was theoretically solved. This was a very important discovery— in fact, an essential prerequisite to the development of the telephone, both in respect to the reproduction of harmonic musical tones and of articulate speech... [25]

In 1875, Thomas Edison read the 1860 Reis paper "On

Telephony by the Galvanic Current" and conducted his own telephone experiments using a diaphragm and electromagnetism to transmit sound. During the winter of 1876-77, Edison searched for materials whose resistance varied with pressure. He found that carbon was such a material, and he fastened a molded button made of lampblack to a diaphragm for use in a transmitter. In February 1878, he applied for a patent for this transmitter.

Amos Dolbear, who began his experiments with the telephone in August 1876, also benefited from the work of Reis. His transmitter was based on the Reis design, but he substituted carbon for the platinum contact. Dolbear's receiver was of the condenser type (a later design than Reis's) and used a pair of two-inch diameter metallic discs and an induction coil.

Dolbear considered Reis the real inventor of the telephone. In 1883, Professor Silvanus Thompson of University College, Bristol, England, wrote a biography of Reis entitled *Philipp Reis: Inventor of the Telephone*, in which he defended Reis's claim. Dolbear's opinions were discussed by Thompson in that biography:

> Professor Dolbear, the inventor of the "static receiver" form of telephone, is still more explicit in avowing Reis's claim. In the report of his paper on "The Telephone," read March 1882, before the Society of Telegraph Engineers and of Electricians we find: "The speaker could testify that the instrument would talk, and would talk well. The identical instruments employed by Reis would do that, so that Reis's transmitter would transmit. Secondly, his receivers would receive; and Reis did transmit and receive articulate speech with such instruments."

As far as Professor Dolbear is concerned,

therefore, he admits in unequivocal terms the whole claim of Reis to be the inventor of the telephone.[26]

Even after his death, Reis continued to be a significant influence on the development of telephone technology. We can only speculate what he would have accomplished had he lived. Regardless of whether or not he deserves to be called "the" inventor of the telephone, his contribution to its development was crucial. Reis expressed his viewpoint in his autobiographical notes: "As I look back upon my life I can indeed say ... that it has been 'labour and sorrow.' But I have also to thank the Lord that He has given me a blessing in my calling and in my family, and has been known to bestow more good on me than than I have known to ask of Him."[27]

Alexander Graham Bell

CHAPTER 8

ALEXANDER GRAHAM BELL

Inventor of the Telephone II

"Don't keep forever on the public road, going only where others have gone, and following one after the other like a flock of sheep. Leave the beaten track occasionally and dive into the woods. Every time you do so you will be certain to find something that you have never seen before. Of course it will be a little thing, but do not ignore it. Follow it up, explore all around it; one discovery will lead to another, and before you know it you will have something worth thinking about to occupy your mind. All really big discoveries are the results of thought."

Alexander Graham Bell

On March 3, 1847, Alexander Graham Bell, the second of three sons of Alexander Melville Bell and Eliza Symonds Bell, was born in Edinburgh, Scotland. Graham, as he was called in his youth, was the third generation in succession of Alexander Bells. Bell's grandfather Alexander was a Shakespearean actor who knew how to project his voice and to enunciate his lines clearly. After mastering his own speech, his goal in life was to teach others what he had learned, particularly the optimum use of lips, mouth, tongue, and larynx in speech. He gave up acting and moved to London, where he became an instructor of elocution.

Bell's father, Alexander Melville Bell, extended the work of his father by developing "visible speech" and by studying the "anatomy of speech." He studied the use of the lips and tongue in speaking and singing as well as the contribution of breathing and the roof of the mouth to the formation of sounds. He made drawings of the mouth to illustrate how sounds were made in English and other languages. His work was highly regarded; he was a popular teacher of elocution and a university lecturer. His book, *Bell's Standard Elocutionist*, was a best seller.

Bell grew up surrounded by the studies of his father and grandfather and was profoundly influenced by them. He loved music and studied the piano in his early teens. Young Bell taught elocution and music at a boys' school, the Weston House Academy at Elgin, Morayshire, prior to enrolling at the University of Edinburgh. His work with deaf students was rewarding; while still a young man, he decided to spend his life teaching the deaf to speak.

Alexander Ellis, a friend of Bell's father and a specialist in acoustics, familiarized Bell with Hermann von Helmholtz's work in Germany. Helmholtz had used a tuning fork and electromagnets to experiment with vowel sounds by breaking them down into their components. Bell knew about tuning forks from his piano tuner, but electromagnets were a mystery to him. Bell's German wasn't very good; he thought

Helmholtz was writing about telegraphing speech over a single wire. He obtained a translated version of Helmholtz's book and realized his mistake; however, the idea stayed with him and contributed to his understanding of the subject.

While in his early twenties, Bell's older brother, Melville James, and his younger brother, Edward Charles, died of tuberculosis within three years of each other. Bell also had symptoms of the disease. A Canadian friend of his parents suggested that the dry cold of southern Ontario would be a better climate for their surviving son than the damp cold of London. Bell's father had to leave many professional contacts developed over the years, but he didn't hesitate. In August 1870, the family moved to Brantford, Ontario.

Away from the dampness and fog of London, Bell regained his health and was happy in the home on Tutelo Heights overlooking the Grand River. He did much of his dreaming and thinking in a sunken spot shaped like a sofa in the lawn near the orchard. In later years, when asked where his ideas originated, he acknowledged that on many occasions inspiration came to him while he sat in his "sofa seat."

Sarah Fuller, principal of the Boston School for the Deaf, heard that Alexander Melville Bell had immigrated to Canada and invited him to teach his visible speech concepts to her instructors. He declined because he had accepted a position with a Canadian university; however, he informed Miss Fuller that his son was trained in his concepts and would like to come to Boston in his place. Bell started his assignment at the Boston School in April 1871 at the age of twenty-three. He was successful from the beginning, not only because of his knowledge of visible speech, but also because of his patience and deep concern for the children.

Fathers of two deaf children asked Bell for special help with their daughter and son. Mabel, the daughter of Cambridge lawyer Gardiner Hubbard, had lost her hearing at age four from scarlet fever. She seemed to have regressed in her ability to talk since then. Boston had no schools for the deaf, so Hubbard could either send her to Germany to learn the "oral method" of speaking or enroll her in the American Asylum in Hartford, Connecticut, to learn sign language. He sent Mabel to Germany where she learned to speak, not well, but well enough to be understood.

Thomas Sanders's five-year-old son, George, had been born deaf. The wealthy businessman asked Bell to educate his son and arranged for Bell to board with them. In addition to his assignment at the Boston School, Bell was professor of vocal physiology in the School of Oratory at Boston University and director of his own School of Vocal Physiology and Mechanics of Speech.

Fortunately, Bell had boundless energy and was able to do several tasks in parallel; also, he didn't require much sleep. When he wasn't teaching, Bell experimented with electrical equipment. Electricity was a popular subject in the 1870s, and the young teacher educated himself in the subject. Hubbard and Sanders didn't understand Bell's experiments, but they were so grateful for the progress their children made under his tutelage that they offered to pay for his laboratory work.

Bell was extremely fortunate to have the part-time services of a bright, young technician, Thomas Watson, to make equipment for him. Watson worked in Boston at the shop of Charles Williams, who made experimental equipment for tinkerers and serious inventors. Williams also repaired annunciators, barometers, compasses, galvanometers, gauges, magnets, and relays. Williams and his staff provided equipment for chemical, electrical, and mechanical experiments, but their speciality was electricity. Williams's workmen weren't specialists; they were expected to be familiar with all equipment. Bell was given a workbench at Williams's shop.

Watson was unsuccessful in his first assignment for Bell, who was attempting to develop a harmonic telegraph device to send multiple messages simultaneously over a wire. In this experiment, electromagnets triggered tuning fork vibrations that were transmitted by electric current to tuning forks at the

other end of the wire. Electric current would then be interrupted by the dots and dashes of a telegraph key. Each fork at
the receiving end was supposed to vibrate in sympathy with
only its counterpart at the sending end; thus multiple messages could be sent simultaneously. Later designs used steel
springs or reeds instead of tuning forks. Unfortunately, none
of the early designs worked.

Bell adapted the device to use an undulatory or wave current, instead of an interrupted direct current. He intended to
use an "induced" current, as described by scientists Michael
Faraday and Joseph Henry—one that would be alternately a
strong and a weak current. Bell described his idea to Watson
when his tired assistant was at the end of a sixteen-hour day;
the young technician was concerned that he was too weary to
generate interest in Bell's latest scheme. Instead, Watson's
"nervous system got such a shock that the tired feeling van-
ished."

Bell told Watson that "If I can get a mechanism which will
make a current of electricity vary in intensity, as the air varies
in density when a sound is passing through it, I can telegraph
any sound, even the sound of speech."[28] Bell provided
Watson with diagrams of the apparatus he had in mind.
Unfortunately, Bell's sponsors, Hubbard and Sanders, wanted
him to continue to develop the harmonic telegraph. Bell and
Watson were unable to send and receive multiple messages
simultaneously. However, Bell couldn't get his idea out of his
head.

Bell's work with deaf students was excellent preparation
for his experimentation. He had studied the human ear and
realized that air waves striking the eardrum were converted to
impulses that the brain interpreted as sound.

Bell used two instruments in his experiments in visible
speech that helped him develop the telephone. The manomet-
ric capsule was a box divided by a stretched membrane. A
speaking tube was attached to the box on one side of the
membrane, and on the other side was a gas-filled chamber

with a pipe leading to a gas flame whose height varied as one spoke into the speaking tube.

The phonautograph sketched vibrations of the membrane using a bristle attached to a lightweight wooden arm connected to the membrane. Lines made by the bristle on a smoked pane of glass were photographed. Bell tried to use these two instruments in his work with his students, but the concepts were too complicated for them. Nevertheless, the experiments were invaluable to him in evolving a design for a working telephone.

Bell admitted his lack of knowledge about electricity when he visited Joseph Henry, the secretary of the Smithsonian Institution and the discoverer of induction. Bell described his experiments to Henry, who asked if he could repeat Bell's experiments and have the Smithsonian Institution publish the results. Bell conducted the experiments for Henry, who "thought it was 'the germ of a great invention' and advised me to work at it myself instead of publishing. I said that I recognized the fact that there were mechanical difficulties.... I felt that I had not the electrical knowledge necessary to overcome the difficulties. His laconic answer was 'Get it.' I cannot tell you how much these two words have encouraged me...."[29]

Bell returned to Boston to prepare a patent application for a harmonic telegraph that could not only send multiple telegraphic signals on a single line simultaneously but also musical tones. Lawyers assisting him with his patent application suggested that he obtain patents on all of the novel devices he was using in his experiments.

The moment of epiphany occurred on the afternoon of June 2, 1875. Bell and Watson were working in two rooms sixty feet apart on the top floor of Williams's shop. Watson was working with the transmitters in one room; Bell was adjusting the receivers in the other room. The garret was hot, and the experiment wasn't going well. Watson's temper was rising, and his enthusiasm was dropping. Bell, as usual, was full of energy. In Watson's words:

> One of the transmitter springs I was attending
> to stopped vibrating and I plucked it to start it
> again. It didn't start and I kept plucking it,
> when suddenly I heard a shout from Bell in the
> next room, and then he came out with a rush,
> demanding "What did you do then? Don't
> change anything. Let me see!" I showed him.
> It was very simple. The contact screw was
> screwed down so far that it made permanent
> contact with the spring so that when I snapped
> the spring the circuit had remained unbroken
> while that strip of magnetized steel by its
> vibration over the pole of its magnet was gen-
> erating that marvelous conception of Bell's—
> a current of electricity that varied in intensity
> precisely as the air was varying in density
> within hearing distance of the spring.
>
> That undulatory current had passed through
> the connecting wire to the distant receiver
> which, fortunately, was a mechanism that
> could transform that current back into an
> extremely faint echo of the sound of the vibrat-
> ing spring that had generated it, but what was
> still more fortunate, the right man had that
> mechanism at his ear during that fleeting
> moment, and instantly recognized the tran-
> scendent importance of that faint sound thus
> electrically transmitted. The shout I heard and
> his excited rush into my room were the result
> of that recognition. The speaking telephone
> was born at that moment.... All the experi-
> menting that followed that discovery, up to the
> time the telephone was put into practical use,

was largely a matter of working out the details.[30]

The breakthrough was, to an extent, the result of an accident. The contact screw was screwed down so far that it made permanent contact with the spring, allowing the circuit to remain unbroken and an "undulatory" current of varying intensity to move from the transmitter to the receiver. Another year of experimentation was required before they could send the first clear sentence over the wire.

Initially, the undulatory current was too weak. Bell strengthened it by designing a plunger that moved vertically in a container of weak sulphuric acid activated by an arm attached to a diaphragm that expanded and contracted when spoken into. On February 14, 1876, he filed his application for a patent accompanied by a diagram of his device; the patent was granted on March 7, 1876.

On March 10, Bell was setting up the equipment for an experiment when he spilled some of the weak sulphuric acid on his clothes. He knew that even though it was diluted, it could burn a hole in his clothing if it wasn't washed off quickly. He summoned Watson to help, saying, "Mr. Watson, come here, I want to see you."[31] Watson heard him in the next room on the receiver. The first complete sentence transmitted over a telephone line wasn't as memorable as Samuel Morse's first message on the telegraph: "What hath God wrought?" However, Bell's message wasn't contrived; it was an unrehearsed request.

Frequently, inventors encounter resistance to the acceptance of their discoveries. Bell encountered considerable resistance; many people couldn't see the practical use of his invention. However, timing worked to his advantage. On May 10, 1876, the Centennial Exhibition, commemorating the hundredth year of the America's independence, opened in Philadelphia; forty-nine countries participated in the Exhibition. President Grant asked Emperor Dom Pedro of

Brazil to help him pull the levers to start the impressive Corliss steam engine in the Machinery Building to open the Exhibition.

Bell was invited to display his invention at the Exhibition, but he arrived in Philadelphia too late to be included in the electrical exhibit section. Bell was stuck in a corner of the main building alongside a Swedish glass exhibit. His exhibit didn't receive any attention until Emperor Dom Pedro saw him. The Emperor had met Bell in Boston; he was not only familiar with visible speech, but also he had introduced it in Brazil's schools.

Emperor Dom Pedro showed Bell's display to the committee of judges, including President Barnard of Columbia University, Joseph Henry of the Smithsonian Institution, and Professor James Watson of the University of Michigan. The committee, particularly the chairman, British scientist Sir William Thompson (Lord Kelvin), was impressed with Bell's telephone exhibit. Newspaper reports quoted Lord Kelvin liberally and were extremely favorable. Bell won Centennial prizes for both the multiple telegraph and the telephone.

Bell conducted one of the first successful one-way distance conversations on the telephone between his parents' home in Brantford, Ontario, and the neighboring town of Mt. Pleasant. Earlier experiments between Boston and New York and between Boston and Rye Beach hadn't been successful. The first successful two-way conversation between Boston and Cambridge was followed by a two-way conversation over a sixteen-mile-long line between Boston and Salem.

Bell and his former student, Mabel Hubbard, became engaged shortly after the Exhibition in Philadelphia. Mabel's intelligence helped to minimize the handicap of her deafness. Her training in Germany and in visible speech permitted her to communicate effectively. They were very much in love, and Bell wouldn't have participated in the Centennial Exhibition without prodding from Mabel. Bell, ever the inventor, thought he should stay in Boston to develop the equipment further. Bell said, "I was not much alive to commercial matters. So I went to Philadelphia, growling all the time at this interruption."

When the telephone became commercially successful, Bell and Mabel set their wedding date, July 11, 1877. They were married in Cambridge, honeymooned at Niagara Falls, and visited Bell's parents in Brantford before returning home.

On July 9, 1877, Bell and his partners formed the Bell Telephone Company, dividing 5,000 shares of stock. Bell gave all but ten of his shares to Mabel as a wedding present. When the newlyweds returned to Boston three weeks later, 600 telephones were in use, and Williams's shop was producing twenty-five a day.

Bell and Mabel went to England to promote the telephone there. In October 1877, he lectured at a meeting of the Society of Telegraph Engineers in London. He also lectured on visible speech at Oxford University and was awarded an honorary degree. His effort to promote the telephone in Britain was successful in terms of disseminating information, but it wasn't commercially successful. Bell hadn't filed a patent in Britain, and an English Company used Bell's patents to produce telephones there. Technically, his patent wasn't infringed upon, but it cost Bell and his associates substantial loss of revenue.

The first telephone exchanges were established in New Haven, New York, and Philadelphia. As the Bell Telephone Company grew, revenue didn't increase fast enough to finance growth. The Company offered to sell the Bell patents to the Western Union Telegraph Company for $100,000. William Orton, president of Western Union, answered their offer with a question: "What use would this company make of an electrical toy?"

Later, Western Union answered their own question by convincing Professor Dolbear, owner of a competing design, to assign his telephone patent to their company. Western Union also purchased licenses to Elisha Gray's and Thomas Edison's telephone patents and organized the New England Telephone Company to enter the telephone business. In September 1878, Bell filed suit for infringement, beginning eighteen years of litigation; he didn't lose a suit.

On a business trip, Gardiner Hubbard met a young man employed by the U.S. Post Office, Theodore Vail, whom Hubbard chose to guide the expansion of the Bell Telephone Company. Vail had made many improvements in the postal service; his organizing strengths were immediately obvious as the new general manager of the Bell Company. He standardized the equipment, implemented policies and procedures for running the organization, and rejected selling the patents. Vail insisted on receiving royalties from the independent telephone companies established around the country.

The Bell Company considered the Edison transmitter used in Western Union's telephones superior to theirs. Vail bought an improved transmitter designed by Francis Blake, whom he paid with stock in the Bell Company. Bell continually strived to improve its designs.

Litigation in the courts dragged on. George Gifford, Western Union's patent attorney, advised company management that they couldn't win their suit against Bell. Finally, Frank Pope, senior electrical scientist for Western Union, suggested buying the Bell patents instead of suing Bell for infringement of the Elisha Gray patents.

The agreement reached by the two companies astounded everyone. Western Union agreed to recognize the Bell patents and retire from the telephone business; Bell bought the Western Union telephone system (55,000 telephones in fifty-five cities) and consented to stay out of the telegraph business. Bell paid Western Union twenty percent of all telephone rentals because of its subsidiary, the Western Electric Manufacturing Company. Bell bought that subsidiary from Western Union and renamed it the Western Electric Company in 1882, the year that Bell became a naturalized U.S. citizen.

Bell wasn't a businessman. His principal interests were

working with deaf children and inventing. His associate, Thomas Watson, observed, "Bell was a pure scientist. Making money out of his idea never seemed to concern him particularly." The Bells bought a large property near Baddeck, Nova Scotia, and built a hilltop vacation house, which they named Beinn Bhreagh ("beautiful mountain" in Scottish Gaelic). Beginning in 1893, the Bells lived in Washington, D.C., during the winter and at Beinn Bhreagh the rest of the year.

Bell had a lifelong interest in flight, and he frequently experimented with kites. In 1905, he built a kite large enough to carry a passenger into the air. Two years later, he founded the Aerial Experimental Association with four other men interested in flying. The Association built and tested four airplanes at Beinn Bhreagh. The first pilot to fly was Tom Selfridge in the *Red Wing*. Another member, Glenn Curtiss of Hammondsport, New York, built the *June Bug*, with which he won a prize from *Scientific American* by flying over one kilometer in a flight witnessed by the public.

Bell suffered from diabetes in his later years. As he lay dying after a prolonged illness, Mabel said to him, "Don't leave me." Bell was unable to speak, but he signed the word "no" and passed away.

Bell died on August 1, 1922, at the age of seventy-five. All telephone service was suspended for one minute that day in his memory. Mabel died five months later. Bell was buried on the hilltop at Beinn Bhreagh. Inscribed on his headstone are the words "Citizen of the United States and Teacher of the Deaf." No reference to the invention of the telephone was inscribed.

CHAPTER 9

INVENTION OF THE TELEPHONE

SUCCESS VS. FAILURE—SUMMARY AND ANALYSIS

"Somebody said it couldn't be done, but he with a chuckle replied that 'maybe it couldn't,' but he would be one who wouldn't say no 'til he tried."

Edward Albert Guest

Philipp Reis and Alexander Graham Bell were pure inventors who weren't interested in the business aspects of financing, marketing, and promoting their invention. Reis was an introvert who worked alone. He had neither a technician to assist him nor a sponsor. Bell had both.

Reis and Bell were highly motivated individuals. However, Reis was burdened by the lack of recognition for his development efforts. Initially, Reis's work received some attention, but, eventually, the local technical society lost interest. He began to think that his work was premature, that he was ahead of his time, and that others would have to carry his work to its completion.

During the last two years of his life, Reis was unable to work or to talk. He was only forty-one when he died. One wonders what he might have accomplished had he lived. He persevered in his efforts, but he lost his drive toward the end of his life. Without the treatment available today, tuberculosis was usually a progressive disease, which provides at least a partial explanation. He wasn't around in the late 1870s when interest in the telephone increased exponentially.

Bell came from a family of achievers. His father and grandfather, experts in speech and hearing, influenced him greatly. Family friends, such as Ellis with his interest in acoustics, provided Bell with built-in consulting support. Bell was a well-liked extrovert. He was the type of individual who could have been a superior marketer and promoter, but those weren't his priorities. His interests were the inventor's interests of developing and improving the product. He even begrudged the time taken to attend the Centennial Exhibition in Philadelphia where the exposure his exhibit received significantly increased public interest in the telephone.

Reis's principal shortcomings were his inability to market and promote his ideas on the development of the telephone. He couldn't convince the scientific community of the value of his invention. Inventors are usually the ones who push their concepts the hardest. Reis was unsuccessful in doing this, even though he was able to demonstrate his device successfully.

Reis's development work was on such a small scale that he didn't need large amounts of money to finance it. He financed his work out of his teacher's salary. His family had to live on less to support his work. The highly energetic Bell always had several jobs at one time, and initially he financed his own work. As the demands for development funds increased, Bell was fortunate to have the support of Hubbard and Sanders.

However, they wanted him to develop the multiple telegraph instead of the telephone; he resisted their pressure to work on the telegraph. His focus on the development of the telephone wouldn't allow him to place that effort second. He couldn't push his ideas about transmitting sound along a wire to the back of his mind, so he persevered in developing a telephone that worked.

Neither Reis nor Bell can be evaluated on their organizational ability. Reis worked alone, and when an individual was needed to manage the Bell Telephone Company, Vail was recruited for the job. Bell had no interest in the position, and his mentor, Hubbard, knew better than to push the job on him. Hubbard made the correct decision in hiring Vail for the position.

Reis's contributions to the development of the telephone can't be considered a failure. His small-scale effort was one of the key steps along the way in the evolution of the telephone. His contributions would have been even greater had he been a stronger promoter and had lived longer. He didn't consider himself a failure.

Again, we can ask what are the criteria for success. Financially, Reis wasn't successful in his development work, since he received no income from it. Nevertheless, he contributed to society, and he considered himself a success.

Bell was a success by any yardstick by which success is measured. He was financially secure. He received worldwide recognition and many honorary degrees. He was a successful family man, and his work with deaf children ranked him high as a teacher and as a humanitarian. Bell's motivation and perseverance were two components of his success. He knew that his idea was a breakthrough, and he wouldn't give up until he had demonstrated that his invention was practicable.

REVOLUTIONARY DEVELOPMENT

Introduction of the Mainframe Computer

CHAPTER 10

JOHN MAUCHLY / PRESPER ECKERT

Developers of the UNIVAC

"The secret of the true love of work is the hope of success in that work; not for the money reward, for the time spent, or for the skill exercised, but for the successful result in the accomplishment of the work itself."

Sidney A. Weltmer

John Mauchly and Presper Eckert were two key members of the team that designed and built the ENIAC, the first electronic digital computer, at the Moore School of Electrical Engineering at the University of Pennsylvania during World War II. Computers had been developed earlier, such as Vannevar Bush's Differential Analyzer in the 1930s at M.I.T., an analog machine designed to solve differential equations. In 1944, Howard Aiken's Automatic Sequence Controlled Calculator (ASCC), also called Mark I, was completed at Harvard University. It was the first automatic digital computer, but it wasn't electronic. It was electromechanical; its design relied heavily on relays.

John Mauchly was born on August 30, 1907, in Cincinnati, Ohio. In 1916, his family moved to Washington, D.C., when his father was appointed chief of the Section of Terrestrial Electricity and Magnetism at the Carnegie Institution. In 1925, Mauchly enrolled at Johns Hopkins University in Baltimore in electrical engineering. In September 1927, he was awarded a state scholarship in the graduate school of physics, from which he graduated with a doctorate in 1932. In 1933, he was appointed head of the department of physics at Ursinus College in Collegeville, Pennsylvania.

At Ursinus, he conducted research on the calculation of energy levels and in meteorology. His assistants manipulated weather data using adding machines. Mauchly knew that electronics was the key to faster computing, but he couldn't afford the components to build an electronic computer. However, he built a gas-tube counter that operated at a rate of 500 calculations per second; he also built a harmonic analyzer, which was an analog device.

In 1942, Mauchly joined the faculty of the Moore School of Electrical Engineering at the University of Pennsylvania. The Moore school had used a differential analyzer to solve differential equations since the mid-1930s, and Mauchly hoped that he would be asked to help develop the next generation of computers. He met Presper Eckert at the Moore

School; they shared a common interest in developing an electronic computer. During 1942, they compared notes on the theory and application of an advanced computer.

Presper Eckert was born on April 9, 1919, in Philadelphia; his father was a building contractor and real estate developer. Eckert attended the William Penn Charter School in Germantown and the Moore School of the University of Pennsylvania. When he graduated in 1941, he accepted a teaching position at the Moore School where he did applied development work in measuring the concentration of napthalene vapor using ultraviolet light, in determining the fatigue limit in metals, and in measuring the strength of small magnetic fields. In June 1943, he received a M.S. in electrical engineering from the Moore School and accepted a position working for John Mauchly.

Computation needs increased dramatically in early World War II. The U.S. Army Ordnance Department's Aberdeen Proving Ground in Maryland received requests for six new ballistics tables per day; each table required the calculation of hundreds of trajectories. Scientists from Aberdeen used the Moore School's differential analyzer, which had reached the limit of its usefulness. Mauchly and Eckert pushed for the development of an electronic digital computer. Many scientists advised against the use of vacuum tubes for reliability reasons. Mauchly prepared a five-page memorandum, "The Use of High-Speed Vacuum Tube Devices for Calculating," for Dr. John Brainerd, director of research at the Moore School.

Specialists spent seven hours at a desk calculator to compute a single trajectory for a ballistic table. The Aberdeen Proving Ground's liaison with the Moore School, Lt. Herman Goldstine, had been challenged by his superior, Col. Paul Gillon, to reduce ballistics calculation time. Enthusiastic about Mauchly's proposal for developing an electronic computer, Goldstine convinced the Army Ordnance Department to fund the project on April 9, 1943; expenditure of $400,000 was authorized for the development of the Electronic Numerical Integrator and Computer (ENIAC).

A development team of fifty was formed. Mauchly, although he had a full teaching load, directed the project, and Eckert was the chief engineer. Eckert increased the reliability of the vacuum tubes by operating them below their rated voltages. Building ENIAC required 200,000 man-hours over a thirty-month period. It had forty nine-foot-high panels that occupied 1,500 square feet of floor space, weighed thirty tons, and contained 17,468 vacuum tubes, 10,000 capacitors, 70,000 resistors, 1,500 relays, 6,000 switches, and 500,000 solder joints. The electronic ENIAC was much faster than the electromechanical Mark I developed at Harvard.

Even before ENIAC was completed, Mauchly and Eckert planned improvements for the next machine, particularly increased memory and faster input / output. In the fall of 1944, the U.S. Army Ballistics Laboratory funded the development of the Electronic Discrete Variable Automatic Computer (EDVAC). EDVAC, unlike the decimal-based ENIAC, was based on the binary numbering system.

In 1944, Goldstine informed mathematician John Von Neumann of the work of Mauchly and Eckert. Von Neumann was a member of the Institute for Advanced Study at Princeton and a consultant to the Army Ordnance Department. Von Neumann supported computer development enthusiastically and participated in the development of EDVAC. Von Neumann promoted the "stored program" for EDVAC instead of ENIAC-type wired electrical panels to provide the program instructions.

Because the development of the ENIAC was classified and was completed on an army contract during wartime, no patent applications were made. In 1944, Mauchly and Eckert decided to apply for a patent for ENIAC. Dean Pender of the Moore School told them that the University of Pennsylvania had no formal patent policy and suggested that they hire their own patent attorney. On September 27, 1944, Eckert told the other engineers on the project of their intentions and asked them to notify him of their patentable contributions.

On June 30, 1945, Von Neumann's paper, "First Draft of a Report on the EDVAC," was received at the Moore School. It contained an explanation of all of the thinking at the University of Pennsylvania about the next computer, including a discussion of its stored, programmable memory, but contained no reference to Moore School contributions.

Goldstine distributed copies of the paper to scientists around the United States and in Great Britain. Mauchly and Eckert hadn't published a paper about their work because ENIAC was still classified. Furthermore, their application for a patent could be affected by Von Neumann publishing first, even though they had an agreement signed by the president of the University of Pennsylvania granting them the ENIAC patents.

The new director of research at the Moore School decided that Mauchly and Eckert should sign over their patents for ENIAC to the University. When they objected, they were told that it was a requirement for their continued employment by the School. In a single stroke, the new research director required university scientists to give up all of their rights to an invention, caused the university to lose millions of dollars in licensing fees and royalties, and eliminated the Moore School's lead in computer science.

Mauchly and Eckert received offers to join IBM, but they were concerned about making the transition to a large corporation and the loss of independence in their development efforts. Instead, they formed a partnership and sought government funding for development of an EDVAC-like computer. They lost a contract to add rudimentary storage capability to ENIAC, even though they were the most qualified individuals to perform the work.

Mauchly and Eckert had difficulty raising money for their partnership, the Electronic Control Company, to develop the next generation of electronic digital computers. Eckert's father invested $25,000; friends around the Philadelphia area contributed "a few hundred thousand." Eckert named the new machine the "Universal Automatic Computer (UNIVAC)." Their lawyer assured them that, although UNIVAC was the name of an English vacuum cleaner and an adhesive for false teeth, there should be no legal problems.

Mauchly and Eckert signed a fixed-price contract to develop a computer for the Census Bureau and the National Bureau of Standards for $255,000, even though their estimated cost was $400,000. To raise money for their fledgling company, Mauchly and Eckert signed a $100,000 contract with Northrop Aircraft to build a general purpose computer called Binary Automatic Computer (BINAC) for use with the Snark missile. Unfortunately, this contract cost them $278,000 and diverted them from working on UNIVAC.

The Eckert-Mauchly Computing Corporation (EMCC) was incorporated by Eckert and Mauchly, who received 6,750 shares worth $1.00 each. They tried unsuccessfully to obtain funding from a venture capital firm. Eckert was responsible for the technical part of the company; Mauchly managed the business side.

Eckert and Mauchly needed a financial "angel," and they found one in Henry Straus of the American Totalizator Company, manufacturer of parimutuel betting machines for thoroughbred tracks. American Totalizator needed computers to calculate the odds, total the bets, and compute the winnings at horse races.

Straus paid $500,000 for forty percent of EMCC stock; unfortunately, he was killed in a plane crash, and EMCC had to find other sources of income. EMCC incurred cash flow problems and applied unsuccessfully for a loan from the Reconstruction Finance Corporation.

Demand for computers was created when Congress passed the Guertin Act, which required the computation of more complex actuarial tables. Prudential Insurance initially paid EMCC $20,000 for consulting and ordered a $150,000 UNI-

VAC. Nevertheless, orders from Prudential, from A. C. Nielsen Company, and from a few other customers weren't enough to save the company.

On February 1, 1950, James Rand of Remington Rand purchased American Totalizator's shares of EMCC stock and established the company as an independent subsidiary. Mauchly and Eckert each received $70,000 for their patents and $18,000 per year in salary. Their lawyers encouraged them to take Remington Rand's offer, which wasn't favorable to them. Mauchly became director of UNIVAC applications research for Remington Rand, and Eckert was appointed director of engineering for the UNIVAC Division.

In March 1951, the first UNIVAC was delivered to the Census Bureau. By the end of 1952, UNIVAC I was a huge success, and Rand knew that he had made a good decision in buying EMCC. Remington Rand sold the only commercial general-purpose electronic digital computer in the world, owned the principal computer patents, and employed several of the world's foremost computer scientists.

However, the slumbering giant, IBM, was awakening to the threat of competition in the calculator / computer business. In 1951, IBM hired Von Neumann as a consultant. Early work on model 600 electronic calculators was followed by the IBM 701, the first IBM electronic computer. The machine sold well, even though its design wasn't state of the art like the UNIVAC. The first IBM commercial computer, the IBM 702, which followed the scientific IBM 701, was also technologically inferior to the UNIVAC.

Dissension slowed research and development at Remington Rand. Its marketing organization, notably inferior to IBM's, was comprised of shaver and typewriter salesmen who weren't trained in computers. Remington Rand salesmen weren't concerned that they didn't understand their product. In 1953, UNIVAC was the only commercial computer. By 1955, IBM made over fifty percent of the computers sold in the United States, and Remington Rand's share had dropped below forty percent. Remington Rand never regained the lead.

Mauchly and Eckert didn't benefit from their ENIAC patents to the extent they should have. They delayed too long in filing their patent application in 1947, and it wasn't well written. In 1952, the federal government filed an antitrust suit against IBM. IBM lost, and the resulting consent degree required IBM to permit any competitor to receive a license to build computers as long as IBM was paid.

Remington Rand filed a brief requesting complete access to IBM patents. IBM attorneys countered by demanding access to ENIAC and UNIVAC patents by offering a cross-licensing agreement and $2 million if Remington Rand would drop its suit. Remington Rand's attorneys were outmaneuvered by IBM's and agreed to cross-licensing. Remington Rand patents were far more important to IBM than IBM patents were to Remington Rand. As a result, IBM obtained access to Remington Rand's superior technology.

IBM agreed to pay royalties of one percent for all machines built after October 1, 1956. Because Remington Rand considered these payments "damages," not royalties, and payments were spread out over a long period of time, Mauchly and Eckert each received only $300,000 for their patents.

Mauchly left Remington Rand, which in 1955 had merged with Sperry Gyroscope to become Sperry Rand, in 1959 to form a computer consulting firm, Mauchly Associates. Eckert became vice president and director of research of Sperry Rand in 1955, and vice president and technical advisor for computer systems in 1963.

Although Eckert and Mauchly didn't receive substantial sums for their development efforts, they were the recipients of many awards. In the early 1960s, they received the John Scott Medal for "adding to the comfort, welfare and happiness of mankind." In February 1965, Eckert and Mauchly were given the Institute of Electrical and Electronic Engineers

Philadelphia Section Award for "their fundamental concepts and contributions to electronic computers," and in 1966, they received the Harry Goode Award for "contributions to, and pioneering efforts in, automatic computing."

In May 1964, Eckert received an honorary degree of doctor of science in engineering from the University of Pennsylvania and was awarded the National Medal of Science in 1969. Mauchly's consulting firm, Mauchly Associates, became Scientific Resources, which wasn't financially successful.

On October 19, 1973, Judge Earl R. Larson ruled against Mauchly and Eckert as well as Remington Rand in the ENIAC patent suit. Judge Larson decided that the original patent was invalid because ENIAC was used in hydrogen bomb development work for over a year before the patent was applied for. A patent application must be made within a year of the existence of the invention. Larson also claimed that Mauchly and Eckert had learned the concepts of the computer from John Vincent Antanasoff.

Antanasoff, an Iowa State College mathematician and physicist, developed a protype of a computer in 1939 with the help of Clifford Barry, a graduate student in electrical engineering. Their prototype was the first machine to perform arithmetic calculations electronically. Their goal was to develop a device to solve differential equations.

Antanasoff and Berry didn't assemble a complete working computer. Later, it was claimed that they "had succeeded in designing and building an electronic computer whose computing system worked." However, the binary card input device didn't work.

Isaac Aurerbach, who publicized Antanasoff's work thirty years later, provided a more accurate description of his invention: "Antanasoff built pieces. They talked about components of the computer. He built a memory drum; he built arithmetic units. He never built a computer ... it was never assembled into a computer. Antanasoff joined the legions of inventors

105

who were close to success but never achieved it."[32]

Bitter about the treatment that he and Eckert had received with respect to their patents, Mauchly suffered from poor health in his later years. Mauchly and Eckert may not have received the financial remuneration that they deserved for their development work, but their place in history is assured.

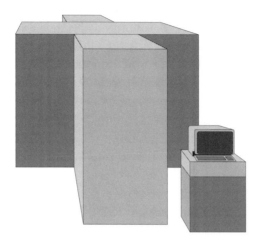

CHAPTER 11

THOMAS J. WATSON

Founder of IBM Corporation

"Within us all there are wells of thought and dynamics of energy which are not suspected until emergencies arise. Then oftentimes we find that it is comparatively simple to double or treble our former capacities and to amaze ourselves by the results achieved. Quotas, when set for us by others, are challenges which goad us on to surpass ourselves. The outstanding leaders of every age are those who set up their own quotas and constantly exceed them. The great accomplishments of man have resulted from the transmission of ideas and enthusiasm."

Thomas J. Watson

Thomas J. Watson, founder of the IBM Corporation, was born on February 17, 1874, in Campbell, New York, the first of five children of Thomas Watson and Jane White Watson. Watson's father, who was in the lumber business, wanted his son to study law. Watson didn't want to pursue a legal career; he applied for a temporary teaching certificate for three years and enrolled at the Albany Teachers' College. However, one day of teaching changed his mind: "I can't go into a classroom with a bunch of children at nine o'clock in the morning and stay until four."[33]

Watson enrolled at the Miller School of Commerce in Elmira, New York, and, in May 1892, completed the accounting and business program. He accepted a position as a bookkeeper in Painted Post, New York, but soon decided that "I couldn't sit on a high stool and keep books all my life."[34] He formed opinions early about what he didn't want to do, but he wasn't yet sure what he wanted to do.

Willard Bronson, a neighbor of the Watsons, operated a hardware store and consignment business. Bronson acquired Estey organs, pianos, and sewing machines and sold them on consignment from a wagon. Watson went on the road selling for Bronson; it was the first of his many sales jobs.

Watson learned the importance of a neat appearance and of making a good first impression. He sold for Bronson for two years without a raise and without many kind words of encouragement from his boss. Bronson was astounded when Watson quit after two years. Only then did Bronson offer him a raise; he even offered to sell him the business. Watson's father advised his son to find a position outside the region. He suggested the Buffalo area.

Watson accepted a position selling sewing machines for the Wheeler and Wilson Company in Buffalo. After a short time, he lost his job, not because of any shortcoming on his part, but because they had too many salesman. C. B. Barron, a coworker who lost his position at the same time, accepted a job selling shares in the Buffalo Building and Loan

Association and invited Watson to join him. Watson sold shares in the Building and Loan Association until Barron ran off with all of the building and loan funds, including Watson's commissions.

Watson applied for a job with the National Cash Register Company (NCR) and met the manager of the Buffalo office, John J. Range. Range wasn't interested in hiring him, but Watson persisted until he did. Watson made no sales during the first two weeks, and Range made his disappointment clear. Watson absorbed Range's constructive criticism and, within a year, was one of the most successful NCR salesmen in the East. By the time he was twenty-five, Watson was the top salesman in the Buffalo office.

John Henry Patterson, chief executive officer of NCR, made the cash register virtually indispensible to businessmen and then monopolized its manufacture and distribution. Patterson was a successful manager because he combined paternalism with an emphasis on training. He realized that salesmen responded to the fear of punishment and the promise of reward. Patterson knew just how hard he could push Watson. He became the shaper of Watson's life over the next eleven years.

In the summer of 1899, Patterson promoted Watson to manager of the Rochester office. Watson moved the sales of the Rochester branch from near the bottom of all NCR's offices to sixth from the top within several months. He used ruthless techniques to beat his main competitor, the Hallwood Company, and his performance was followed closely by Hugh Chalmers, the Company's general manager, and by Patterson.

NCR had between eighty and ninety-five percent of the sales of new cash registers. Patterson decided to be aggressive in reducing the impact of sales of used cash registers. Patterson gave Watson $1 million to set up a company to front for NCR in driving out used cash register competition in the United States. When told by his son that he had been given $1 million to establish a business, Watson's father advised him: "Before you spend a dollar of your company's money, consider it as your own dollar. Do not spend any of your company's money when you would not spend your own money."[35]

Watson established Watson's Cash Register and Second Hand Exchange in Manhattan, undercut the prices of his main competitor, and bought him out. He repeated this activity in Philadelphia and Chicago. He made the second-hand machine business a profitable unit of the company and was offered a position at NCR headquarters in Dayton.

Eventually, Chalmers could no longer tolerate Patterson's dictatorial style and, as the number two man in the company, disagreed with some of Patterson's non-business decisions. Chalmers was fired; Watson was promoted to general manager in his place.

Patterson went to Europe for two years, and, by the time he returned, Watson had doubled the sales volume (to 100,000 cash registers in 1910). The increase in sales was due partly to the redesign of the cash register by Charles (Boss) Kettering, who replaced the manual operation of the machine with an electric motor. Kettering moved on to General Motors where he designed the self-starter for automobiles.

NCR management's monopolistic practices in the second-hand cash register business caught up with them. On February 22, 1913, Patterson, Watson, and twenty-eight other company managers were indicted on three counts of criminal conspiracy and were placed on trial in Cincinnati for restraining trade and maintaining a monopoly.

While awaiting trial, Watson met Jeanette Kittridge, whose father was president of a railroad car manufacturing company. The Kittridges were friends and neighbors of Patterson; Jeanette was Patterson's choice of a wife for Watson. The two young people fell in love.

Patterson, Watson, and all but one of the other senior NCR managers were found guilty as charged. Patterson was released on $10,000 bail, and Watson was released on $5,000 bail. Watson suggested postponing the wedding until the results of the appeal were known. Jeanette disagreed. She was as strong-willed as he was; together they made a powerful team. Shortly after their marriage, Watson was fired, just as Chalmers had been abruptly dismissed earlier. Upon leaving his office for the last time, he observed to friends: "I've helped build all but one of those buildings. Now I'm going out to build a business bigger than John H. Patterson has."

Watson received a job offer from Charles Flint, who had assembled a company called the Computer-Tabulating-Recording Company (CTR) by combining a computing scales company, a time recorder company, and the Tabulating Machine Company. CTR was unprofitable, and Flint wanted a new manager. Watson accepted Flint's offer; however, he wasn't elected to the board of directors because of the pending NCR lawsuit. On March 13, 1915, the District Court verdict was set aside and a new trial granted. No new trial was conducted, and Watson was cleared of any wrongdoing. CTR promptly elected Watson president and general manager.

Watson authorized the redesign of the Hollerith (punched card) tabulator, and the Tabulating Machine Company became the premier unit of CTR. From 1914 until 1920, CTR's gross income increased from $4 million to $14 million. The recession of 1921 curtailed CTR's expansion plans, and sales that year were $3.5 million instead of the projected $15 million. All salaries, including Watson's, were cut by ten percent. Watson had difficulty meeting payments on CTR's loans. The president of the Guaranty Trust Company, holder of CTR's debt, told him, "I believe so much in the future of your business and in you as the head of it that Guaranty Trust will go along with you, and don't worry about it."[36]

In 1924, Watson renamed the company International Business Machines (IBM). He was appointed chief executive officer and, for the first time, was really in charge of the company. IBM's revenues increased from $19.7 million to $39.5 million from 1928 to 1939. IBM was a tough competitor; by

1935, IBM had 85.7 percent of all leased tabulating machines.

An important source of IBM's profits was from sales of punched cards used in tabulating machines. Passage of the Social Security Act in 1935 and the Wages-Hours Act in 1937 contributed heavily to IBM's growth. Businesses were now required to record wages paid, hours worked, and overtime earned. The company's revenues grew from $39.5 million in 1939 to $141.7 million in 1945.

IBM's competitors in business machines were Burroughs, NCR, Remington Rand, and Underwood-Elliott-Fisher. IBM's principal competitor was Remington Rand. James Henry Rand had formed Remington Rand by merging companies that manufactured adding machines and typewriters to his original company that produced Kardex systems. In 1927, Rand acquired the Powers Accounting Machine Corporation, a respected manufacturer of tabulating equipment.

Remington Rand's revenue decreased from $59.6 million in 1928 to $43.5 million in 1939 mainly because of the stiff competition from IBM in tabulating machines. However, from 1939 to 1945, Remington Rand's net sales increased from $43.2 million to $108 million, principally due to sales of material to support the war effort.

In the 1930s, IBM funded university research in computing, including development of a mechanical calculator for astronomers by Wallace Eckert at Columbia University. The calculator had no commercial value, but IBM's support was widely recognized. In 1939, Howard Aiken of Harvard University entered a joint agreement with IBM to build an automatic computer, the Automatic Sequence Controlled Calculator (Mark I), at the IBM plant at Endicott, New York. Four IBM engineers participated in the development of the machine, an electromechanical device with 760,000 components.

In 1944, the Mark I was completed and shipped to Harvard University where it was demonstrated by Aiken, who took all of the credit for its development. IBM and Watson weren't mentioned, even though they had participated heavily and contributed $500,000 to its development. Watson had involved IBM more from a public relations than from an earnings point of view; he was furious with Aiken. Aiken's betrayal motivated Watson to develop a machine that could outperform the Mark I. In 1948, the first step was taken with the introduction of the Selective Sequence Electronic Calculator (SSEC), IBM's first commercial electronic computer. The SSEC contained 12,500 vacuum tubes and 21,400 relays.

In June 1950, communist forces crossed the thirty-eighth parallel into South Korea. Watson immediately sent a telegram to President Truman offering the services of the IBM Corporation. A team was formed to plan IBM's contribution during the Korean conflict. The team foresaw a need for "more computational power," so the Corporation developed the "IBM Defense Calculator," later renamed the IBM 701. In March 1953, the first IBM 701, which leased for $24,000 per month, was installed at the Atomic Weapons Development Center at Los Alamos, New Mexico.

In 1952, Thomas Watson, Jr., became president of IBM; his brother Arthur was appointed general manager of the IBM World Trade Corporation. From 1914 through 1953, assets had grown by twenty-four times, employees by thirty-four times, the data processing business by 316 times, and development expenditures by 500 times. On May 8, 1956, Thomas Watson, Jr., became chief executive officer of the IBM Corporation. Just over a month later, on June 19, Thomas Watson, Sr., died of a heart attack.

IBM's founder definitely made his mark on U.S. industry. The New York *Herald Tribune* called Watson "a man who could well stand as a symbol of the free enterprise system." *Time* magazine called him "one of the first of a new breed of U.S. businessmen who realized that their social responsibilities ran far beyond their own companies." President Eisenhower considered his friend "an industrialist who was first of all a great citizen and a great humanitarian."

Thomas Watson, Jr., maintained the growth that was the legacy of his father. The IBM 701, a scientific computer, was followed by a commercial version, the IBM 702. In 1954, the IBM 704, the successor to the IBM 701, was placed on the market. The IBM 705, the successor to the IBM 702 and the first commercial computer with magnetic memory, was introduced in 1956.

In the early 1960s, IBM spent $5 billion developing the IBM 360 series of computers in the first development activity that used all international units of the company. It was considered a "you bet your company" effort; it was a phenomenally successful family of computers.

Note: This profile of Thomas J. Watson, with additions, is reprinted from *People of the Finger Lakes Region.*

CHAPTER 12

INTRODUCTION OF THE MAINFRAME COMPUTER

SUCCESS VS. FAILURE—SUMMARY AND ANALYSIS

"Whether you want to make money, or write a book, or build a bridge, or run a streetcar—or do anything else successfully—you'll do well to remember that in all the world there is no more important word than—'Think.'"

Edwin Baird

Thomas J. Watson was an entrepreneur, and John Mauchly and Presper Eckert were inventor / entrepreneurs and scientists. A more appropriate comparison might be made between Watson of IBM and James Rand of the Remington Rand Corporation, than between Watson and Mauchly / Eckert. Rand was as capable and intelligent as Watson, but the environments within which they operated were very different.

Watson was a visionary, although he was slow to perceive the potential market for mainframe computers. He organized his company to meet the demands of the time and prepared strategies to grow rather than just react in response to changing market conditions. In the early days of IBM, it was referred to as "make your plans and then work your plans."

In 1915, James Rand left his father's bank-ledger manufacturing company because his father wouldn't expand aggressively. Rand was viewed as "shrewd, ruthless, persistent past the point of obstinacy." He borrowed $10,000 and developed and marketed a filing system, Kardex, that he had invented. He borrowed another $50,000 and joined with his father in forming the Rand Kardex Company. They borrowed $25 million to establish "the greatest office supply company the world has ever seen."

On January 25, 1927, Remington Rand was formed by consolidating thirteen companies into five that were merged to form the new company. It included the Kardex Company, the Powers Tabulating Machine Company, the Remington Typewriter Company, the Dalton Adding Machine Company, and the Library Bureau of Boston. By 1932, the company had 11,000 employees and 3.8 million square feet of manufacturing space.

However, the principal comparison here is between the individuals involved in the development, manufacture, and marketing of the first commercial mainframe computers. James Rand wasn't a dominant factor in the development of the UNIVAC computer.

Remington Rand's research and development activities

weren't on the same high level as IBM's. Remington Rand scrimped on R & D expenditures and continued to market equipment long after it was out of date because they had few new products in the pipeline. This carried over from the 1930s and 1940s when IBM converted to electrical tabulating machines and Remington Rand stayed with mechanical technology. Remington Rand's development effort was consistently undercapitalized.

A principal difference between the two companies was the superiority of IBM's sales force. IBM salesmen were highly trained in the use of the equipment that they sold, and they specialized in a particular industry. They knew their customer's business as well as the customer did. Remington Rand's salesmen weren't well trained in the use of the equipment that they sold; usually, they were former typewriter and electric shaver salesmen. An example of their lack of marketing discipline was their negligence in following up on a contact with a potential customer. Even salesmen hired away from IBM were ineffectual because they lacked the support organization that they were accustomed to at IBM.

In 1953, Remington Rand had the only commercial electronic computer on the market. The IBM 701 and 702 were a generation behind the UNIVAC. The next generation of IBM computers, the IBM 704 and 705, were still technologically inferior to the UNIVAC. The early IBM computers sold because of the letters "IBM" on the cover of the machine.

By 1956, IBM had delivered 76 mainframe computers; UNIVAC had delivered 46. IBM had orders for 193; Sperry Rand had orders for 65. Gilbert Burck wrote in *Fortune* magazine: "Few enterprises have ever turned out so excellent a product and managed it so ineptly. UNIVAC came out too late with good models, and not at all with others; its salesmanship and software were hardly to be mentioned in the same breath with IBM's. The upper ranks of other computer companies are studded with ex-UNIVAC people who left in disillusionment."

IBM continued to improve the design of its mainframe computers until it caught up with and passed UNIVAC. Then, with its strengths in marketing, training, software, and support, IBM became the notable success in the mainframe computer business. Remington Rand / Sperry Rand became not so much the failure of the industry as a classic example of lost opportunity. However, the principal architects of the UNIVAC, Eckert and Mauchly, are considered by biographers to be successes because of their contribution to the development of the electronic digital computer.

ENGINEERING ENTREPRENEURS

Introduction of the Minicomputer

CHAPTER 13

EDSON DE CASTRO

Founder of Data General Corporation

"There is only one failure in life that is possible, and that is not to be true to the best one knows."

Farrar

Edson de Castro was born in 1938 in Plainfield, New Jersey. In 1960, he graduated from the University of Lowell with a B.S. degree in engineering. He became employee number 100 at the Digital Equipment Corporation (DEC), founded in 1957 by Ken Olsen and Harlan Anderson. By 1960, DEC had two successful minicomputers on the market, the PDP-1 and the PDP-4, and had been profitable since the end of its first year.

De Castro worked under the tutelage of Gordon Bell, the chief architect of DEC's computers from 1960 through the mid-1980s. De Castro successfully introduced the PDP-5, a low-priced, general-purpose computer designed as a front-end for the larger PDP-4. He was ambitious and strong-willed, but he didn't always say what was on his mind. He was moody, quiet, and considered difficult to manage. Nevertheless, because of his success on the PDP-5, he was given the opportunity to develop the next generation of computers, the PDP-8.

When the PDP-8 was being developed, DEC's president, Ken Olsen, suggested that de Castro use a new diode chip, called a flip-chip, with a thin-film capacitor. Flip-chip technology was unproven, and, on his own initiative, de Castro asked circuit-designer Dick Sogge to develop a backup circuit. When the untried flip-chip didn't perform well, de Castro stayed on schedule by using his alternate design. When hailed as a hero, he asked, "That's what a good engineer is supposed to do, isn't it?"

By 1967, de Castro and two of his friends, Henry Burkhardt and Dick Sogge, were frustrated working in the large organization that DEC had become. Burkhardt had dropped out of Princeton University at the age of nineteen to become a programmer and computer-checkout technician at DEC and had been a project development engineer on the DEC10. Both Burkhardt and Sogge had worked with de Castro on the development of the PDP-8.

De Castro was frustrated by the rejection of his design

ideas. He pushed the design of a 16-bit machine to replace DEC's earlier 12- and 18-bit architecture. He agreed with the IBM architecture of multiples of 8-bit computers. In late 1967, he presented his proposal for a 16-bit PDP-X design that could evolve into a 32-bit machine. Users would be able to expand their machines instead of replacing them. In his proposal, he suggested that DEC redesign its entire product line, eighty-five percent of the minicomputer market. He made recommendations outside his area of responsibility. De Castro's idea was ahead of its time, and he was viewed as a troublemaker. The operations committee rejected his proposal.

De Castro attempted to keep his company at the cutting edge of the technology. Competitors had leapfrogged ahead of DEC with 16-bit minicomputers. Computer Controls Corporation was a significant threat until they merged with Honeywell and slowed down technologically. Hewlett-Packard also had a 16-bit entry in the minicomputer market.

De Castro admitted later that he didn't have the breadth of experience to obtain buy-in within DEC to develop the PDP-10. The business plan was poorly written, and benefits weren't clearly defined. The technical portion of the effort was the only part that he knew was right for DEC: "From the technical point of view, I sure thought it was. But what it meant in terms of customer migration, revenue streams, and all that was far beyond my ken at the time."[37]

Earlier, Olsen and de Castro had had a confrontation. In addition to being president of DEC, Olsen was the company's chief packaging engineer. His specialty was the human engineering of products, such as their appearance and use. Olsen saw the power supply that de Castro had designed for the PDP-5 and was unimpressed. At the next PDP-5 progress review, Olsen threw the power supply on the conference table and said, "This is ridiculous. This could be smaller. The thing is a kluge."

De Castro didn't respond to Olsen's attack. He didn't

defend his design either in the meeting or afterwards. He absorbed the ridicule quietly, knowing that he was a talented engineer who didn't need Olsen to tell him how to design products. Olsen wasn't known around the company for his interpersonal communication strengths.

De Castro was a highly regarded engineer who was valued for his creativity. Nevertheless, he wanted to control his design activities, and he didn't like being manipulated in a large organization. Eventually, he was accused of not communicating within the engineering organization. Also, de Castro was disappointed at being bypassed for product line manager for the PDP-8, even though he had played a significant role in its success. His manager recommended de Castro for the product manager's job, but Olsen vetoed the suggestion.

De Castro considered starting his own business: "The idea of starting my own company was in my bones for a long time, even before I went to DEC. Having been in the small computer area and seeing it from multiple points of view—the marketplace, sales support, product design—I felt there was going to be a real growth opportunity in the business. That combined with the frustrations with some of what I tried to do at DEC led me to think more seriously about it." De Castro, Burkhardt, and Sogge stayed at DEC for three months while seeking capital to start their own company.

Herb Richman, a salesman for Fairchild Semiconductor who had sold computer chips to de Castro, heard that the PDP-10 project hadn't been approved. He had a high opinion of de Castro and encouraged him to seek venture capital and start his own company. Subsequently, Richman joined de Castro's new company, Data General Corporation.

De Castro, Burkhardt, and Sogge were unable to raise $300,000. Venture-capitalists were more receptive when they asked for $800,000. Finally, venture-capitalist Fred Adler provided funds for their start-up.

While still at DEC, they had designed an 8-bit minicomputer that became the first product of their new company. De Castro wasn't concerned about proprietary issues with DEC; the new machine wasn't a copy of any DEC computer and much of the design was in the public domain. Olsen was irate at the defection of three of his key engineers. The configuration of the 8-bit machine that de Castro had designed while at DEC was replaced within a year, but Olsen was understandably bitter.

In 1979, eleven years after the incident, Olsen told *Fortune* magazine: "What they did was so bad, we're still upset about it." As late as 1986, Olsen was still emotional in discussing their defection: "We've never had vindictive or vicious feelings about them, never threatened them. All that was made up by the press, or maybe them ... "[38] "The wisest thing we ever did was not sue Data General."[39] Olsen's brother, Stan, observed:

> In this business, you have to be prepared for people to leave. When you're dealing with people with an entrepreneurial spirit, they're going to go on their own. And we specifically selected people with that capability. But we also like to have complete honesty and integrity in our people, and we don't believe what they did was the most straightforward act. It became clear that they were not working for the same company, that they were pulling in a different direction.[40]

Olsen predicted that de Castro's new start-up, Data General Corporation, would fail. DEC's salesmen told the company's customers: "Don't talk to Data General." DEC's customers called Data General to ask why they weren't supposed to talk with them. Rumors of DEC suing de Castro's start-up increased Data General's visibility with potential customers and with the public. Finally, Olsen realized that by putting Data General in the spotlight, he was supporting its cause.

The first day after leaving DEC in 1968, de Castro and Burkhardt began to design their first product, the 16-bit NOVA minicomputer, on Burkhardt's dining room table. Fred Adler, their major venture capitalist, was named president for the first six months; Burkhardt and Sogge convinced de Castro that, after six months, he should be president.

De Castro undertook the responsibilities of president reluctantly; his quiet, aloof personality didn't inspire his development teams. Data General was fortunate to have had an extremely successful first product. The company concentrated on developing, building, and shipping NOVAs instead of stressing the people side of the operation. Data General shipped 200 NOVAs in its first year and was in the black in just over a year.

NOVA used the latest advances in chips; the manufacturing cost was low. Its design was considered elegant for its time. The circuit boards in which the chips and other components were inserted were large, reducing the amount of hardware in the computer. An engineer observed, "The NOVA was a triumph of packaging."

Good hardware is only one of the factors of success. Xerox Data Systems, formerly Scientific Data Systems, made good hardware and went out of business doing it. In Richman's opinion: "We did everything well." The quantity discounts offered to customers peaked at forty percent, twice that offered by the rest of the industry.

Data General's founders didn't keep large blocks of stock for themselves; it was used as fuel for growth. They even made the company lawyer invest in the company, telling him: "We don't want you running away if we get in trouble. We want you protecting your money." At Data General's second public stock offering, the company's legal department requested each founder to sell $1 million of their personal stock to allow them to negotiate without fear of losing everything they had invested.

Data General's first location was in rented space with linoleum on the floor in Hudson, Massachusetts. When corporate headquarters was built in Westboro, Massachusetts, its architectural goals were to be functional and inexpensive. One contractor, who said he would never work for Data General again, said, "What they call tough auditing, we call thievery."

The Westboro headquarters cost nineteen dollars per square foot when Massachusetts's average was thirty-four dollars per square foot. Expansion was accommodated by tacking building 14B onto building 14A. When Data General management was asked to identify the architect for buildings 14 A and 14 B, they said they didn't have one. In *Soul of a New Machine*, Tracy Kidder described the utilitarian lobby: "The lobby could belong to a motor inn. It has orange carpeting and some chairs and a sofa upholstered in vinyl ... "[41]

From 1973 to 1979, Data General's revenues increased forty-five percent per year. The company reached annual sales of $100 million within seven years; it had taken DEC thirteen years to reach that level. Data General, at that time, was only one-fifth the size of DEC, but represented a loss of $100 million in sales for Ken Olsen's company.

The goal of the minicomputer industry was to sell some machines and service to end users, but to sell most of the computers to original equipment manufacturers (OEMs). Because they incorporated a minicomputer into their products, such as film processors, OEMs didn't need much support from the manufacturer. The OEM's engineers provided the necessary support, allowing minicomputer manufacturers to spend less on marketing. Richman managed the Data General sales force, which was considered aggressive by some and the "Darth Vader of the industry" by others.

During its first ten years, Data General focused on financial performance. A security analyst observed, "Data General is usually the last company to come out with a new product.

But they design their machines for ungodly manufacturing profits and allow for incredibly tight control over costs. And then the salesmen go to work. What it comes down to at Data General is that the whole army gets the right marching orders." Data General employees' requests for magazine subscriptions had to be approved by the vice president of finance. The company didn't pay for the spouses of sales personnel to attend national sales meetings, and Data General had no company airplanes.

In 1979, Data General's first major setback occurred when fourth quarter earnings declined due to to several factors:

- The service organization had hired to many people. Although service was growing faster than product sales, service margins were adversely affected by hiring and training new people.
- The component market had become less predictable. Supplies of memory chips and related components were irregular and prices were increasing. Passing price increases on to the customers, particularly in peripherals, was delayed.
- Prices increases of software offerings weren't timely.

Data General's first drop in earnings was a harbinger of things to come. Profits decreased from $54.7 million in 1980 to $40.9 million in 1981 and to $19.9 million in 1982. In early March 1982, Data General announced that it expected sharply reduced near-term profits. On March 4, Data General stock dropped twenty-two percent in six hours, representing a paper loss of $106 million.

In the early 1980s, Data General hired many ex-IBM salesmen and entered typical IBM markets, such as direct sales to large end-user customers, and launched a new word processing and electronic mail system. In 1983, sales increased to $1.6 billion, a gain of forty percent over the previous year.

To prepare for anticipated increased in demand, de Castro added 3,000 employees in 1984 and increased capital spending the following year by seventy-eight percent. The expected increase in sales didn't happen. Data General's plans were affected by an industry slump, and its new strategy of being a market leader, such as IBM, rather than a market follower, like Data General had been, didn't work. De Castro said, "We tried to penetrate large accounts, but, during a downturn, people are averse to risk."

Entering the laptop computer market with a product made in Japan was another poor decision. Data General, which didn't have a track record with consumer products, was unable to penetrate a new market with a laptop computer handicapped by a dim screen. Data General sold only 35,000 laptops out of a total market of 550,000.

Also, Data General's Eagle minicomputer encountered heavy competition from DEC's VAX line of machines. While Data General struggled, eight vice-presidents and many middle managers left the company. De Castro, who had delegated running day-to-day operations for the previous five years, took over management of the company and brought Richman back from semi-retirement to rejuvenate marketing and sales. John McCarthy of Forrester Research considered Data General "too big to be a niche player and too small to be a [large-scale] system supplier."

By February 1985, Data General's orders had declined significantly. The company notified security analysts that actual earnings would be half of projected earnings. De Castro announced the closing of three facilities and the layoff of 1,000 employees to reduce overhead $100 million a year, ensuring that "we can be profitable even if revenues stay flat." Data General planned to refocus on selling value-priced minicomputers to OEMs. The company incurred a $29 million loss in 1986, followed by a $127 million loss in 1987.

Revenues reached $1.4 billion in 1988, but Data General's woes continued. Workstation manufacturers, such as Sun Microsystems, had made inroads into Data General's traditional markets. De Castro acknowledged that he missed the personal computer revolution. He also missed the move to open systems, including those that used the Unix operating system.

In 1989, de Castro was forced out as chief executive officer of the company that he founded. He was replaced by a financial man.

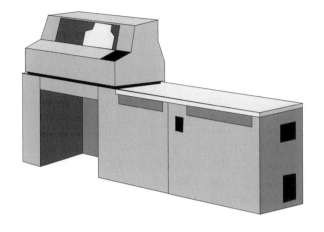

CHAPTER 14

KEN OLSEN

Founder of Digital Equipment Corporation

"Success is probably the worst problem for an entrepreneur. Someone who is successful finds it all too easy to believe that he can do anything. He confuses responsibility with authority. He forgets that power doesn't come from telling people what to do; it comes from learning what goes on."

Ken Olsen

Ken Olsen, the second child and oldest son of Oswald and Elizabeth Svea Olsen, was born on February 20, 1926, in Bridgeport, Connecticut. Oswald and Elizabeth, the children of Norwegian and Swedish immigrants, were born in New York City. Olsen's father was an engineer and machine tool designer who, later in life, became a machine salesman in Stratford, Connecticut.

After graduating from high school, Olsen joined the U.S. Navy as an electronics technician. When he completed his enlistment in the Navy, he majored in electrical engineering at M.I.T. Olsen joined the team designing the Whirlwind computer at M.I.T.'s Lincoln Labs after receiving his degree. Jay Forrester managed the development of the Whirlwind, the brains of a sophisticated air defense system. Olsen took graduate courses in engineering at M.I.T. while working at Lincoln Labs. He and his team amazed Forrester by designing and building a "memory test computer" in nine months.

Lincoln Labs was a subcontractor on the project, which became the Semi-Automatic Ground Environment (SAGE) defense system. In 1953, Olsen was selected as the Lincoln Labs engineer to work with IBM, the prime contractor, at Poughkeepsie, New York. This experience taught him the difference between the modus operandi of a large organization, such as IBM, and a small organization, like Lincoln Labs. Olsen preferred the atmosphere of a small organization.

In 1957, Olsen and his partner, Harlan Anderson, established a company to make interactive computers similar to those they had developed at M.I.T. However, they didn't have sufficient capital to start a company, so they approached a venture-capital firm, American Research & Development Corporation (ARDC), headed by General Georges Doriot. ARDC was willing to provide Olsen and Anderson with $70,000, but the price was high—seventy percent interest in the new enterprise. Doriot also promised to loan them $30,000 in the first year. In 1987, *Fortune* magazine estimated that Olsen's decision to give up seventy percent of the venture cost him a five-billion-dollar personal fortune.

Olsen and Anderson were engineers, not businessmen; nevertheless, they prepared a four-page business plan for ARDC. Olsen wanted to design and build computers that users could interact with. He disliked the remoteness of submitting batch jobs to a mainframe computer, such as those made by IBM. He planned to use the latest transistor technology in his computers. ARDC discouraged the use of the word "computer" in the company name, so they called their company the Digital Equipment Corporation.

The entrepreneurs rented 8,680 square feet in an old woolen mill in Maynard, Massachusetts, about twenty minutes from Lincoln Labs. Later, the use of this facility brought new meaning to the words, "It's in the mill." In addition to the floor space, they received heat, parking space, and the services of a watchman for twenty-five cents a square foot. Olsen's younger brother, Stan, joined the enterprise on its first day of business. Stan, who had an engineering degree from Northeastern University, had been a technician at Lincoln Labs.

Of the $70,000 provided by ARDC, they spent $12,500 for 1,000 transistors. The $12.50 unit price dropped to $8.00 before they used any of them, incurring a $4,500 inventory loss. For office furniture, they used Anderson's lawn furniture and an old roll-top desk that came with the floor space. Circuits were printed with silk on wooden frames and etched in fish tanks bought at the local five and dime store. On several occasions, the etch solution spilled onto furniture of the tenants below them.

As promised, they produced a profit in their first year. Doriot said, "I'm sorry to see this. No one has ever succeeded this soon and survived." An early Digital Equipment Corporation (DEC) philosophy was: "He who proposes does." In other words, be prepared to implement your suggestions. Another rule was: "When dealing with a customer, vendor, or an employee, do what is 'right' in each situation."[42]

Their first product, other than circuit boards, was the PDP-1, a general-purpose computer for scientists and engineers that sold for $120,000. It had a 4,000-word memory, a cathode ray tube display, and operated at 10,000 additions per second. In 1962, DEC received its first multiple order—from ITT for fifteen PDP-1s to control its message switching system. That year DEC had net profits of $807,000 on sales of $6.5 million.

Both a 24-bit machine, the PDP-2, and a 36-bit machine, the PDP-3, were planned but never built. The chief PDP architect was Gordon Bell, who had joined DEC from M.I.T. in 1960 as the company's second computer engineer. He was pursuing a Ph.D. degree when he visited DEC and decided that it was the place for him. Bell's decision to join DEC was a stroke of good fortune for the company; he played a key role in DEC's growth for twenty-three years.

One of Bell's early decisions was only a limited success. He envisioned a significant market for a machine with five-eighths the performance of a PDP-1 at one-half the price, $65,000. Only fifty-four PDP-4s were sold.

By 1963, DEC, with sales of $10 million and a profit of $1.2 million, had reached the size at which its highly centralized decision-making was no longer efficient. Olsen made all of the major decisions, and he was being spread thinner and thinner. He was being forced to operate as a nay-sayer with veto power. Without an organizational structure, manufacturing and order processing were problem areas. Engineering and manufacturing weren't communicating, and product shipments were late. Anderson, who was responsible for the financial side of the company, was overcommitted and was struggling.

In addition, the company was going through some technological growing pains. In 1963, DEC designed the PDP-5 as a low-priced, general-purpose computer to be used as a front-end for the larger PDP-4. In parallel, Bell was designing the

PDP-6, a large-scale 36-bit computer targeted to sell for $300,000. In 1964, DEC began to ship the PDP-6; initially, it had many technical problems.

Finally, Olsen decided to reorganize the company. Each product line would be the responsibility of one senior manager. The manager was responsible for development, marketing, manufacturing, and profit and loss for his or her line of products. Olsen said, "Each of you is responsible for your part of the company. You are now entrepreneurs, and everybody else is a service."

In effect, he had created a matrix organization, where everyone had two managers, a project (or product) manager and a functional manager (e.g. manufacturing, marketing, etc.). Olsen didn't like the word "matrix," but he liked the form of organization because it encouraged creativity and enabled them to handle explosive growth. The matrix organization was successful beyond Olsen's dreams. Profit doubled in the first year it was used.

In Anderson's opinion, he had been demoted. He was given the responsibility for the PDP-6 line of computers, a problem area. He thought he was being made a scapegoat. Strain developed between the two founders, and Anderson pleaded his case before Forrester, who was a consultant to DEC, and to Doriot. Believing that Anderson was trying to outmaneuver him, Olsen transferred resources from the PDP-6 to the PDP-5 line of products. Only twenty-six PDP-6s were sold. In 1966, Anderson left the company; Olsen's control of DEC was clear and uncontested.

The PDP-8, aggressively priced at $18,000, was the machine that established DEC in the computer industry. The company sold over 50,000 PDP-8s in the product's fifteen-year life span. The PDP-8 formed a new market in the industry—sales to original equipment manufacturers (OEMs). OEMs used a PDP-8 as a component on their own products, such as typesetting equipment. DEC assisted the OEM in integrating the PDP-8 into their design, but the OEM was responsible for service and maintenance.

DEC revenues grew from $15 million in 1965 to $23 million in 1966; from fiscal year 1966 to 1967, profits increased by a multiple of six. By 1970, DEC had seventy competitors in the minicomputer business. Olsen received many offers to sell DEC, including offers from Control Data Corporation, Harris Corporation, Hewlett-Packard, Singer, and Xerox.

In August 1966, DEC had an initial public offering of its stock. Olsen's shares, 350,000 (thirteen percent), were worth over $7 million. He didn't change his lifestyle; he still drove his economical Ford. The outdoorsman said, "Now I can afford a second canoe." ARDC owned 1.75 million shares, or sixty-five percent of the company, worth $38.5 million. In nine years, ARDC's investment had multiplied over 500 times.

In late 1966, the 36-bit architecture of the PDP-6 was resurrected and renamed the PDP-10, later called DECsystem 10. Bell didn't participate in its redesign; he was on a leave of absence at Carnegie-Mellon University. The high-end, modular DECsystem 10 came with scientific programming languages, such as Fortran and Lisp, and was an active product for sixteen years.

In 1967, DEC had revenues of $39 million. The company's profits doubled from 1967 to 1968, and sales and profits doubled from 1968 to 1970. DEC's entry in the 16-bit market was the PDP-11. DEC's design engineers visited Bell, who directed the design of the machine from Carnegie-Mellon. On January 5, 1970, the PDP-11 was announced with a selling price of $10,800. By mid-1971, DEC was selling 100 PDP-11s a month and was back on top of the minicomputer market. Eventually, more than 250,000 PDP-11s were sold.

Competing projects were a way of life at DEC. Two similar development projects were allowed to run in parallel until, eventually, one of them was cancelled. A key part of the process was "buy-in," which was described in a company manual as "the process of talking with interested parties to gather support for a project. When a party expresses interest in the job, buy-in can be achieved. Buy-in can be more powerful if the interested party provides 'real' support by being a part of a committee, providing resources, or working difficult political situations. Sometimes buy-in involves horse trading."

From 1971 to 1975, DEC sales grew from $146 million to $533 million, and profits quadrupled. In March 1974, the company shipped its three-millionth computer system. By June 1977, DEC passed $1 billion in revenues, employed 38,000 people, and had a market share of forty-one percent of the computer business.

In 1972, Bell returned to DEC as vice president of engineering. On April 1, 1975, he formed a team called VAX-A to develop a new family of computers. The VAX (Virtual Address Extension)-11 provided virtually unlimited address space built into its architecture. Compatibility with the PDP-11 was a design criteria. Bell's vision was larger than just compatibility or ease of use, he wanted to leapfrog existing designs in a way that would carry DEC into the mid-1980s and beyond. He said that VAX "will merge systems development into a single system to cover a large range."

In parallel with the hardware development effort was a software development project to create DECnet, a proprietary network to connect DEC machines together. The federal government had pioneered the concept by developing ARPANET to link Department of Defense computers into a network. DECnet networks connecting individual VAXs was a landmark decision within DEC. Bell called it a "major architectural triumph." DECnet became so effective that not only did the company become known for networking its own computers, but for its ability to link DEC computers with IBM computers better that IBM could network its own machines.

In addition to the DECnet software, a means of cabling together the machines in a network was needed. Bell had a high opinion of Ethernet, developed by Bob Metcalfe of

Xerox's Palo Alto Research Center. Metcalfe searched for a semiconductor chip on which to base Ethernet technology. He called a meeting attended by DEC, the chip-maker Intel, and Xerox. In May 1980, the three companies announced their Ethernet plans. Later, Metcalfe observed, "I believe the company's [DEC's] focusing on networking explains DEC's success and IBM's relative failure."

During the 1970s, Stan Olsen attempted to steer DEC into commercial markets such as word-processing. However, the DECmate word-processor wasn't based on current PDP-11 technology but on PDP-8 technology, which was almost fifteen years old. Wang Laboratories dominated the word-processing market. Stan's venture into small business centers in the late 1970s and early 1980s wasn't successful.

In 1980, Stan advocated moving into personal computers. His brother wasn't sure than Stan was the manager to lead DEC in this area. Stan increasingly became the target of his brother's ire in operations committee meetings, and he was left out of the decision-making process of Olsen's inner council. Stan had invested heavily in real estate with his earnings from DEC, and, in early 1981, he requested a leave of absence to attend to his real estate holdings. His brother didn't encourage his return to DEC.

In August 1981, IBM introduced its personal computer (PC). On May 10, 1982, DEC announced its entries into the personal computer market: the Professional models 325 and 350 and the Rainbow. IBM's one-year lead was insurmountable. In January 1983, IBM cemented their lead over DEC when Lotus Development Corporation introduced the Lotus 1-2-3 integrated spreadsheet that ran on the IBM PC. Also, IBM began its immensely successful "Little Tramp" television advertising campaign based on a Charlie Chaplin lookalike. IBM's PC strategy overwhelmed DEC's approach, which provided little software for its products.

By the early 1980s, the matrix organization that had worked so well initially had become less effective. Finally,

Olsen decided to replace the product line structure. In July 1982, he consolidated engineering and manufacturing. A year later, the twelve product groups were combined into three regional management centers, and 200 members of the corporate staff were reassigned to the field. He replaced the operations committee with three committees: product strategy, marketing and sales, and management. A four-person executive committee was formed, and thirty line executives and middle managers were added to the organization chart.

The changes were very disruptive. Product managers thought they had been stripped of their power; many left the company. The company struggled because the administrative systems to accompany the organizational changes weren't in place. Forecasting, order processing, and production scheduling were in a state of chaos. Customers received either no shipments or incorrect shipments. Olsen's wife, Aulikki, asked him, "How can you lose orders?" Earnings dropped seventy-two percent from the previous year, and in one day DEC stock dropped twenty-one points.

In March 1983, Bell suffered a serious heart attack while skiing in Colorado. He had experienced angina attacks, but he had ignored them. When he returned to work, he had lost much of his fire. He wasn't happy with the consolidation of engineering and manufacturing because he had to share responsibility with the vice president for manufacturing. Bell, the principal designer of DEC's architecture on virtually all machines except the PDP-1, left the company in 1983 to join a start-up, Encore Computer.

In 1985, the first of the second generation of VAX machines, the VAX8600, was announced. It was four times as powerful as the largest first-generation machine. History was repeating itself. DEC was poised to exploit a large market overlooked by IBM: the concept of networking. Sales of the VAX8600 took off, and DEC's problems of the early 1980s had been overcome.

In October 1986, *Fortune* magazine put "America's most

successful entrepreneur," Ken Olsen, on the cover. "A few like Teledyne's Henry Singleton or Wal-Mart founder Sam Walton, have done better for their shareholders or made themselves richer than Olsen. But none has created as mighty or important an industrial enterprise as DEC. And on that basis, *Fortune* considers him the greatest success."

In 1992, at the age of sixty-five, Ken Olsen stepped down as chief executive officer of DEC. He had guided DEC through the first thirty-five years of its existence, and it was time to retire and to do other things, such as fishing and other outdoor activities. In the opinion of Jack Shields, a DEC vice President, "Olsen will go down in American corporate history as the industrialist of the century. Unlike the laissez-faire environment that spawned the empires of Henry Ford and Thomas Watson, Sr., Olsen created his entrepreneurial masterpiece in an age of heavy government regulation."[43]

CHAPTER 15

INTRODUCTION OF THE MINICOMPUTER

SUCCESS VS. FAILURE—SUMMARY AND ANALYSIS

"You can do what you want to do, accomplish what you want to accomplish, attain any reasonable objective you may have in mind.... Not all of a sudden, perhaps, not in one swift and sweeping act of achievement.... But you can do it gradually—if you *want* to do it, if you *will* to do it, and if you *work* to do it, over a sufficiently long time."

William Holder

A comparison of Ken Olsen of the Digital Equipment Corporation and Edson de Castro of Data General Corporation isn't as much a comparison of success vs. failure as it is a comparison of degrees of success. In terms of the relative size of the companies that Olsen and de Castro created, DEC grew to be significantly larger than Data General. However, the first ten years in the life of Data General must be viewed as a resounding success by any criteria used to measure success.

Olsen definitely underestimated the ability of Data General to compete with the Digital Equipment Corporation. Olsen admitted: "If we made one mistake with Data General, it's that we ignored them. We never thought that they'd succeed."[44]

Many similarities existed between de Castro and Olsen. Both were technical people, and neither was particularly good at interpersonal relationships. Early in the life of their companies, both exercised strong central control of decision-making. At times, both were considered to be good choices to start an enterprise, but not necessarily good candidates to manage a company once it had grown to a certain size. They were considered to be strong entrepreneurs, but less strong at being chief executive officers of medium-sized or large corporations.

In 1984, which wasn't a spectacular growth year for sales and earnings at DEC, one of Olsen's employees agreed with Wall Street's concerns: "Personally, I thought Ken had lost it. You always hear about these entrepreneurs who can manage a company up to a certain size, and then lose control and don't have the skills to run a really large company. I thought, here's an engineer who is losing control of the company."

Fortune magazine asked: "DEC's troubles raise a difficult management question faced at many corporations that started small, grew fast, and became giants: Are the engineering and entrepreneurial skills displayed in abundance by the man who founded the company the kind of skills needed to keep it growing in a changed competitive environment?" Olsen had once observed, "Entrepreneurs do not make good businessmen."

For the first ten years in the life of Data General, de Castro's suitability as chief executive officer was rarely questioned. However, from the time of Data General's difficulties in the early 1980s until he stepped down as CEO at the end of that decade, his ability to manage the company was often questioned. He was considered by some analysts the classic case of the entrepreneur who was effective in starting an enterprise, but wasn't the right person to run the organization when it became a large corporation.

As DEC grew, Olsen made fewer major decisions. The company wasn't a highly disciplined organization, and several competing projects were allowed to survive until, ultimately, one was permitted to proceed. The environment was considered by some employees to be "controlled chaos." *Fortune* magazine observed that "DEC's organization, policies, and management style are aimed at developing as many new products as possible. To achieve its long-term goal, DEC is willing to accept some internal disorder and sacrifice immediate profits ... "[45] DEC placed great emphasis on the treatment of its customers. An overarching goal of the company was to "do the right thing" by their customers. DEC was considered the gentleman of the minicomputer industry.

Data General, on the other hand, was seen as a feisty company, reflecting the personality of its founder. De Castro was a strong believer in tight controls. He set all prices and made all of the major decisions affecting profit and loss. He had a reputation for toughness. Richman said of de Castro, "I've never seen anybody so tough in a negotiation. He's brutal."[46]

Rowland Thomas, Data General's vice president of product marketing observed: "We are bastards—but fair bastards. We treat everybody the same." Data General had a reputation for squeezing margins to accommodate shareholders by concentrating on short-term profits instead of long-term gains.

DEC and Data General also differed in the way they compensated their salespeople. Initially, DEC salespeople were paid a salary with no commissions and no bonuses for exceeding their quota. However, the top salespeople were rewarded with trips to Europe or the Far East. DEC's goals for its sales force were customer satisfaction and low turnover; those goals were accomplished without paying commissions early in the history of the company. Subsequently, the policy was changed.

Data General salespeople were paid half salary and half commission. Their commissions increased with their sales, and there was no cap on commissions. Data General salespeople earned more than their counterparts at DEC in a good year, but did poorer in a depressed economy.

On several occasions, Olsen created an environment that motivated a potential competitor for his CEO job to leave the company. The first high-level person to leave DEC was its cofounder, Anderson. On at least two other occasions, a high-level DEC manager was perceived to be positioning himself to overthrow the throne. On both occasions, the real or imagined competitor moved on. De Castro, in contrast, was willing to give up the day-to-day running of the company to others for five years during the 1980s.

The critical factors in comparing success and failure in managing a company include:
- the ability to deal with downturns in the economy
- the faculty to survive downturns in the industry (influenced by the economy)
- the capacity to provide a vision for the future, e.g. to foresee the demand for new products
- the aptitude for selecting individuals with strengths that management lacks.

During the 1980s, de Castro had difficulty with the first three of these factors, and his company encountered financial trouble.

On at least two occasions during the first thirty years of

DEC's life, Olsen encountered these difficulties also. At the first significant low point, he restructured the company into a matrix organization. His delegation of authority to product line managers proved extremely successful when the company was medium-sized.

At the second low point, the introduction of the VAX line of computers with its emphasis on networking and communications pulled DEC out of its doldrums. On this occasion, the efforts and vision of Gordon Bell were herculean. Tom West, Data General's architect for a 32-bit machine designed to compete with the VAX-11/780, led a notable development effort, but Bell's efforts at DEC were of hall-of-fame proportions.

Data General was strongly influenced by bottom-line financial pressure to make short-term gains. Usually, this can be done best by modifying existing products. DEC, on the other hand, concentrated on introducing large numbers of new products. More risk is inherent with this approach, and an established company has a few advantages over a start-up. Two advantages of a large company compared with a start-up are existing distribution channels and access to capital to develop new products.

The elements of Olsen's success included his assertive leadership in crises. He believed that his key people should accept responsibility and "do the right thing." As the founder and long-term CEO, he provided stability for his relatively undisciplined organization. He became an enforcer who provided leadership. Also, he recognized the importance to DEC of Bell's VAX strategy, even though he didn't personally participate in its creation.

By comparison, after a decade of dramatic success, de Castro faltered during Data General's second decade. He admitted that: "We have made some strategic mistakes. We have focused in some of the wrong places." He didn't have the equivalent to DEC's VAX strategy to carry Data General through the 1980s. However, de Castro's accomplishments at

Data General shouldn't be considered a failure. As observed earlier, it's a matter of measuring relative success.

PERSONAL COMPUTING

Introduction of the Personal Computer

CHAPTER 16

XEROX'S PALO ALTO RESEARCH CENTER

Personal Computer Pioneer

"Many blunder in business through inability or an unwillingness to adopt new ideas. I have seen many a success turn to failure also, because the thought which should be trained on big things is cluttered up with the burdensome detail of little things."

Philip S. Delancey

In 1973, over three years before Steve Wozniak of Apple Computer designed and built the Apple I, Xerox's Palo Alto Research Center (PARC) created the first computer dedicated to the use of one person. PARC did more than design and build a computer. Its developers introduced a comprehensive system of hardware and software that changed the computing environment.

PARC created an astounding list of "firsts" in digital computing, including:

- The first graphics-based monitor
- The first local area communications network
- The first "mouse" input device
- The first object-oriented programming language
- The first word processing program not designed for the use of experts

PARC called its computer Alto and its environment "personal distributed computing." "Personal" because it was designed for use by an individual and "distributed" because it was connected via a network to shared resources, such as printers and other computers.

PARC was unable to convince Xerox management to exploit the technology. PARC was a development and research center, not a manufacturing and marketing organization. The technology languished. Xerox failed to capitalize on PARC's dramatic developments.

Apple Computer promoted the technology and became associated with the introduction of the personal computer. After Apple's initial success, Xerox introduced the Star computer, which was too late and too expensive. Xerox had missed the window of opportunity.

Xerox established PARC in 1970 as part of the company's plan to acquire or develop digital capability. IBM was entering the copier business, and Xerox knew that it had to expand into the computer business to remain competitive.

However, Xerox didn't want to take on IBM in large mainframe computers. Its goal was to fight it out with IBM in developing products for the "office of the future." In other words, it would develop and market equipment and systems to be used by managers and secretaries as well as by production and sales personnel.

Peter McColough, founder Joe Wilson's successor as CEO of Xerox in 1968, decided to buy and expand an existing computer company rather than form a start-up. He approached Control Data Corporation, Digital Equipment Corporation, and the Burroughs Corporation, but no mutually-beneficial agreements could be reached.

In 1969, Xerox paid $900 million for Scientific Data Systems (SDS), a California-based company with sales of $100 million the previous year. Most of the SDS customers were in technical computing, but McColough planned to shift his new acquisition to commercial computing markets.

SDS had no independent development laboratory. Jack Goldman, who had succeeded John Dessauer as director of research at Xerox in 1968, recommended to McColough that Xerox establish a digital research and development center. McColough approved the request, and a talented team of scientists and engineers was assembled at Palo Alto to provide Xerox with future-oriented digital capability. Goldman chose George Pake, a well-regarded physicist with experience in both academia and industry, to establish and manage the new center.

Both Goldman and Pake believed in hiring highly-capable people and then following a "bottom up" rather then a "top down" approach to research. Overall goals were conveyed to the researchers, but it was left up to them to tell their managers what they had to do to accomplish them. After all, development of the "architecture of information" involved in moving to the "office of the future" wasn't immediately obvious to high-level managers.

Pake divided the lab into three components:
- The General Science Laboratory (GSL)—conducted research in physics and other basic sciences

- The Systems Science Laboratory (SSL)—was responsible for broad "systems" research in engineering, information, mathematics, operations, and statistics
- The Computer Science Laboratory (CSL)—focused on computer systems

Pake managed the GSL in addition to the laboratory as a whole. Bill Gunning, who had twenty years of computer science experience, was appointed to manage SSL. Jerry Elkind was selected to head CSL. Elkind had worked for NASA and for the computer consultant who designed ARPANet, the first nationwide computer communications network, for the Advanced Research Projects Administration (ARPA) of the Department of Defense. Bob Taylor, who had served as ARPA's chief administrator of computer funding, was named associate director of CSL.

With the cost of mainframe computers and minicomputers exceeding $100,000, time-sharing was a popular tool. Users at many terminals were connected to one central computer and shared its use. Computers were considered fast and people slow, so this was viewed as a good arrangement. However, it caused many computer scientists to work odd hours, such as the middle of the night, to gain access to the central computer. Developers' schedules were slaves to the computer's schedule. As the cost of computers came down due to the increased use of integrated circuits and microprocessors, an alternative to time-sharing was sought. Taylor recommended a "one computer, one person" solution to the problem.

CSL computer scientist Alan Kay described a tool called FLEX in his 1969 doctoral dissertation that fit Taylor's concept:

> ... an interactive tool which can aid in the visualization of and realization of provocative notions. It must be simple enough so that one doesn't have to be a systems programmer to

use it. It must be cheap enough to be owned. It must do more than just be able to recognize computable functions; it has to be able to form the abstractions in which the user deals. FLEX is an idea debugger and, as such, it is hoped that it is also an idea media.[47]

Kay proposed that PARC develop a FLEX-like computer called "Dynabook," which he referred to as a "dynamic media for creative thought." When the Dynabook project was turned down, he countered with a project called "interim Dynabook."

Interest in the project began to build within CSL, and Taylor obtained approval to develop a computer that met the "one person, one computer" criterion. It was called Alto. CSL scientist Butler Lampson described it as having an enhanced display monitor, being almost as powerful as a minicomputer, operating in a network of distributed machines, and being affordable. He referred to the use of such a computer as "personal computing." Computer scientist Chuck Thacker had some ideas on developing it. Their goals were to make it both better and cheaper than a minicomputer.

Lampson and Thacker used some of the tools developed by Douglas Englebart, an early advocate of interactive computing, including an input device called a "mouse" and displays that could be divided into multiple "windows." Englebart's mouse was a bulky analog device that was converted into a digital tool and made smaller and more reliable.

Lampson and Thacker planned to improve Englebart's displays. They favored a technique called bit-mapping, which associated each picture element (pixel) with a specific bit of computer memory. Specific binary bits are programmed to be "on" (one) while others are "off" (zero); in combination, the bits create a character on the screen and retain it in memory for later use. Unfortunately, this one-to-one relationship of pixels on the screen with bits in the computer's memory

149

required a large storage capacity and therefore was expensive.

Another Alto innovation was multitasking, which allowed one processor to operate as many. A task was performed according to its priority. Multitasking slowed Alto down because the bit-mapped display used the processor two-thirds of the time, but it provided more functionality for less cost. In April 1973, after four months of work, the first Alto was completed. Ten Altos were built by the end of the year, and forty were completed by the following summer.

However, hardware alone doesn't make a computer system. Still needed to obtain benefit from the machine were an operating system, programming languages, and application software. As the software became available, three functions were emphasized: communications, printing, and word-processing.

PARC developer Robert Metcalfe's communications tool, Ethernet, didn't use telephone lines but relied on local cable runs within a building. Ethernet connected an Alto to shared equipment, such as printers and other Altos. PARC also developed the xerographic laser printer. Laser printers were expensive, but sharing them reduced the cost to individual computer users.

Lampson and CSL scientist Charles Simonyi developed a word-processing application called "Bravo," which allowed the word image on the screen to be the same as that output by the printer. This feature, called "wysiwyg" for "what you see is what you get" wasn't available on earlier word-processing packages. Subsequently, a more user-friendly version, called "Gypsy," was developed. Alto was used successfully in an experiment at Ginn & Company, a Xerox textbook publishing subsidiary, to streamline the publishing process.

The Alto personal computer seemed prepared for takeoff. Thacker observed, "It was certainly from my own experience the largest piece of creative effort I have seen anywhere. And it was like being there at the creation. A lot of people worked harder than I have ever seen, or have seen since, doing a thing they all felt was worthwhile, and really thought would change the world." However, no attempt was made to translate PARC's developments into successfully marketed products.

Xerox faced many challenges at the time. In 1972, the Federal Trade Commission (FTC) claimed that the company was monopolizing the plain paper copier market. The FTC accused Xerox of manipulating patent laws, setting prices that were discriminatory, insisting on leases over sales of equipment, and exploiting the market by using joint ownership arrangements with Rank in England and Fuji in Japan. In July 1975, the FTC discontinued the antitrust action. In order to comply with FTC demands, Xerox had to give up its patents, change its pricing policies, and allow supplies such as toner to be sold by other companies.

In late 1973, CEO McColough and president Archie McCardell, a Ford Motor Company financial executive who had joined Xerox in 1971, formed a team of four people to map the future strategy of Xerox. The team was headed by corporate planner Michael Hughes and included George Pake, who had been assigned to corporate headquarters after directing PARC for three years. The team evaluated four distinct strategies for Xerox and recommended the "office of the future" alternative. They suggested combining computers, copiers, and word-processing typewriters with PARC's innovations in communications, microcircuitry, and software. No action was taken on their recommendation.

Originally, Xerox research director Goldman thought that PARC's inventions would be brought to market by Scientific Data Systems. When SDS hemorrhaged severely during the first half of the 1970s, he realized that another avenue was needed to capitalize on PARC's innovations. As the emphasis on financial analysis practiced by ex-Ford executives became prevalent at Xerox, Goldman's influence as the senior technical person waned.

In January 1973, Bob Potter became the general manager of Xerox's Office Products Division, responsible for developing and manufacturing office products other than copiers. The division had few successes other than the development of a popular facsimile machine. Potter wanted to move the division from Rochester, New York, to another location. Dallas and Silicon Valley were two of the favored locations.

Goldman lobbied strongly for Silicon Valley because PARC was located there. However, Dallas was chosen for strictly financial reasons, including lower costs for labor, taxes, and transportation. The financial types had won again; PARC was to remain isolated from the rest of the company. In Goldman's opinion, this decision had the greatest negative impact of any single decision on the future of digital technology at Xerox.

Potter visited PARC and observed the Alto technology, but he decided to concentrate on word-processing. Although his background was in both technology and operations, he thought that PARC's ideas were too futuristic. Also, he was influenced by Xerox financial people, who emphasized short-term profits.

PARC was disappointed that software didn't enter into Potter's plans for Dallas. They thought that products that weren't programmable, such as Potter's electro-mechanical devices, would fail. Within a year and a half of entering the market, Potter's word-processing typewriter was out of date because of its display and communications shortcomings.

Xerox's Display Word Processing Task Force recommended a new Alto-based word-processor. However, a team from Dallas recalculated PARC's estimates for the new product and concluded that the Alto would take longer to build and cost more than the estimates. The task force's recommendation was ignored. Next, Goldman proposed the formation of a small entrepreneurial team to produce a general-purpose workstation using the Alto. That proposal was also rejected.

The recession in 1974-75 impacted Xerox severely. The company found that customers made as many copies in bad times as in good times, but they made them with existing machines. They didn't buy or lease new copiers during a slowed economy. However, the greatest negative impact on Xerox was the staggering losses from the Scientific Data Systems acquisition. SDS lost $71 million in 1970-71, $47 million in 1972, $45 million in 1973, and $42 million in 1974. Taking on IBM head-to-head in the "office of the future" wasn't working.

Combining the copier and the computer businesses in a functional organization grouped by design and manufacturing, marketing and service, and planning had removed the focus of the computer business. In effect, SDS drifted without a general manager. In July 1975, CEO McColough admitted that the SDS acquisition had been a mistake. No buyer for SDS could be found. Xerox took a write-off of just under $1.3 billion and left the computer business.

In 1975-76, the Office Products Division began to manufacture the laser printer developed at PARC; a patent was received for Ethernet; and the Systems Development Division (SDD) was formed to translate PARC inventions into products. Some PARC-developed products were finding their way to the marketplace. However, Xerox still wasn't prepared to exploit the advances made on the Alto.

In 1976, PARC researcher John Ellenby was authorized to produce hundreds of Altos for use with laser printers within Xerox. He thought that at last technology transfer from the lab to the user was beginning to happen. In August 1976, Ellenby submitted a proposal on Alto to the Xerox task force determining new product strategies for the company. No action was taken on his proposal.

Ellenby was pleased when he was asked to organize the 1977 "Futures Day" at which Xerox showcased its new products within the company. His team worked hard and thought they had made a strong case for proceeding with the Alto. By this time, McCardell had left Xerox to become CEO of International Harvester, and David Kearns from IBM had replaced him as president and chief operating officer. Kearns decided not to go into production with the Alto.

In 1979, a Xerox investment unit contacted Steve Jobs about a possible joint venture. Jobs requested and received a tour of the PARC facility. Larry Tesler demonstrated Alto for Jobs, who saw its potential immediately. He asked, "Why isn't Xerox marketing this? You could blow everybody away."[48]

Once Jobs knew that it could be done, he set out to duplicate it at Apple. He hired Tesler immediately and later Alan Kay, who eventually became an Apple Fellow. Most of the "look and feel" of the Alto that provided its ease of use eventually was incorporated into the Apple Lisa and Macintosh. Xerox was amazingly open with its technology.

In 1978, Xerox combined the Office Products Division in Dallas with other non-copier units. General manager Potter left to join McCardell at International Harvester as chief technical officer.

In 1979, the Office Products Division was again made independent, and Don Massaro was hired from Shugart Associates to replace Potter as general manager. Massaro, an entrepreneurial type, announced a new word-processor, readied two facsimile machines for the market, announced PARC's Ethernet as a product, and started an electronic typewriter project within the first year. Soon he became interested in Star, a product that had evolved from the Alto.

He asked for $15 million to make and sell Star and was turned down. He scaled down his request and was turned down again. He proceeded on his own using his division's budget. Star's strength, like Alto's, was its "user interface," including the contents of the screen and the tools provided to work with the display. Star used icons, action-choice menus, and multiple screen windows along with electronic file cabinets, in and out boxes, and wastebaskets. However, Star was designed to be used by managers.

Much of the software had already been designed when a decision was made to replace the processor. Hardware is usually designed before software, and compromises had to be made that slowed the speed of the machine to incorporate the new processor. It was the first personal computer to offer the bit-map screen, a laser printer, the mouse, combined text and graphics in the same document, and "what you see is what you get" word processing.

However, it had limitations in addition to its slow speed:
- Because it was a distributed system, it was more expensive than a stand-alone computer. ($16,595 for the workstation, five times the cost of a stand-alone personal computer).
- It didn't offer a spreadsheet.
- Its design was based on a closed architecture, not an open architecture; suppliers couldn't make and sell components to be used with it.
- Its programming language wasn't available to the public (only Xerox employees could write application software for it).
- It wasn't compatible with other computers.

In April 1981, Star was introduced—eight years after the invention of the Alto. It wasn't a successful product; nevertheless, Star (Xerox 820) was the first personal computer introduced by a *Fortune* 500 corporation.

Xerox's mishandling the introduction of the personal computer was a classic case of missing an opportunity. Unfortunately, the technology developed at PARC was exploited by others; Xerox didn't receive the benefit of its labors. An incredible body of talent had been assembled at PARC during the 1970s. Key PARC people seeded the laboratories of other companies; for example, Charles Simonyi joined Microsoft Corporation.

Butler Lampson, Bob Taylor, and Chuck Thacker joined the Systems Research Center of the Digital Equipment Corporation. In 1984, they received the System Software Award from the Association of Computing Machinery for the invention of personal distributed computing. In 1987,

President Reagan awarded George Pake the National Medal of Science for the notable accomplishments of the Palo Alto Research Center.

CHAPTER 17

STEVE JOBS / STEVE WOZNIAK

Founders of Apple Computer Corporation

"If you want to succeed you should strike out on new paths rather than travel the worn paths of accepted success."

John D. Rockefeller

Steve Jobs was born on February 24, 1955, in San Francisco. Shortly after his birth, he was adopted by Paul and Clara Jobs. Paul Jobs worked for a finance company in Palo Alto; the family lived in nearby Mountain View.

Steve Jobs was smart but was known as a loner. He wasn't subjected to much discipline as a child, and he became used to getting his own way. He didn't have much interest in team sports so he became a swimmer, where the emphasis was on individual contribution. Paul Jobs's hobby was buying and fixing up old cars. He took his son with him when he negotiated for cars and for parts. This experience helped young Jobs to develop his strengths as a negotiator.

Jobs became interested in electronics at the age of ten. Many Hewlett-Packard engineers lived in the neighborhood, and he was intrigued with the variety of electronics projects assembled in neighborhood garages. A neighbor instructed Jobs in electronics and enrolled him in the Hewlett-Packard Explorer Club, where he learned about calculators, diodes, holograms, and lasers.

Jobs's father accepted a position as a machinist in Los Carlos and moved the family to Los Altos because his son didn't like the school in Mountain View. Through a mutual friend, Jobs met Steve Wozniak, who was four years older than Jobs. Jobs knew the Wozniak family through Steve's younger brother who swam on the Mountain View swimming team. Jerry Wozniak, an electrical engineer at Lockheed, instructed his sons in electronics.

Steve Wozniak was only eighteen when he met Jobs, but his knowledge of electronics was advanced for his age. He had won prizes in local electronics fairs against tough competition. He had already expanded his design for a one-bit adder-subtractor into a ten-bit parallel adder-subtractor, a precursor to a computer.

One of Jobs's first projects for the Explorer Club was building a frequency counter. He needed parts and obtained them with the chutzpah for which he later became known: "I picked up the phone and called Bill Hewlett of Hewlett-Packard. He was in the Palo Alto phone book. He answered the phone and was real nice; he chatted with me for twenty minutes. He didn't know me at all, but he ended up giving me some parts, and he got me a job that summer working at Hewlett-Packard on the line, assembling frequency counters.... " Later, when Jobs needed another part, he called the Burroughs Corporation in Detroit, collect, and asked them to donate it to him.

During high school, Jobs worked at a surplus electronics warehouse store in Sunnyvale, where he learned electronic part pricing. He purchased capacitors, resistors, and microchips at flea markets and resold them at a profit.

Wozniak enrolled at the University of Colorado but returned to San Francisco after one year. He took programming courses at the local community college and later enrolled at the University of California at Berkeley.

Jobs and Wozniak cultivated their skills at designing, assembling, and selling electronics by becoming "phone phreaks." Wozniak designed and assembled and Jobs sold "blue boxes" to place calls that circumvented the telephone company's billing system. They learned from phone phreak Cap'n Crunch, who used a toy whistle from a cereal box to simulate the telephone company's tones. Wozniak's "blue box" used a digital design instead of an oscillator. It required forty dollars worth of parts, took four hours to assemble, and sold for $150. Jobs and Wozniak stopped making and selling blue boxes when other phone phreaks, including Cap'n Crunch, were caught.

Despite his parents' objections, Jobs enrolled at Reed College in Portland, Oregon. Reed was a liberal school; its students considered themselves anti-establishment. Jobs and a fellow student, Daniel Kottke, studied Buddhism, Yoga, and Zen. They became vegetarians and visited the Hare Krishna temple frequently. Jobs dropped out of school but stayed on the periphery of Reed. He lived in an unheated room and supported himself by maintaining electrical equipment. He usually went barefoot and only wore sandals when it snowed.

In 1974, Jobs returned home and interviewed for a job at Atari as a technician. He insisted that they hire him, so they did. Nolan Bushnell had founded Atari in 1972 to develop video games. His first big success was the game, Pong.

Jobs wanted to travel to India, as one of his Reed friends had done the previous summer. Jobs asked Atari's chief engineer to pay his way to India "to see his guru." The chief engineer laughed at him but thought of a way to give him time off. He asked Jobs to stop in Germany on his way to India.

Atari had a grounding problem with circuit boards in the games they sold in Germany, partly due to the difference between sixty-cycle and fifty-cycle power. The chief engineer gave Jobs a short course in ground loops. In Germany, Jobs solved the problem in two hours by ensuring that the chassis in which the board was inserted was properly grounded.

Jobs's friend Kottke joined him in India. They were moved by the poverty, which was greater than they had expected. Jobs's summer in India caused him to question many of his beliefs. His friends thought his disillusionment with India made him seem detached. In the fall of 1974, Jobs returned home and resumed contact with Wozniak.

Wozniak had dropped out of Berkeley during his junior year, married Alice Robertson, and taken a position as a engineer in Hewlett-Packard's calculator division. He became a regular attendee at meetings of the Homebrew Computer Club, a gathering place for computer hobbyists, engineers, programmers, and suppliers.

Attendance at club meetings increased exponentially after the January 1975 issue of *Popular Electronics* was circulated. It included an article about the Altair 8800 computer kit produced by MITS in Albuquerque, New Mexico. The Altair, based on the Intel 8080 central processing unit, was a collection of parts with meager documentation and little input / output capability. It required substantial knowledge of electronics to assemble and was usually missing parts. It cost $495. Hobbyists couldn't write checks fast enough to buy this first mail-order computer. The Altair software, written in BASIC programming language, was developed by Bill Gates and Paul Allen, who later founded Microsoft Corporation.

Wozniak decided to design his own computer. Initially, he based his design on the Motorola 6800 microprocessor, but later replaced it with the MOS Technology 6502. He drew on his previous experience in building a computer with limited capability in a neighbor's garage and in designing a "Computer Converser" for Call Computer. Wozniak was adept at designing efficient circuit boards with a minimum of components; the circuit board for this computer was no exception.

Wozniak took his computer to meetings of the Homebrew Computer Club, but they weren't interested in it because it wasn't based on the Intel 8080 used in the Altair. He offered to give away circuit diagrams of his computer to club members, until Jobs suggested that they sell them. Better yet, Jobs recommended that they make the circuit board computers and sell them.

On April 1, 1976, Jobs and Wozniak formed a partnership called Apple Computer to make and sell computers. Jobs chose the name because it came before Atari in the phone book and because he liked the Beatles. Apple was the name of the Beatles' record label.

Jobs invited Ron Wayne, Altari's chief field service engineer, to join the partnership to do artwork, advertising layout, and documentation. Wayne was given ten percent of Apple Computer and Jobs and Wozniak each took forty-five percent. Wayne, a conservative engineer in his forties, favored low-risk investments such as precious metals and stamps. He became nervous when Apple Computer committed substantial amounts of money for circuit board parts. He withdrew from the partnership, a move he regretted later.

Jobs found a source of economical circuit boards. He had

gained experience in dealing with circuit board manufacturers when he negotiated circuit board work for Wozniak's Computer Converser. Jobs developed a reputation of being a tough negotiator. He was called "the rejector," because he usually turned down early designs and estimates.

Jobs met an electronics retailer at a Homebrew Club meeting who offered to buy fifty circuit board computers, later called Apple I, for $500 each. Apple Computer needed start-up capital, but no one was willing to lend it to them. Jobs had $1,000 from the sale of his van plus a small nest egg from selling Atari a video game called Breakout that Wozniak had designed. Jobs's loan requests were turned down by banks and by his previous employer at the electronics warehouse store.

Finally, Jobs found a supplier of electronics parts in Palo Alto who would sell them $20,000 worth of parts on credit with no interest if they paid within thirty days. Patty, Jobs's sister, had married and moved out of their parents' home, so they used her bedroom to assemble the circuit boards. The Jobs' garage is usually noted as the first location of Apple Computer. The garage was used when the work volume overflowed Patty Jobs's bedroom. Their customer was unhappy with the first delivery of the Apple I because it lacked a display, a keyboard, a power supply, and software. Nevertheless, he paid in cash.

Jobs hired his old friend, Kottke, and his sister, Patty, to insert components into circuit boards. A Reed classmate kept the company's books. Wozniak obtained a $5,000 loan from friends to keep the enterprise going. In the fall of 1976, Jobs and Wozniak took Apple I to a computer fair in New York City. Commodore Business Machines offered to buy Apple Computer, but they thought that $100,000 and annual salaries of $36,000 a year for Jobs and Wozniak was too much to pay for a garage-based operation.

Jobs offered to sell Apple Computer to Nolan Bushnell of Atari and was turned down; Bushnell saw no future in microprocessors. Wozniak approached Hewlett-Packard about buying Apple, but they didn't want to get into that "dubious" market. Finding no buyers for the company, Jobs and Wozniak addressed the shortcomings of the Apple I.

Wozniak had already started to design the next generation computer, so Jobs farmed out the design of the power supply. Jobs insisted on a power supply that required no cooling fan. After another designer failed with a cassette interface, Wozniak designed a straightforward interface for use in loading the BASIC programming language into the computer. Jobs devised a wooden case for the Apple I made by a local cabinet maker. However, it was heavy and didn't dissipate heat well; it cost almost as much as the circuit board.

When they outgrew their bedroom / garage operation, Jobs contracted out the insertion of components into circuit boards. The company he chose didn't want the work, but Jobs succeeded with his "I'm not going to leave here until you agree" approach. Wozniak's next-generation computer incorporated a case, a keyboard, and a power supply. It was designed to be used a with a standard television as the display, both to hold down the cost and because it was less intimidating to the user.

Wozniak added expansion slots to the Apple II to be used by suppliers of add-on circuit boards. This important feature started a new industry when other vendors realized how easy it was to design and build products for the Apple II. Wozniak also designed a read-only memory chip to hold the BASIC programming language, thus eliminating the cassette interface. Jobs found a designer for Apple II's plastic case through contacts at Hewlett-Packard.

Until this point in his life, Jobs had been an individual in search of a cause. In promoting the personal computer, he found his cause. He was still a pushy, abrasive person who "didn't know what he didn't know," but he had a knack for convincing talented people to undertake projects for Apple.

One of Jobs's important early decisions was his choice of an advertising / public relations firm. He asked Intel who had handled its recent advertising campaign and was told it was the Regis McKenna Agency. McKenna turned Jobs down. Jobs persisted; he called McKenna three or four times a day until he agreed to take on Apple as a client. McKenna's first action was to change the logo. Wayne had designed the original black and white logo with Isaac Newton sitting under a tree with one apple on a limb. McKenna redesigned the logo using an apple with multicolored bands and a bite, or byte, taken out of it. Apple used that multi-colored logo until it was replaced in 1998.

The fledgling enterprise needed capital to expand. Jobs asked Nolan Bushnell of Atari to recommend a venture capitalist. Bushnell suggested Don Valentine of Sequoia Ventures, but Valentine wasn't interested. Valentine told Jobs and Wozniak they weren't thinking big enough; he suggested they talk with Mike Markkula, who made his first million when Intel went public. Markkula, who had retired at the age of thirty-three, offered to devote four years to Apple and provide $250,000 to develop and manufacture the Apple II in return for a one-third ownership in the company.

Markkula's offer was dependent upon Wozniak leaving Hewlett-Packard and working for Apple full-time. Wozniak refused, even though his division of Hewlett-Packard was moving to Oregon, and he didn't want to move. He changed his mind when a friend told him that he didn't have to become a manager; he could continue as an engineer.

Markkula helped Jobs and Wozniak prepare a business plan. On January 3, 1977, Apple Computer Corporation was incorporated and, within three months, bought out the partnership for $5,308.96. Jobs, Wozniak, and Markkula each owned thirty percent and Rod Holt, designer of the power supply and finisher of Wozniak's projects, owned ten percent.

Markkula's strengths were business planning and marketing strategy. He had no desire to be president of Apple; he recommended his friend, Michael Scott, who was responsible for producing $30 million worth of components a year at

National Semiconductor. Scott was an aggressive manager who could make tough decisions, in contrast with the diplomatic, mild-mannered Markkula.

As on the development of Apple I, Jobs worked closely with the circuit board contractor on the Apple II. The circuit board, due to Wozniak's original design of sixty-two chips and ICs and to Jobs's efforts as the "rejector," was a work of art. It was easy to produce and it looked good when the cover was raised. Jobs persisted in negotiating bargain-basement prices for the Apple II's components.

Neither Markkula nor Scott could get along with Jobs; daily confrontations occurred between Scott and Jobs, partly because Markkula pushed off all of his dealings with Jobs onto Scott. Jobs was openly critical of the work of the young employees; no one could mistake him for a diplomat. As the business increased and company operations became more formal, Jobs continued going in several directions at once.

Wozniak fit less well with the expanding environment and wasn't consulted as often as he had been. The close working relationship between the two Steves began to change. Wozniak spent so much time at Apple that his marriage broke up. He gave his wife fifteen percent of his Apple stock in the divorce settlement.

In early 1977, Apple II was demonstrated in a classy booth at the West Coast Computer Faire in San Francisco. Jobs bought his first suit to wear at the Faire. Apple II captivated the 13,000 attendees; 300 orders were taken.

During 1977, Markkula worked hard to obtain additional capital to fuel Apple's growth. He was astoundingly successful. In January 1978, financing arrangements were completed, and Apple was valued at $3 million. Venrock Venture, a firm that invested Rockefeller money, invested $288,000; Don Valentine, who earlier had declined investing in Apple, invested $150,000; Arthur Rock, who made millions on Intel and Scientific Data Systems stock, invested $57,600. Rock also became an important advisor to the fledgling enterprise.

Henry Singleton of Teledyne invested $108,000 and agreed to serve on the board.

In early 1978, Wozniak completed his design for a floppy disk drive, and it went into production. Wozniak considered this his best design; it added important functionality to the Apple II by allowing programmers to produce software that could be transferred from computer to computer reliably.

Also in 1978, Markkula suggested that Apple enter the education market. His daughter was learning grade school math, and he could see the enormous potential of the market. His efforts ultimately led to the establishment of the Apple Education Foundation. Education became a lucrative market for Apple.

The next product was an enhanced Apple II, Apple Plus, that had an improved start-up routine and an updated version of BASIC software. Memory was doubled to forty-eight kilobytes. However, enhancement wasn't enough; the company provided additional features requested by customers and dealers, such as:

- Increasing the width of the display from forty to eighty characters
- Providing lowercase as well as uppercase letters
- Providing additional memory to accommodate more sophisticated programs
- Ensuring compatibility between the Apple II and new machines
- Bundling the software and providing it with the purchase of the hardware

Wozniak wasn't directly involved with the next machine, the Apple III, as he had been on earlier products. Jobs designed the case first and then made the designers fit within the case as best they could. The designers didn't have enough space, but Jobs wouldn't enlarge the case. As a result, they designed a circuit board to piggyback onto the motherboard. To save money, they didn't use gold contacts (that don't corrode) to connect the two boards. The connectors corroded, and the Apple III wasn't reliable.

Fortunately, sales of Apple II, which had little competition in 1979, were strong. Apple sold an additional $7,273,801 worth of stock that year. 1979 was also the year that the spreadsheet application entered the marketplace. Dan Fylstra, a Boston software entrepreneur, developed VisiCalc on an Apple II and offered it to Apple for $1 million. Apple declined; however, when VisiCalc was shipped in the fall of 1979, it only ran on the Apple II. The availability of a spreadsheet application and of Wozniak's floppy disk drive spurred Apple II sales.

Following Apple III's limited success, Jobs needed a new goal. He hired two Hewlett-Packard managers, one to manage software development and the other to manage engineering. Jobs's goal was a machine based on 16-bit architecture, rather than the Apple II 8-bit architecture, to sell for $2,000. The new machine, Lisa, was large, awkward-looking, and based on the 68000—the new microprocessor from Motorola.

Lisa was slow in both processing and in screen refreshment speed, but the software group had been innovative in using bit-mapping that provided a one-to-one correspondence between the bits in the computer memory and the picture elements (pixels) on the screen. Screen resolution was considerably higher than that of the Apple II and III. Jobs didn't think that Lisa was "sexy" enough; also, he didn't think it was the right product for the office environment. In seeking a partner, he considered IBM and Xerox. However, at Apple, IBM was considered the enemy.

Xerox had invested in Apple's second private investment placement. Jobs contacted the Xerox Development Corporation, the company's venture capital unit, and offered to let them invest $1 million in Apple if they would give him a tour of their Palo Alto Research Center (PARC). PARC had a talented staff of computer scientists who had made many breakthroughs that Xerox had failed to exploit. Xerox purchased 100,000 shares of Apple at $10.00 a share and opened their doors to Jobs. The twenty-five-year-old entrepreneur had gotten his way again.

Larry Tesler of PARC demonstrated the Alto personal computer to Jobs and seven Apple developers, who salivated when they saw Alto's potential. User interaction with the Alto was revolutionary through the use of icons, menus (action lists), partitions of the screen (windows), and a "mouse." Jobs was moved by what he saw. He shouted: "Why aren't you doing anything with this? This is the greatest thing! This is revolutionary!" After the demonstration, Jobs hired Tesler to work for Apple. Later, Alan Kay, one of PARC's principal computer science visionaries, joined Apple and eventually became an Apple fellow.

In August 1980, Markkula reorganized Apple into three divisions:

- Personal Computer Systems (Apple II and III)
- Professional Office Systems (Lisa)
- Accessories (add-on circuit boards, disk drives, printers, etc.)

Jobs had hoped to be given line authority of a division; instead, he was named chairman of the board.

On December 12, 1980, Apple Computer Corporation went public. Apple's 4.6 million shares sold out within the first hour in the most oversubscribed initial public offering since Ford Motor Company had gone public in 1956. Apple was worth $1.778 billion on the stock market. The company had reached the *Fortune* 500 faster than any company in history. Forty new millionaires were made that day, including:

- Jobs, whose fifteen percent of the outstanding shares was worth $256 million
- Markkula, who owned $239 million of Apple stock
- Wozniak, who was worth $135.6 million
- Scott, the president, who owned Apple stock worth $95.5 million
- Holt, a key designer, who was worth $67 million
- Wozniak's ex-wife, whose divorce settlement stock was

worth $42 million[49]

Without line responsibility, Jobs was again without a project. He needed a subject for his evangelism. Macintosh was the next project to provide an outlet for his zeal. Macintosh was in the R & D phase and had already survived one attempt by Jobs to kill it. Scott had rescued the project. Jef Raskin and his team of two developers planned a "luggable" machine that would be easy to use and would sell for about $1,000. Hardware and software designers would work together from the beginning, and software would be offered as part of the purchase price of the machine.

Jobs promoted the Macintosh within Apple, and three developers were immediately added to the team. Jef Raskin had based the design on the Motorola 6809 microprocessor. Jobs insisted that the 6809 processor be replaced with the faster Motorola 68000; Raskin was overruled.

Jobs challenged Burrell Smith to redesign the Macintosh based on the 68000 by the end of 1980. Smith was a Wozniak-type designer who liked simple designs and worked on a project night and day until it was done. He also had Wozniak's ability to evaluate the elements of a complex design in his head.

The Macintosh design had one circuit board that used off-the-shelf parts, compared to the Lisa's five circuit boards with some custom components. Furthermore, it was twice as fast as the Lisa and could be produced at one-third the price. Jobs took over the project and brought in developers from the successful Apple II, including Wozniak and Holt. Jobs headed the Macintosh Division when it was formed.

Wozniak had taken up flying as a hobby and, in early February 1980, was seriously injured taking off from a local airport. While hospitalized, he moved in and out of consciousness; his friends at Apple waited anxiously for news of his condition. His recovery was slow, and he suffered from amnesia.

As the Macintosh development effort expanded, Jobs

pulled talent from the rest of the company. In fact, he frequently and loudly announced that the future of the company was with the Macintosh "pirates." Ultimately, however, this split between Macintosh developers and other Apple developers divided the company in two. The development deadlines for the Macintosh were so tight that they considered contracting the writing of programs outside of Apple.

The first software developer Jobs sought out was Bill Gates of Microsoft, who wrote the first BASIC programs for personal computers. Gates and his partner, Paul Allen, provided the operating system software (eventually called MS / DOS) for IBM's venture into personal computers. Gates negotiated a non-exclusive agreement with IBM that allowed Microsoft to license IBM's operating environment to other customers.

Jobs and Scott, Apple's president, had a tempestuous working relationship. Scott was one of the few people that Jobs couldn't intimidate. Scott's abrasive personality took a toll on the younger employees. Scott fired the vice president of engineering and was attempting to do that job in addition to his own. Finally, he was edged out by Markkula, who had brought him into the company.

Markkula was in a difficult position because his four-year contract with Apple was almost over. He looked outside Apple for a new president. He wanted John Sculley, who, as president of Pepsi-Cola USA, had taken significant market share from Coca-Cola. Initially, Sculley wasn't interested in joining Apple.

Jobs flew to New York City and courted Sculley. After many long conversations about the future of Apple, Jobs asked Sculley, "Are you going to sell sugar water to children for the rest of your life when you could be doing something really important?" Also, the financial package Apple offered to Sculley was difficult to turn down.

Sculley spent many hours learning the technology. Within his first year on the job, he realized that cuts would have to be made. Apple II was carrying the company, and Lisa was a distinct disappointment. He streamlined the organizational structure and eliminated 1,200 jobs to keep the company profitable. For the time being, Jobs managed the Macintosh Division in addition to serving as chairman of the board. Sculley also redirected the company from producing all of its own software to sponsoring outside software developers, an approach similar to IBM's.

The first disagreements between Jobs and Sculley occurred in 1983. By 1984, when Macintosh sales were considerably below Jobs's estimates, the rift was obvious to everyone. Apple lowered the price of Macintosh from $2,495 to $1,995, but sales continued to be disappointing.

The initial demand for the Apple IIc had declined; eventually, 200,000 machines had to be sold through a liquidator. An attempt to market Lisa as the Macintosh XL wasn't successful. In 1985, Wozniak left the company. He was unhappy with Apple's direction, particularly the lack of recognition of Apple II's contribution to the company's bottom line and the dearth of Apple II development funds.

At the board meeting on April 11, 1985, Sculley removed Jobs as manager of the Macintosh Division and replaced him with Jean-Louis Gassee, the successful head of Apple France. Jobs then attempted to have Sculley removed as president and CEO. However, he misjudged Sculley's support on the board of directors. Finally, their disagreements became so disruptive that the board suggested that Sculley force Jobs out of the company.

When Jobs left Apple, he formed a new computer company called NeXT. He attracted many key Apple developers to his start-up. Apple was alarmed by the loss of critical personnel and was concerned about a potential loss of technology. Jobs sought start-up capital for NeXT; Ross Perot invested $20 million for sixteen percent of the company. Jobs was only moderately successful with NeXT, which generated some income by selling software to Apple. In 1997, Apple's sales and earnings plummeted, and Jobs returned to Apple Computer as "interim" CEO.

Steve Jobs and Steve Wozniak made significant contributions to the computer industry. Working out of a garage, they succeeded where large corporations had failed; they pioneered the personal computer revolution. In 1985, President Reagan awarded National Technology Medals to Steve Jobs and Steve Wozniak at the White House. Together, they provided the technology, drive, and vision to found an industry within an industry. In doing so, they changed the home and workplace environment forever.

CHAPTER 18

INTRODUCTION OF THE PERSONAL COMPUTER

SUCCESS VS. FAILURE—SUMMARY AND ANALYSIS

"Dreamers and doers—the world generally divides men into those two general classifications, but the world is often wrong. There are men who win the admiration and respect of their fellow men. They are the men worthwhile. Dreaming is just another name for thinking, planning, advising—another way of saying that a man exercises his soul. A steadfast soul, holding steady to a dream ideal, plus a sturdy will determined to succeed in any venture, can make any dream come true. Use your mind and your will. They work together for you beautifully if you would only give them a chance."

B. N. Mills

The Palo Alto Research Center (PARC) of the Xerox Corporation was a resounding success at what it was established to do: to perform research and development in digital science and related areas. Developing the Alto personal computer with its advanced capabilities by 1973 was an outstanding accomplishment. The failure was the Xerox Corporation's inability to recognize the Alto's potential and to exploit it.

Xerox missed at least eight opportunities to capitalize on the development of the first comprehensive personal computer at PARC:

- In April 1973, the first Alto was completed. Ten were assembled by the end of the year, but the company didn't promote the product.
- In late 1973, Alto technology was demonstrated to the general manager of the Office Products Division (OPD). He considered PARC's ideas too futuristic. OPD concentrated on word processing typewriter technology.
- In 1974, Xerox's future strategy team suggested combining computers, copiers, and word processing typewriters with PARC's innovations in communications, microcircuitry, and software. No action was taken on their recommendation.
- In 1975, Xerox's Display Word Processing Task Force recommended a new word processor based on Alto. OPD recalculated PARC's estimates for Alto and increased the cost estimates, thus killing the project. The task force's recommendations were ignored. Wang Laboratories capitalized on this concept.
- Later in 1975, Xerox's director of research proposed the formation of a small entrepreneurial team to produce a general-purpose workstation using the Alto. The proposal was rejected.
- In August 1976, PARC developer John Ellenby submitted a proposal on the Alto to the Xerox task force determining new product strategies for the company. No action was taken on Ellenby's proposal.

174

- In 1977, the Alto was showcased at the Xerox "Futures Day" for company employees. PARC researcher Ellenby proposed to Xerox CEO David Kearns that he authorize production of Alto. Kearns decided not to go into production with the Alto.
- In 1978, Don Massaro became general manager of OPD and immediately requested $15 million to produce Star, a networked Alto with additional features. His request was turned down, as was a lower-cost proposal. He proceeded on his own using his OPD budget.

However, Xerox wasn't the only company that failed to foresee the personal computer revolution. In Apple Computer's infancy, Steve Jobs tried to sell the company; Atari, Commodore Business Machines, and Hewlett-Packard rejected his offer.

The dramatic drop in the cost of microprocessor chips during the 1970s is clear in hindsight but wasn't foreseen at the time. Early in that decade, envisioning "computers for one user" affordable to home users was difficult. By the end of the decade, the trend was obvious.

Entrepreneurship within a larger organization is called intrapreneurship. In the 1970s, Xerox wasn't organized to operate entrepreneurially; now, the "American samurai" is set up to reap the benefits of intrapreneurship. Xerox learned the lesson the hard way.

Xerox failed to capitalize on its lead in the development of the personal computer for a strategic reason—the decision to base the Office Products Division in Dallas instead of Silicon Valley. OPD was the obvious choice to exploit the Alto when the acquisition of Scientific Data Systems didn't succeed. Geographic remoteness from the rest of the Corporation contributed to PARC's problems.

If OPD had been located near PARC in Silicon Valley, the synergy between the two units could have made Xerox the leader in personal computers, assuming that OPD would have looked beyond the next quarter's and the next year's bottom line. This short-sightedness wasn't just a Xerox shortcoming; it was recognized as a shortcoming of U.S. industry in general. Xerox financial control analysts, many of whom were Ford alumni, were powerful enough to chose a Dallas location for OPD and to convince management that Alto's potential profits didn't justify proceeding with its production.

Xerox's environment at the time negatively influenced management's willingness to spend sizable sums to enter a "dubious" market. The Federal Trade Commission claimed that Xerox was monopolizing the plain-paper copier market, and the energy of the CEO and many other key managers was diverted to address FTC charges.

During the recession of 1974-75, Xerox's sales and earnings were depressed; many copies were being made on old copiers, but few new copiers were being sold or leased. In 1975, Xerox wrote off just under $1.3 billion on Xerox Data Systems and left the computer business. The Company had many distractions during the time that Alto was struggling for recognition.

Nevertheless, by not exploiting the introduction of the personal computer, Xerox failed conspicuously. The Ford Motor Company's Edsel was another notable corporate failure. However, the Edsel was only one car model; Ford didn't miss out on founding a new industry within an industry.

The founding of Apple Computer with the introduction of the Apple II and the Macintosh is one of the success stories of American industry. Growing from a bedroom / garage operation to a $1.778 billion enterprise in six years was an enviable accomplishment. Apple Computer reached the *Fortune* 500 in less than five years, faster than any company until that time.

The factors of Apple's success included Wozniak's superior designs and Jobs's inspired promotion of their products. The company's timing couldn't have been better. Customers had expressed a need for a one-user computer at a time when the cost of microprocessor chips was dropping dramatically. Apple's location in Silicon Valley was also fortuitous. Area computer hobbyists were pushing the leading edge of the technology, and both microchip manufacturers and high-tech component contractors were located there.

Although Jobs was in his early twenties when the partnership started, his job performance was that of a more experienced individual. Some of his personal characteristics, such as perseverance and determination, were key components of Apple's early success. At times, Jobs was just not willing to take "no" for an answer.

Another element of Apple's success was identifying the need for and hiring managers critical to the growth of the enterprise, such as Mike Markkula and Michael Scott in the business arena and Rod Holt and Burrell Smith in the technical area.

Jobs can be viewed as the catalyst who brought the technical ability of Steve Wozniak and the business acumen of Mike Markkula together to create Apple Computer. Markkula immediately recognized the commercial potential of the personal computer that Wozniak had designed.

Hiring John Sculley at a crossroads in the life of the company was crucial. Sculley had no technical background and, initially, was out of his element at Apple. However, he was a quick study, and he worked hard to learn about the fledgling industry. Application of his management skills and his focus on marketing Apple's products came at a critical time.

Ability to obtain financing was also vital to the company's early success. Like many start-ups, Apple was on the verge of failure several times in its early life. The infusion of capital from sources like Mike Markkula, Venrock Ventures, Don Valentine, Arthur Rock, and Henry Singleton was important to the well-being of the enterprise. Of course, these investors were amply rewarded for the risks they took.

The overriding factor in the success of Apple Computer in introducing the personal computer was a strategic one. Its time had come. The market demanded a one-user computer; Apple provided it. Fortunately, the cost of key components, such as integrated circuits, had dropped, allowing the price of personal computers to be within the budget of the consumer.

RUBBER MADE PRACTICAL

Development of Vulcanization of Rubber

CHAPTER 19

CHARLES GOODYEAR—Developer of Vulcanization

" ... Charles Goodyear was a man who, having undertaken a thing, could not give it up. He struggled for ... years—in debt, with a family to support, and exposed to the derision or reproaches of his friends. Several times he was in debtors' prison. He sold his effects, he pawned his trinkets, he borrowed from his acquaintances, he reduced himself and his young family to the severest straits. When he could no longer buy wood to melt his rubber with, his children used to go out to the fields and pick up sticks for the purpose. Always supposing himself to be on the point of succeeding, he thought the quickest way to get his family out of their misery was to stick to India rubber."

Cyclopedia of Biography

179

In 1834, Charles Goodyear inspected an inflatable rubber life preserver in a store operated by the Roxbury India Rubber Company of Roxbury, Massachusetts, and realized that he could improve the design of the life preserver's inflation valve. He described the new valve design to the store manager, who agreed that Goodyear had invented a better valve. However, he pointed out that unless the quality of rubber products could be improved, the new valve design had no value because rubber products were returned daily. The Roxbury India Rubber Company was struggling financially.

Natural rubber products melted and became sticky and odoriferous in warm weather and were very hard and unyielding in cold weather. In Goodyear's opinion: "Rubber is such a wonderful substance. If only a way could be found to keep it from melting in the summer and getting brittle in the winter, it would be useful to mankind in a thousand ways."[50]

While living in Philadelphia, Goodyear began working with rubber using his wife's pots, pans, rolling pin, and oven in the kitchen of their rented home; he couldn't afford to rent a shop to use for his experiments. After several months of experimentation, he was sent to debtors' prison. The laws of the United States, modeled on English law, punished debtors by putting them in prison. A man who owed you money was jailed, thus preventing him from earning money to repay you. However, Goodyear was permitted to have his equipment in jail to conduct his experiments.

When released from jail, Goodyear attempted to manufacture several hundred pairs of crude rubber shoes. He made them during the winter and stored them to determine what effect the summer heat would have on them. Equipment for controlled temperature experiments didn't exist at that time. He had to wait for the change of season to check his results. The smell of the sticky, melting lumps was obvious to the entire neighborhood that summer.

Shortly after this failure, Goodyear, with his wife, Clarissa, and their children, moved to New York. He sold his household furniture to pay his creditors and used his wife's chest of fine linen as security at their boarding house. A friend let him use a room as a laboratory, and another friend, a druggist, provided him with chemicals on credit. Rubber was shipped in turpentine, and Goodyear thought that turpentine might be the problem. He tried coating some material with pure latex, but noticed no improvement.

Goodyear concluded that the process for which he was searching involved adding a substance to the raw rubber, so he experimented with additives. He commented, "I was encouraged in my efforts by the reflection that what is hidden and unknown, and cannot be discovered by scientific research, will most likely be discovered by accident, if at all, and by the man who applies himself most perseveringly to the subject and is the most observing.... "[51]

To promote rubber products, Goodyear wore clothing made from rubber and carried a hard rubber cane. A person who inquired how to find him was told: "If you see a man in an India-rubber coat, India-rubber shoes, and India-rubber cap, and in his pockets an India-rubber purse with not a cent in it, that is Charles Goodyear."[52]

Goodyear tried mixing the rubber with magnesium salts, which converted the mixture into a hard, dry material. He tried to bind a book with this material, but it became soft and sticky in warm weather. Goodyear boiled his batches in quicklime and water; he could make thin rubber sheets using this process, but not thick rubber products. Goodyear obtained a patent and began to manufacture rubber products. In 1835, he won an award from the American Institute of New York for his development efforts.

Goodyear's perceived success was premature. Any acid, even a mild acid such as vinegar or fruit juice, dropped on the rubberized material caused it to dissolve and become sticky. Goodyear used nitric acid to dissolve some ornamental designs made with bronze paint on a rubberized material. The acid discolored the fabric, so he threw it away. Several days later, he retrieved it, realizing that he hadn't checked the changed appearance of the material sufficiently. He found that the rubber surface was smooth, and it had lost its stickiness. He followed up on these findings and filed a patent for what he called his "acid gas process."

Goodyear rented a factory in New York to produce life preservers and shoes. Even before his factory had produced any products to display, he rented a display room on Broadway. His rubber products sold well, so he rented a larger factory on Staten Island. The business of one of Goodyear's major backers failed in a recession; Goodyear was forced again into poverty.

The Goodyears moved into a shack on Staten Island. The entire family worked in an abandoned rubber factory producing piano covers, table covers, and aprons. Many rubber companies went out of business. The Roxbury India Rubber Company survived despite a significant reduction in sales. Goodyear moved to Roxbury to use a portion of their factory that wasn't being used.

In 1838, Goodyear reached a turning point when he met Nathaniel Hayward, who had lost his job when a Woburn shoe factory closed. Hayward used the empty shoe factory for his rubber experiments. He tried sulfur as an additive and achieved the same results as Goodyear's acid process in drying the rubber and removing the stickiness. Hayward agreed to work as Goodyear's assistant. Goodyear encouraged Hayward to obtain a patent on his sulfur additive process; he bought Hayward's patent rights in 1839.

Goodyear tried unsuccessfully to combine his acid process and Hayward's sulfur process. Goodyear's next break was a U.S. Government contract to make 150 waterproof mailbags. He produced the mailbags, hung them up by the handles, and went away during a summer hot spell. Upon his return, he found the handles stretched and the bags on the floor in a softened, smelly mess. He had received considerable publicity on his government contract; however, he was disappointed again. He concluded that his current process worked well on the surface of his rubber products and on thin rubber, but it failed with thicker rubber.

Goodyear had similar results with other rubber products. His commercial reputation suffered; consumers wouldn't buy his products, and he was penniless again. The Goodyears sold their household possessions one more time. His friends advised him to give up his pursuit of rubber as a usable, practical material. Goodyear had discovered only half of what became known later as the vulcanization process for rubber; he was about to discover the other half of the process.

In January 1839, Goodyear heated mailbag rubber on a wood stove in a house in Woburn, Massachusetts. He shifted the rubber from one hand to the other while talking with his brother, Nelson, and two friends. In gesturing, he accidentally dropped a piece of the rubber on the stove. It hardened like leather instead of melting, as rubber usually did. Goodyear became very excited when he saw the result; he realized that he had discovered a key step in his ultimate process. In his words:

> While on a visit to Woburn (1839) I carried on at my dwelling place some experiments to ascertain the affect of heat on the compound that had decomposed in the mailbags and other articles. I was surprised that a specimen, being carelessly brought into contact with a hot stove, charred like leather. I directly inferred that if the charring process could be stopped at the right point, it might divest the compound of its stickiness throughout, which would make it better than the native gum. Upon further trials with high temperatures I was convinced that my inference was sound. When I plunged India rubber into melted sulfur at great heats, it always charred, never melted.

> What was of supreme importance was that
> upon the border of the charred fabric there was
> a line which had escaped charring and was
> perfectly cured.[53]

Goodyear had made a major breakthrough, but he faced an uphill struggle. He and others had announced product improvements in the past, and the public had been disappointed repeatedly. Consumers weren't willing to buy rubber goods.

Goodyear tried varying the temperature of the rubber. Initially, he used small kitchen stoves for his work, but they were inadequate. Then he used furnaces in nearby factories in Woburn and Lynn. The Goodyear family again relied upon friends and neighbors for gifts of food and of heating fuel in the winter. He also depended on others to provide the raw materials for his work.

Goodyear and his sons built a crude brick oven so they wouldn't have to beg foremen to use their furnaces at times that were unpredictable. He traded rubber products, such as rubber aprons, for the bricks and mortar, since he had no money.

Goodyear moved to Springfield, Massachusetts, where he rented a factory to produce sheet rubber products. Again, he got into financial difficulty and was thrown into debtors' prison. While in prison, he tried unsuccessfully to interest potential backers in his development efforts. When he left prison, he was given financial support by his brother-in-law, William DeForest, enabling him to open a factory in Naugatuck, Connecticut. In 1844, Goodyear applied for a patent in the United States for his 1839 discovery.

Goodyear wanted to apply simultaneously for patents in the United States, England, and France, but he couldn't afford to make all of the samples to apply for the patents. Also, he didn't have the money to travel to England and France to apply; nevertheless, he was awarded a patent in France in

1844, the same year that he was awarded his U.S. patent.

When Goodyear applied for a patent in England, he was told that an English rubber experimenter, Thomas Hancock, had applied for a patent earlier. In his struggle to promote rubber, Goodyear had given away many samples. A sample had been taken to England, where it was examined by Thomas Hancock. It wasn't difficult for him to determine that Goodyear's rubber contained sulfur. In effect, Hancock, who had worked with rubber for years, rediscovered the vulcanization process. Goodyear unsuccessfully contested Hancock's patent in the English courts.

Goodyear could have been a wealthy man if he had been a shrewder businessman. He let money flow through his hands by licensing his process to other manufacturers for a pittance and by spending excessively to display rubber products at expositions and exhibits. However, he was aggressive in protecting his patents against theft, and several of his cases went to the Supreme Court. A well-known case was against Horace H. Day of New Jersey, who used Goodyear's patent without remuneration and claimed to have discovered vulcanization. Daniel Webster took a leave of absence as Secretary of State to defend Goodyear's interests. Webster won "The Great India Rubber Suit" in court after a skillful two-day defense.

Goodyear's exhibit at the "Exhibition of the Works of All Nations" at the Crystal Palace in London was elaborate. He spent $30,000, all of his savings plus borrowed money, on the exhibit, which was centrally located in the main hall and was made entirely of rubber, including sofas, chairs, trays, fans, buttons, canes, combs, and brushes.

In 1854, Goodyear had a more elaborate exhibit at the world's fair in Paris than he had in London. Through a technicality in the French law, his French patent was declared invalid. He had sold licenses for his process to French manufacturers, and he was asked to return their money. Unable to return it, he was imprisoned at Clichy jail. While in jail, he was awarded the Cross of the Legion of Honor by Louis

Napoleon. He was released after a short stay and was treated with respect for the remainder of his stay in France.

Charles Goodyear was $200,000 in debt when he died on July 1, 1860. He considered his life a success; he didn't die a bitter man. His life's work generated many fortunes for others, and his lack of financial success didn't bother him. He wrote, "Life should not be estimated exclusively by the standard of dollars and cents. I am not disposed to complain that I have planted and others have gathered the fruits. A man has cause for regret when he sows and *no one* reaps."[54]

Much of Goodyear's recognition came after his death. In 1939, a statue of Charles Goodyear was unveiled in Akron, Ohio, the rubber capital of the United States, to commemorate his discovery on the wood stove in Woburn in 1839. The Goodyear Tire and Rubber Company was named for him, although it was incorporated many years after he died.

Although synthetic rubber derived from petroleum is used today in making tires, a vulcanization process similar to the one discovered by Goodyear is still in use. In 1976, Goodyear was inducted into the National Inventors' Hall of Fame. He was a member of a select group honored for their technological advances generated through the patent system.

CHAPTER 20

THOMAS HANCOCK

Founder of the Rubber Industry in Great Britain

"Life affords no higher pleasure than that of surmounting difficulties, passing from one step of success to another, forming new wishes and seeing them gratified. He that labors in any great and laudable undertaking has his fatigues first supported by hope and afterwards rewarded by joy."

Dr. Johnson

In 1820, Thomas Hancock established the world's first rubber factory in England and founded the modern rubber industry. As a London coach maker, he had used rubber as a waterproofing material in clothing for his coach passengers. He made his first rubber products by dissolving rubber in turpentine; they weren't successful. His next products were made by using rubber as elastic in articles of clothing such as suspenders, garters, gaiters, gloves, stockings, trousers, and waistcoats.

Hancock discovered the importance of heat in treating rubber in making the "rubber springs" (rubber bands) for these products. The rubber springs tended to pull away from the stitches attaching them to the article of clothing. Hancock exposed the ends of the springs to boiling water to harden them and to prevent the stitches from pulling out of the rubber. He also applied thin pieces of rubber compressed by heat and pressure to both the inside and the outside of shoes and boots to make them waterproof. On April 29, 1820, he was granted English patent no. 4451 for this use of rubber.

Hancock cut strips of rubber for use as elastic bands from blocks of rubber and from rubber bottles imported from South America. Many odd-sized chunks and strips of rubber resulted from this process. To use these scrap pieces, he invented a "masticator," a hollow wooden cylinder with teeth on the inside surface within which a spiked roller was turned by hand. The mechanical action of the roller forced scrap pieces against the cylinder wall and, with no additional ingredients, formed a rubber ball that could then be reused.

Hancock didn't patent his invention because he didn't want others to become familiar with his concept. He and his workers referred to it as a "pickle" to conceal its use. Hancock kept the concept of his masticator secret until 1832, when it was divulged by one of his workmen.

Hancock experienced many setbacks in the early development of the masticator. He improved the process of obtaining reusable rubber by heating the scraps of rubber prior to placing them in the device. From 1820 to 1847, Hancock was awarded sixteen English patents for rubber processes and products, several of which involved mixing another component with rubber. He used oil of turpentine in manufacturing sheet rubber, and he discovered that pitch and tar could also be combined with rubber. A mixture of rubber and pitch was used under the copper sheathing of ships' bottoms as protection against worms attacking the wooden hulls.

Charles MacIntosh, inventor of waterproof fabrics, was an early contemporary of Hancock in the rubber business. MacIntosh started as a chemist looking for uses for the waste products of the Glasgow Gas Works. He used coal naptha, a by-product in the manufacture of coal gas, as a solvent for rubber used to coat fabrics. He overcame the problem of rubber becoming sticky in warm weather by placing it between two fabrics. In 1823, he was granted English patent no. 4804 for raincoats made this way.

Initially, his raincoats leaked through the holes made by the needle in sewing the garment together; the use of double rows of stitches alleviated this problem. MacIntosh called his raincoats "waterproof double textures," but his customers called them "macintoshes." MacIntosh joined the company of individuals for whom an article of clothing is named, including Chesterfield (coats), Derby (hats), and Raglan (sleeves).

In 1825, Hancock became familiar with Charles MacIntosh & Company and was licensed to manufacture macintoshes. In 1830, Hancock began to manufacture his rubber products at the MacIntosh plant in Manchester from masticated rubber shipped from his factory in London. Later in the 1830s, Hancock and MacIntosh became partners.

In 1840, Hancock described in his book, *Personal Narrative of the Origin and Progress of the Caoutchouc or India-Rubber Manufacture in England*, the first rubber samples he had seen that were treated with sulphur:

As nearly as I can remember, about 1840, a

gentlemen from Paris gave me a small kind of doily, or small piece of cambric, covered on one side with rubber of a dingy yellow color, on which was the print, I think, of a female. He also gave me a map printed on rubber without cloth, which would expand by the elasticity of the material. These were the only articles, as far as I can recollect, that I had seen that were not of English or French manufacture. The yellow tinge in the rubber was produced by the use of sulphur, and the appearance of the article was by no means good.[55]

Hancock's second encounter with sulphur-treated rubber samples occurred in 1842:

Some time in the early part of the autumn of 1842, Mr. Brockedon (coiner of the term "vulcanization" based on Vulcan, the god of fire from Roman mythology) showed me some small bits of rubber that he told me had been brought by a person from America, who represented himself as an agent of the inventor; it was said that they would not stiffen by cold, and were not affected by solvents, heat, or oils....

Mr. Brockedon cut, from two of the small pieces that had been given him, two very diminutive bits, and gave them to me; one bit was about one and a half inches long, and one inch and a quarter wide, and perhaps about a twentieth of an inch thick; this bit, on the exterior, was of a dirty yellowish grey colour, and had a little dusty powder upon it; when cut across, the cut edge appeared of a dark colour;

the other bit was of a dark reddish brown throughout, with a clean surface without any dusty appearance. The first named had a slight smell of sulphur, and I thought that a little sulphurous powder had been rubbed on to mislead. On stretching them out thin, I observed that they were both quite opaque. I found they were, as stated, not affected by cold.[56]

Hancock's 283-page book contains no mention of Charles Goodyear.

In late 1842 and early 1843, Hancock conducted experiments treating rubber to prevent its stiffening in cold temperatures. He attempted to produce a "single texture" raincoat with just one layer of fabric and one layer of rubber. He had tried similar experiments twenty years earlier without success.

Goodyear's discovery of the vulcanization process for rubber occurred in early 1839 when he observed the effect of heat applied to rubber in combination with sulphur and lead salts. Goodyear submitted his specification for the process to the U.S. Patent Office in December 1841. Goodyear gave samples of his vulcanized rubber to Stephen Moulton, a young Englishman visiting the United States, and asked Moulton to find a British manufacturer willing to buy the process.

Goodyear wasn't alone in thinking that the secret of the process by which he "changed" rubber couldn't be deduced by studying the samples. Moulton showed the samples to William Brockedon, an inventor who had contacts with the MacIntosh Company. Moulton returned to America without obtaining the agreement from the MacIntosh Company to buy the process for the requested £50,000.

Unfortunately, Moulton left samples with Brockedon, who passed them on to Hancock. Hancock realized the importance of the samples and conducted experiments to duplicate them immediately. It wasn't difficult for him to detect that sulphur had been used in the process. Once Hancock had evidence that the "change" in rubber for which he had been searching for twenty years could be accomplished, he attempted to rediscover the process. He worked alone in his laboratory for more than a year, and "resolved, if possible, not to be outdone by any." He did, however, use the advice of experts, such as chemists.

Hancock was close to duplicating the process when he applied for a provisional patent on November 21, 1843, just weeks before Goodyear applied for a patent in England. Since Goodyear didn't have money for samples and for travel to apply for all the necessary patents at one time, he applied for the U.S. patent promptly but delayed in requesting the English and French patents. His French patent was granted on April 16, 1844.

Hancock, according to English law, had six months to complete his process, and, on May 30, 1844, he was granted the patent. When Goodyear applied for an English patent, it was denied even though Hancock later admitted under oath that the first vulcanized rubber he saw was from the United States. Hancock's patent didn't include lead salts in the process; however, this wasn't a requirement. The purpose of the salts was to reduce the amount of heat required in the vulcanization process.

The principles followed by the British patent authorities at this time were different from those followed by the American and German patent offices. The main objective of the British was to register claims to patents, not to guarantee the originality or the validity of the patent. In the United States and Germany, the inventor had to prove that his patent was "novel and deserving." Inequities existed in many of early patent processes. In 1851, Isambard Kingdom Brunel, designer of the first transatlantic steamer, the Great Western railway, and the Thames tunnel, testified before the Select Committee of the House of Lords on Patent Laws:

Q. Speaking of current inventions, you would say that by no means the best invention wins the race?
A. I believe it is rarely so; the chances are entirely against it. I believe it is rare that the man most able to work it out, and who arrived at the best collection of ideas on the subject, is the patentee.
Q. He generally finds himself anticipated by some more rapid projector?
A. Yes.[57]

Another English technologist, Alexander Parkes, inventor in 1846 of a cold process of vulcanization using a chemical process without heat, wrote in his personal copy of Hancock's *Personal Narrative*:

> I think it is a sad thing for Mr. Thomas Hancock to try to claim the discovery of vulcanization from the fact of the vulcanized rubber first being brought by Goodyear from America and pieces given to Brockedon "Hancock's co-partner" and others. These were seen, examined and experimented on by several and it was found to be free sulphur in a heated and molten state that produced the permanent elasticity of rubber. The above facts related to me both by Brockedon and Thomas Hancock. It is quite true that Mr. Thomas Hancock obtained the first patent in England.[58]

The main uses of rubber during the nineteenth century were for clothing and household products. Overshoes, another successful rubber product, were more popular in the United States than in Britain; however, overshoes made in the United States and licensed by Hancock were exported to Britain.

Invention of the pneumatic tire guaranteed the explosive

growth of the rubber industry. Robert William Thomson filed a patent for a "hollow belt" filled with air in England in 1845, in France in 1846, and in the United States in 1847. No use was made of Thompson's "elastic belt" until 1888, when John B. Dunlop, a veterinary surgeon in Belfast, Ireland, used them on his son's tricycle. His son entered a race on a tricycle that used double tube pneumatic tires encased in Irish linen laced to the wheels.

Dunlop was granted a patent for his tire design in England but was denied patents in France and the United States because of the similarity to the Thompson patent granted over forty years earlier. Dunlop began to manufacture tires for tricycles and bicycles and was positioned for the rapid growth of the automotive tire industry beginning in 1898.

The early efforts of Hancock, as well as of MacIntosh and Thompson, formed the groundwork for the modern rubber industry in England. Goodyear's work formed the basis for the rubber industry in the United States, but the patent structure for rubber products and processes in England gave Britain the commercial advantage in the formative years.

CHAPTER 21

DEVELOPMENT OF VULCANIZATION

SUCCESS VS. FAILURE—SUMMARY AND ANALYSIS

"The man who succeeds above his fellows is the one who, early in life, clearly discerns his object, and towards that habitually directs his powers. Even genius itself is but fine observation strengthened by fixity of purpose. Every man who observes vigilantly and resolves steadfastly grows unconsciously into genius."

Edward Bulwer-Lytton

A comparison of the personal characteristics of Charles Goodyear, the pure inventor, and Thomas Hancock, the entrepreneur / inventor, is similar to a comparison between steamboat developers John Fitch and Robert Fulton. Goodyear is another example of a driven individual willing to endure hardships to continue his development activities.

Goodyear was willing to let his family go hungry, wear worn-out clothing, and suffer winter cold due to a lack of heating fuel. At times, his family was totally dependent on relatives and friends for food, clothing, and fuel. Goodyear tolerated these conditions because he thought that, if he continued his experiments with rubber, success was just around the corner. In his opinion, the best way to help his family was to find a way to make rubber a useful product.

With respect to perseverance, Fitch and Goodyear were in a class by themselves. They were so dedicated to their development efforts that they never considered giving up. Goodyear is another example of a highly motivated individual who didn't fit the pattern of Abraham Maslow's hierarchy of needs. He addressed his self-actualization and achievement needs first, finding a way to make rubber useful and to market it successfully. Satisfying his physiological needs, such as food, drink, clothing, and shelter, were a lower priority.

Goodyear's English competitor, entrepreneur / inventor Thomas Hancock, was a more practical businessman than Goodyear. Hancock started manufacturing rubber products in England in 1820, fourteen years before Goodyear became interested in rubber. Hancock was successful in manufacturing and selling rubber products, even with their early shortcomings.

Hancock was satisfied with the profits from his business and didn't actively seek a partner. The partnership he formed with Charles MacIntosh in the 1830s was a partnership of convenience, not of necessity. Hancock was protective of his inventions. He didn't patent his rubber masticator for twelve years, because he didn't want the concept to become public knowledge.

Goodyear, in contrast with Hancock, not only displayed samples of his vulcanized rubber, but left samples with his competitors. He didn't think that anyone could deduce his process from samples. He was wrong. By 1842, Hancock had twenty-two years of experience in the rubber industry. When he realized that rubber could be processed to make useful products in forms other than thin sheets and strips, he focused on rediscovering the process. He was aware of the gaps in his knowledge and was willing to consult with expert chemists to fill those gaps. In 1842-43, he concentrated on duplicating the discovery of the vulcanization process.

Aggressiveness, a key ingredient of success for entrepreneurs as demonstrated by Hancock, is a desirable quality. Entrepreneurs realize that an improved product or process is only one factor contributing to success, although it is a major one. They must also market and promote the product aggressively.

Another quality displayed by Hancock is less desirable. He exhibited ethical shortcomings in his treatment of Goodyear. Hancock didn't do anything illegal in the pursuit of his vulcanization patent in England. In fact, the London patent office operated in a way that favored English inventors over foreign inventors. Nevertheless, Hancock's refusal to acknowledge Goodyear's contribution to his success was the action of a small man.

Hancock was a stronger financial manager than Goodyear. If Goodyear had made better financial decisions, he would have been a wealthy man. The fees that Goodyear charged for his licenses weren't sufficient to recover his development costs and to finance his manufacturing operations. He had the outlook of an inventor, not a businessmen. Promoting the usefulness of rubber was more important to him than making a profit. Earnings weren't a high priority with him.

Goodyear's excessive spending on displays of rubber products is also questionable. He rented a showroom on

Broadway in New York before he had any products to display and went into debt, spending $30,000 for an exhibit at the Crystal Palace in London.

Hancock also had more organizational ability than Goodyear. Hancock was the steady businessman who continually built on an established base. Increases in the size of his business were incremental. Goodyear, on the other hand, managed by fits and starts. Many of his ventures went under; little continuity existed in his business efforts.

Hancock succeeded where Goodyear failed for several reasons, including Goodyear's lack of financial ability. Hancock beat Goodyear to the English patent for the vulcanization of rubber, but Goodyear could have been financially successful with just his U.S. patent. Goodyear did, however, successfully defend his patents in infringement suits in court.

Goodyear, the inventor, was enamored of the product, not the organization, as an entrepreneur would be. A key factor in measuring success is the yardstick used. Should success be measured by the profits made? Should it be measured at some higher level, for example, ethics? Is the opinion of the individual involved a major factor as to whether he or she was a success?

In terms of profits of the enterprise, Goodyear was a failure, and Hancock was a success. On the higher level issue of ethics, Goodyear was a success, and, to an extent, Hancock was a failure. A comparison of Goodyear and Hancock provides us with another example of relative success, not necessarily of success and failure.

EVOLUTIONARY DEVELOPMENT

Invention of the Airplane

CHAPTER 22

SAMUEL LANGLEY

Early Aircraft Inventor

"Because a fellow has failed once or twice, or a dozen times, you don't want to set him down as a failure 'til he's dead or loses his courage—and that's the same thing."

George Horace Larimer

Samuel Pierpont Langley was born on August 22, 1834, in Roxbury, Massachusetts. His parents, Mary Williams Langley and Samuel Langley, a wholesale merchant, were both of English descent. Langley attended private schools, Boston Latin School and Boston High School, from which he graduated in 1851. In his youth, he read extensively in history, literature, and science—particularly astronomy.

From 1851 to 1864, Langley worked as an architect and civil engineer in Chicago and St. Louis. When he returned from touring scientific societies and observatories in Europe in 1865 with his brother John, a chemist, Langley became an assistant at the Harvard University Observatory. In 1866, he was appointed assistant professor of mathematics at the Naval Academy, where he restored the observatory.

In 1867, Langley was appointed professor of astronomy and physics at the University of Western Pennsylvania (University of Pittsburgh) and director of the Allegheny Observatory. Langley, a popular speaker and writer on astronomy, drew classic sketches of sunspots and made observations on the total solar eclipses of 1869, 1870, and 1878. His greatest contributions in astronomy were spectral measurements of lunar and solar radiation.

In 1878, Langley invented the bolometer, an electrical thermometer used to measure the distribution of radiation in the spectrum of the sun. He used the bolometer to measure both the transparency of the atmosphere to various solar rays and their intensity at high altitudes. Langley devised a measure of the intensity of solar heat called the "solar constant of radiation." In 1887, he began research in aerodynamics by measuring "lift" and "drag" on a plane surface inclined to its direction of travel.

In January 1887, Langley was appointed assistant secretary of the Smithsonian Institution and became secretary (director) of the Institution later that year. In 1888, he published *The New Astronomy*, which became a classic in the field. Three of his most important contributions at the

Smithsonian were the establishment of the Astrophysical Observatory, the National Gallery of Art, and the National Zoological Park.

At the Smithsonian Institution, Langley continued his experiments with heavier-than-air aircraft that he had begun in Pittsburgh. The field of aeronautics was ridiculed at the time, and many people, including scientists, thought that humans would never fly. Langley was considered a serious scientist; his peers criticized his studies in aeronautics. From 1891 through 1893, he built and flew thirty-one propeller-driven model airplanes powered by rubber bands. Some of his model aircraft, which he called "aerodromes," flew distances of over seventy-five feet.

In 1891, Langley published *Experiments in Aerodynamics* and two years later published *The Internal Work of the Wind*. He incorporated the principles of flight from these two papers into a series of powered model biplanes with fourteen-foot wingspans. Since there were no lightweight gasoline engines, he built gasoline-heated, flash-boiler steam engines that weighed five pounds per horsepower. In 1891, he predicted that a one-horsepower steam engine weighing twenty pounds could propel a 200-pound airplane at forty-five miles per hour, and, furthermore, that "mechanical flight is possible with engines we now possess."

In May 1896, Langley's model no. 5 was catapulted from a houseboat at Quantico on the Potomac River, flew 3,000 feet, and landed without damage. Later that year, model no. 6 had a successful flight of 4,200 feet at thirty-five miles per hour. In 1898, the Bureau of Ordnance of the War Department appropriated $50,000 for him to design and build an airplane to carry a man aloft.

At the turn of the century, Langley was in his sixties and had a heavy build. He hired an assistant, Charles Manley, to pilot the aircraft. Manley, an engineer, had developed the five-cylinder water-cooled radial engine used to power the manned aircraft. The engine, an advanced design for its time, weighed 125 pounds and generated 52.4 horsepower.

On August 8, 1903, a one-quarter-scale model of the manned aircraft flew 1,000 feet with a smaller engine of similar design. A carpenter at the Smithsonian built the body of the manned machine, and John Wadkins, Curator of Transportation at the National Museum, served as an advisor. Thinly drawn steel tubes were used as structural members because aluminum wasn't yet in use.

On October 8, the full-sized biplane with Manley aboard was catapulted from a houseboat on the Potomac River. Manley wore a cork-lined jacket and was so optimistic that he strapped a compass to his leg to use in finding his way back if he got lost on a lengthy flight. Langley was busy with his responsibilities back at the Smithsonian and wasn't present for the test flight. Manley was headed into a five mile-per-hour wind; however, a part of the aircraft caught on the launching device and the plane was projected downward. It came to rest in sixteen feet of water about 150 feet from the houseboat. Manley was unharmed.

The press was merciless. The New York *Times* editorial was representative:

> The ridiculous fiasco which attended the attempt at aerial navigation in the Langley flying machine was not unexpected. The flying machine which will really fly might be evolved by the combined and continuous efforts of mathematicians and mechanicians in from one to ten million years—provided we can meanwhile eliminate such little drawbacks as the existing relation between weight and strength in inorganic materials. No doubt the problem has its attractions for those it interests, but to ordinary men, it would seem as if the effort might be employed more profitably.[59]

Langley used photographs to evaluate the causes of the failure. The 42-foot wings that provided a wing area of 1,040 square feet were insufficiently braced and showed the strain of attempting to lift the 850-pound load of airplane, engine, and pilot. As suspected at the time of the launch, the main problem was that the launching mechanism snagged the aircraft as it began to take off. Other problems were structural deficiencies and shortcomings with the control mechanisms. With funds almost gone and winter approaching, Langley decided to rebuild the aircraft and try one more test flight.

On December 8, 1903, Langley was present at the second launch of the "Great Aerodrome" from the houseboat on the Potomac. The craft hung up again on the launch rail, and Manley said that "just before the machine was freed from the launching car he felt an extreme swaying motion immediately followed by a tremendous jerk which caused the machine to quiver all over."[60] The support wires connecting the tail and rear wings snapped; the aircraft turned upward and fell backward into the water near the houseboat.

Manley almost drowned. He was pinned under the cockpit, and his cork-lined vest snagged on part of the aircraft. He tore the jacket free, came up under a block of ice, and swam to open water. His frozen clothes had to be cut from him, and he was given a tumbler of whiskey. He wasn't used to drinking; he uttered the "most voluble series of blasphemies" ever heard around the Smithsonian. When asked about this later, Manley had no recollection of it.

Again, the newspapers attacked Langley. One reporter suggested that the aircraft should be sent off the houseboat upside down to improve its chances of getting airborne. The New York *Times* added: "We hope that Prof. Langley will not put his substantial greatness as a scientist in further peril by continuing to waste his time, and the money involved, in further airship experiments. Life is short, and he is capable of services to humanity incomparably greater than can be expected to result from trying to fly."[61] Other columnists called the aircraft a "buzzard" and "Langley's Folly" and accused Langley of wasting public funds.

Langley observed after the December trial: "Failure in the aerodrome [aircraft] itself or its engines there has been none; and it is believed that at the moment of success, and when the engineering problems have been solved, that a lack of means has prevented a continuance of the work." He didn't continue with the aircraft trials. Private individuals, including Jacob Schiff, offered to fund further development work, but Langley refused their support. In his opinion, it was a project from which the nation would benefit, and therefore development support should come from public funds. Unfortunately, the Bureau of Ordnance had lost interest in his experiments.

After deciding not to continue with his aircraft experiments, Langley commented:

> I have brought to a close the portion of the work which seemed to be specially mine: the demonstration of the practicality of mechanical flight. For the next stage, which is the commercial and practical development of the idea, it is probable that the world may look to others ... The great universal highway overhead is now soon to be opened.[62]

Many factors were involved in Langley's giving up his aircraft experiments, including health problems, the burden of the administration of the Smithsonian Institution, and being overwhelmed by the adverse comments of the press. Negative comments about his experiments from other members of the scientific community bothered him most of all. An attempt was made to remove him from his position as secretary of the Smithsonian. He never married, so there was no home life to soften the blows to his career.

In November 1905, Langley suffered a stroke. He recovered partially, but lost the use of his right arm and leg. He suffered a second stroke and died on February 27, 1906, in Aiken, South Carolina. A friend observed that he died "feeling in many ways that his life had been a failure."

Langley wasn't a failure in life. He made significant contributions to the fields of astronomy and aircraft design and was the recipient of many scientific honors, including the gold and silver medals of the American Academy of Arts and Sciences, the gold medal of the National Academy of Sciences, the Janssen medal of the Institute of France, and the Rumford medal of the Royal Society of London. He was a correspondent of the Institute of France and a member of the National Academy of Sciences, the Royal Society of London, the Royal Society of Edinburgh, and the Academia dei Lincei of Rome.

Orville Wright

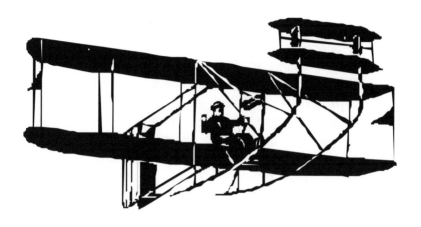

CHAPTER 23

ORVILLE AND WILBUR WRIGHT

Inventors of the Airplane

"These three things—work, will, success—fill human existences. Will opens the door to success, both brilliant and happy. Work passes through these doors, and at the other end of the journey success comes in to crown one's efforts."

Louis Pasteur

Wilbur Wright, born on April 16, 1867, near Millville, Indiana, and Orville Wright, born on August 19, 1871, in Dayton, Ohio, were two of seven children of Milton Wright, a bishop of the United Brethren church, and Susan Koerner Wright. Neither Wilbur nor Orville graduated from high school. Wilbur didn't graduate because his family moved from Indiana to Ohio before he finished his senior year, and Orville took advanced college preparatory courses in his junior year that prevented him from graduating with his class.

Wilbur and Orville were excellent students who took advantage of an extensive family library and expanded their knowledge through private study. They excelled in mathematics and science and benefited from growing up in an inquiring, well-educated family. In December 1892, the brothers opened their first shop to sell and repair bicycles. In 1895, they began to design and build their own bicycles because of increased competition in selling and repairing "safety" bicycles.

Wilbur and Orville worked extremely well as a team; it is unlikely that either would have achieved the success individually that they accomplished together. Wilbur observed that "from the time we were little children my brother Orville and myself lived together, played together, worked together and, in fact, thought together. We usually owned all of our toys in common and talked over our thoughts and aspirations so that nearly everything that was done in our lives has been the result of conversations, suggestions, and discussions between us."

In August 1896, when Orville was seriously ill with typhoid fever, Wilbur heard about the death of aviation pioneer Otto Lilienthal in Germany. Lilienthal's back had been broken when his kite stalled in a gust of wind and fell fifty feet. Lilienthal had added to the body of aeronautical knowledge, but his technique for controlling the craft was limited. He relied on the pilot shifting his weight to control the kite.

On May 30, 1899, Wilbur wrote to the Smithsonian

Institution requesting information about human flight. He wrote that "my observations ... have ... convinced me that human flight is possible and practicable." He intended to "begin a systematic study of the subject in preparation for practical work." The Smithsonian's suggested reading list included *The Aeronautical Annual for 1895, 1896,* and *1897,* edited by James Means; *Experiments in Aerodynamics* by Samuel Langley; and *Progress in Flying Machines* by Octave Chanute.

To test their ideas about control systems, Wilbur built a small two-winged kite with a wingspan of five feet and a chord (wing width) of thirteen inches. They used a canard configuration with the stabilizing surface (elevator) ahead of the wings. With this kite, they tested their concept of "wing warping" that provided control of the craft's roll motion in the air, which, in modern aircraft, is controlled by ailerons in the wings. Wilbur demonstrated the concept with an empty cardboard box that had held a bicycle inner tube. The box retained its lateral stiffness when he twisted it. He showed Orville how the idea could be applied to biplane wings.

In August 1900, Wilbur and Orville started constructing their first full-sized glider capable of manned flight. The metal struts, wing ribs, and metal fittings were made in Dayton. French sateen fabric was used to cover the ash and spruce frame. Wilbur asked Octave Chanute and the National Weather Bureau for recommendations on a site for their test flights. Wilbur selected Kitty Hawk, North Carolina, because of its fifteen- to twenty-mile-an-hour winds, its lack of hills and trees, and its sandy surface. He traveled to Kitty Hawk ahead of Orville and stayed with the Tate family until he selected a site and pitched a tent. Orville arrived in September.

Wilbur had planned to buy eighteen-foot lengths of spruce en route for use as spars, but the longest he could find were sixteen-foot lengths. They modified their kite's wingspan and used a smaller wing surface area, 165 square feet instead of

200, than they had planned. Wooden bows added to the wing tips increased the wingspan to 17 1/2 feet; wing chord was five feet. The total weight of the craft was fifty-two pounds. They didn't seal or varnish the fabric on the 1900 glider as they had on the 1899 kite.

In October, they flew the tethered glider with a man on board. Young Tom Tate did most of the piloting because he weighed less than Wilbur or Orville. The brothers also flew the glider as a unmanned kite using lines to the ground to control it. In addition, Wilbur and Orville tried flying it with a fifty-pound ballast. After several days of tests, the glider was caught in a gust of wind and severely damaged. They considered giving up; instead, they spent three days repairing it.

Wilbur and Orville moved the glider to Kill Devil Hills to take advantage of higher winds. On October 20, Wilbur became the first of the brothers to experience free flight. Wilbur conducted flights of 300 to 400 feet over a duration of fifteen to twenty seconds. The brothers were disappointed with the lift of the glider, but they realized it was at least partially due to the reduced wing area. After completing the trials, they gave the glider to the Tate family to use for materials and left for Dayton on October 23 with plans to build another glider at Kitty Hawk the following summer.

The 1901 glider was a biplane with a wingspan of twenty-two feet, a chord of seven feet, and a wing area of 290 square feet. The camber (curvature) of the wing was increased. The ninety-eight pound craft was the largest anyone had flown up until that time. In Dayton, they hired a machinist, Charlie Taylor, who later designed and built the engine for their 1903 aircraft. In July 1901, Wilbur and Orville traveled to Kitty Hawk, where they constructed a sixteen- by twenty-five-foot hangar for their glider.

Wilbur conducted the test flights. The lift and the speed of the new glider were disappointing. Control of pitch wasn't as responsive as they had hoped, and Wilbur experienced a few stalls in which the forward stabilizer assisted him in making a safe landing. The leading edge of the wing was sharpened to decrease wind resistance, but it provided only a limited improvement. In August, Wilbur made flights of thirteen seconds or more over distances of up to 389 feet.

The wing warping mechanism worked well, but they experienced a reversal in the roll motion of the glider that they couldn't explain. On one flight, Wilbur was distracted when this occurred, and he didn't respond quickly to the controls. He dropped onto the sand abruptly and suffered a black eye and a bruised nose. Soon afterward, they returned to Dayton. On the way back to Dayton, Wilbur told Orville that "men would not fly for fifty years."

The brothers expanded their shop by adding a band saw and a drill press powered by a one-cylinder engine. Charlie Taylor, whose assistance was essential to their experiments, designed and manufactured their first internal combustion engine. With a machinist like Taylor and the additional equipment, the Wrights were now able to make both bicycle and airplane parts of increased complexity.

Octave Chanute invited the brothers to present a summary of their work to the Western Society of Engineers in Chicago. On September 18, 1901, Wilbur presented his paper, "Some Aeronautical Experiments." It was well received, and it supplanted other material as the state-of-the-art reference for aeronautical experimenters.

Wilbur and Orville built a small wind tunnel to use in checking the coefficients required to design their aircraft. The results were so useful that they built a larger wind tunnel, a wooden box sixteen inches square and six feet long with a glass observation window on top. They worked for a month to ensure that the thirty-mile-per-hour wind flowed through the tunnel without turbulence. It wasn't the first wind tunnel, but the discipline they used to apply aerodynamic data directly to the design of aircraft was new. They collected data for a variety of wing configurations to use in lift and drag formulae.

Wilbur and Orville found that the Smeaton coefficient, a factor used in their aerodynamic formula, was off by fifty percent. In addition to studying lift and drag, they also studied the aspect ratio, the ratio of the wingspan to the wing chord. The brothers learned that long narrow wings produce more lift than short wide wings with the same wing area.

In December, they discontinued their experiments and returned to the bicycle business that financed their experiments. Chanute offered to ask Andrew Carnegie to provide financial support for their aeronautical work. However, the Wrights didn't want to be indebted to anyone; they chose to continue to finance own experimental work.

Wilbur and Orville designed the 1902 glider with a wingspan of thirty-two feet and a wing chord of five feet (compared with the 1901 wingspan of twenty-two feet and a chord of seven feet) that doubled the aspect ratio. In February 1902, they added a fixed rudder to address the problem of the reversal of the direction of a roll when the wing warping mechanism was applied.

Wilbur and Orville arrived in Kitty Hawk to find that the force of high winds and wind-driven sand had virtually destroyed their hangar. They rebuilt it sturdier and with more comforts than before. On September 19, the 1902 glider with 305 square feet of wing area was ready for its first test. It had a forward elevator of fifteen square feet and a longer, narrower rudder than the 1901 glider, from which the support struts were reused. The new glider weighed almost 120 pounds. The first tests were unmanned; they made fifty tests covering distances of under 200 feet during the first two days.

In the first manned flights, Wilbur encountered crosswinds that affected the lateral stability more severely than on previous models. They addressed the problem by adjusting the wing trusses and causing the tips of the wings to droop about four inches. A crosswind couldn't catch a wing tip as easily as before. Orville began to make flights at this point. On one of his early attempts, he lost control at an altitude of thirty feet with disastrous results for the glider. Fortunately, Orville was unhurt. They rebuilt the craft in three days.

The reversal of the roll motion when the wing warping mechanism was applied, the cause of Orville's crash, was a recurring problem. It is now called a tailspin. In the middle of the night, Orville thought of a solution to the problem. In the morning, he suggested to Wilbur that they install a movable rudder to compensate for the sudden change in direction. Wilbur agreed with the solution but suggested that the rudder control be coupled with the wing warping mechanism because the pilot already had enough on his mind.

The evolution of the controls of the Wright airplane was now complete. Three-axis motion could now be controlled; that is, they could control pitch, roll, and yaw. They had invented the first truly controllable aircraft and were ready for powered flight. On October 28, they left for Dayton. The Wright's first patent application, which they filed at the end of 1902, was denied because it lacked clarity. They hired a patent attorney to help them; nevertheless, they weren't granted a patent until May 1906. It described the principles demonstrated by the 1902 glider and included no reference to powered aircraft.

During the winter, Wilbur and Orville designed the 1903 powered aircraft that they called the "Flyer." They calculated that the airplane would weigh 625 pounds with a pilot, assuming that the propellers and engine weighed 200 pounds. No commercially-available four-cycle engine met their specifications of eight or nine horsepower with a weight of under 180 pounds. Charlie Taylor designed a twelve-horsepower engine with four cast-iron cylinders in a cast-aluminum crankcase cooled by a water jacket. It had no radiator or water pump; the water didn't circulate.

The Wrights used bicycle sprocket and chain technology to connect two contra-rotating pusher propellers mounted behind the wings with the engine. They were disappointed in the efficiency of existing propellers and realized they would have to design their own. Orville and Wilbur considered propellers as wings that moved in a rotary motion. The propellers were 8 1/2 feet in diameter and were made from three laminations of 1 1/8-inch spruce. The 1903 craft had a wingspan of 44 and 1/3 feet, a 6 1/2-foot chord, and a wing area of 510 square feet.

In September 1903, the Wrights left for Kitty Hawk. Over the next three months, they experienced bad weather, many technical problems, and some disappointing flights with the 1902 glider. The loaded weight of the 1903 aircraft had increased from 625 to 700 pounds. The engine misfired frequently, placing severe strain on the propeller shafts. The damaged shafts had to be returned to Dayton for repair. The reinstalled shafts shook loose the nuts holding the sprockets in position. Bicycle cement on the nuts solved that problem.

The steel-tube propeller shafts broke again, and Orville returned to Dayton to make new shafts out of solid spring steel. He returned on December 11 and three days later, Wilbur won the coin toss to fly the plane on its first lift-off from the sixty-foot-long launching rail.

The "Flyer" lifted off the rail at the forty-foot point, reached an altitude of fifteen feet, stalled, and dropped onto the sand, damaging the forward elevator and one of the skids. This 3 1/2 second flight of 100 feet wasn't considered a real flight. Wilbur hadn't anticipated the sensitivity of the elevator; he had overcontrolled the craft.

On December 17, the temperature was freezing and the wind was blowing at twenty-seven miles per hour. It was Orville's turn to pilot the airplane; the brothers shook hands as though they weren't going to see each other again. At 10:35 a.m., the "Flyer" lifted off after traveling about forty feet and flew 120 feet in twelve seconds.

This flight was considered the first true flight. Orville commented: "The flight lasted only twelve seconds, but it was nevertheless the first in the history of the world in which a machine carrying a man had raised itself by its own power into the air in full flight, had sailed forward without a reduction in speed, and had finally landed at a point as high as that from which it started."[63]

Wilbur flew the second flight of the day over a distance of 175 feet, followed by Orville in a flight of over 200 feet that lasted fifteen seconds. Wilbur flew the "Flyer" on the last flight of the day—a flight of 852 feet with a duration of fifty-nine seconds. While they were discussing the flights, a gust of wind overturned the "Flyer," breaking spars, struts, most of the wing ribs, and the engine crankcase. No more flights were conducted in 1903. However, the Wright brothers had accomplished their goal; they had pioneered powered flight.

In 1904 and 1905, the brothers built two more powered aircraft to continue their experiments. They moved their test flights from Kitty Hawk to Huffman Prairie, eight miles from Dayton. The success of the last 1903 flight wasn't matched until the forty-ninth flight in 1904. On September 20, 1904, they made their first circular flight, which lasted ninety-six seconds and covered 4,080 feet. On October 5, 1905, Wilbur circled the field thirty times in thirty-nine minutes spanning a distance of 24 1/2 miles.

In 1908 and 1909, the brothers successfully marketed their aircraft in the United States and Europe through sales and licensing agreements. In 1910, they established the Wright Company for manufacturing aircraft, conducting exhibitions, and training pilots. Orville ran the company while Wilbur fought the patent infringement suits. Weakened by the strain of the legal process, Wilbur died on May 30, 1912, four weeks after contracting typhoid fever.

Orville brought the suits to successful conclusion in 1914. He sold his interests in the Wright Company in 1915 and retired a wealthy man. Orville lived a long, quiet life in retirement. He suffered a heart attack and died on January 27, 1948.

Wilbur Wright

CHAPTER 24

INVENTION OF THE AIRPLANE

SUCCESS VS. FAILURE—SUMMARY AND ANALYSIS

"The real difference between men is energy. A strong will, a settled purpose, an invincible determination, can accomplish almost anything; and in this lies the distinction between great men and little men."

Fuller

The approaches taken to developing the first heavier-than-air aircraft by Samuel Langley and by Wilbur and Orville Wright couldn't have been more contrasting. Langley was more of a scientist than an inventor; most of his investigations of the principles of flight were conducted in a six-year span ending in 1896. As the secretary (director) of the Smithsonian Institution in Washington, D.C., he had many interests other than developing the first successful airplane.

Although Langley conducted many tests with rubber-band powered models, he conducted few tests with full-sized aircraft. He pinned all of his hopes on two manned test flights conducted from a houseboat on the Potomac River in full view of spectators, newsmen, and photographers. His principal problem was the launch mechanism, not the aircraft, although it had structural shortcomings and control limitations. Langley was in his sixties at the time of his 1903 test flights; he hired a pilot to test fly the airplane for him. Langley wasn't even present at the first manned test flight.

In contrast, Wilbur and Orville Wright were hands-on inventors with years of experience in bicycle design, manufacturing, and maintenance. They had their own machine shop. Their investigation of the principles of aerodynamics was ongoing and extremely focused. The Wrights questioned equations and constants and conducted tests to verify them. They also conducted their own wind tunnel experiments to improve the design of airfoils and propellers.

All of Wilbur's and Orville's focus was on applied development that improved the design and manufacture of a manned craft that could fly. They devoted virtually all of their time for four years to that goal. Although they had to work during the winter season in their Dayton bicycle shop, the source of their income, they devoted their lives to their project.

The Wright brothers conducted a large number of early test flights, including flying their gliders unmanned as kites. Their experiments were conducted in the solitude of the sand dunes in Kitty Hawk, North Carolina, away from newsmen, photographers, and spectators. Area families assisted them with their experiments and the brothers had occasional visitors, but they worked out of the limelight. They piloted their own aircraft. Wilbur did most of the early flying; eventually, Orville became an experienced pilot.

The source of funding was another major difference between the efforts of Langley and the Wright brothers. Langley's work was funded by the War Department because of the potential use of aircraft for aerial reconnaissance. Theodore Roosevelt, Assistant Secretary of the Navy, helped Langley obtain a grant for $50,000.

The Wright brothers paid for all of their development work themselves with earnings from their successful bicycle manufacturing and maintenance shop in Dayton. Octave Chanute, an early mentor, offered to ask his friend, Andrew Carnegie, for money to support the brothers' development work. Wilbur and Orville declined the offer; they wanted to continue as independent developers with no strings attached.

Another key difference between Langley's development and the Wright Brothers' was the environment within which they functioned. Langley never married and didn't have a sounding board off whom to bounce ideas. He had a network of scientific colleagues, but they thought that he was wasting his time and effort developing aircraft. In fact, they suggested that he drop the effort because he was damaging his reputation as a serious scientist. Langley's pilot was an employee, the designer of his engine, which was superior to the Wright engine—particularly the power to weight ratio.

The Wright brothers, on the other hand, had each other. If one of them didn't think of a good solution to a problem, the other one did. One brother would originate an idea; the other brother would improve upon it or enhance it. The Wright family was very supportive of their efforts. The brothers were close to their parents, and, after the death of their mother, their father and younger sister followed their work closely.

The Wrights had helpful mentors and a network of advisors / consultants.

Langley, by doing his experimentation in public, became the target of many jibes and critical newspapers articles. The abuse that he received in the newspapers bothered him. He had been a respected scientist all of his life; he wasn't thick-skinned because he never had to be. Eventually, the controversy surrounding his experiments affected his health. After the two unsuccessful manned flights and the withdrawal of government funding, Langley dropped his effort to develop a manned aircraft because he believed it should be a national effort, not an individual effort. Langley never sought personal recognition for his work.

The Wright brothers, by conducting their work in seclusion, were never a target of the press as Langley was. However, they could probably have handled it better than Langley because of their incredible will to succeed. Their focused determination, coupled with a willingness to modify their designs to incorporate the findings of their test flights, were key ingredients in the ultimate achievement of their goal.

Unfortunately, Langley discontinued his work when he was on the threshold of success. Fortunately, the Wright brothers persevered and launched the aviation age. They significantly affected our lives.

NEW USES OF OLD INVENTIONS

Invention of the Sewing Machine

CHAPTER 25

ELIAS HOWE

Sewing Machine Inventor and Litigant

"I'm proof of the word 'failure.' I've seen behind it. The only failure a man ought to fear is failure in cleaving to the purpose he sees to be best."

George Eliot

Elias Howe was born to Elias Howe, Sr., a farmer and owner of a gristmill and a sawmill, and Polly Benris Howe in Spencer, Massachusetts, on July 9, 1819. Young Howe worked on the family farm until he was eleven, when his father sent him to "live out" with a neighboring farmer. At that time, children were provided with room, board, and clothing in return for doing farm chores. Howe's father arranged for him to work on the neighboring farm until he was twenty-one; however, Howe had a congenital lameness in one leg and wasn't capable of doing heavy farm work.

Howe returned home after two years and worked with his brothers and sisters inserting wire teeth into leather "cards," which were used in carding machines to prepare cotton cloth that his father sold to mill owners. At the age of sixteen, Howe was apprenticed to a machine shop that manufactured and serviced cotton-spinning equipment in the textile town of Lowell. He lost his job when the mills serviced by the machine shop closed in the financial panic of 1837.

Howe found a job in Boston with Ari Davis, a maker of marine instruments and scientific equipment. Davis was consulted by many inventors in the area and was known both for his good advice and for his outspokenness. An inventor brought a knitting machine to Davis's shop to obtain advice and was asked why he bothered with knitting machines when he could be doing something worthwhile, such as inventing a sewing machine. Howe overheard the conversation, including Davis's comment about the fortune that would accompany such an invention. Howe tucked the thought away for future reference.

On March 3, 1841, Howe married Elizabeth Ames of Boston. He struggled to support a wife and three children during the first three years of marriage on his earnings as a journeyman machinist. Howe didn't have a strong constitution; he occasionally missed several days of work at a time. His wife took in sewing jobs to help support the family.

Howe watched his wife sew and became convinced that he

could devise a machine that could duplicate her sewing motions. He had the mind of an inventor, and ideas began to flow. His uncle, William Howe, had designed and built the first truss bridge in the United States, which spanned the Connecticut River at Springfield. Another uncle, Tyler Howe, had invented bedsprings.

In his book, *Eminent Engineers*, Dwight Goddard described a dream of Howe's in which he was challenged by a king to develop a working sewing machine or lose his head. As Howe was being marched to his execution, he noticed that the spears carried by the king's men had holes near their tips. Until this time, Howe had designed his machine with a needle pointed at both ends, but with the hole for the thread in the center. From this time onward, he used a needle design with the hole toward one of the tips, similar to the spears in his dream.

Howe's father moved to Cambridge and opened a factory to split palm leaves for use in making hats. Howe joined his parents in Cambridge and installed a lathe and other tools on the top floor of his father's factory. When the factory burned down, Howe was fortunate to obtain the backing of a old friend and classmate, George Fisher, who had just received a small inheritance. Fisher invested $500 in Howe's effort to develop a sewing machine in return for a fifty percent interest in the patent.

Howe spent several months designing and building his first model of a sewing machine. In July 1845, he sewed two wool suits, one for Fisher and one for himself, using the machine. Howe's machine, which was similar to an earlier machine designed by Walter Hunt, had the needle with the eye near the point and used both a shuttle and an overhanging arm. However, Hunt hadn't been able to demonstrate a machine that worked.

Inventing the sewing machine was an evolutionary process; many inventors added to or improved upon earlier designs. Prior to Hunt's effort, Barthelemy Thimonnier had based his design on the use of a chain stitch made by an over-hanging arm with a hooked needle that sewed material held horizontally. In England, Fisher and Gibbons were the first to use the combination of a needle with the eye near the point and a shuttle to stitch material. Hunt, whose innovations in sewing machine design included the use of a lock stitch instead of a chain stitch, was the first inventor who didn't attempt to duplicate the motion of a hand stitch.

The chain stitch, which used a single thread and caught each loop in the one following it, was easily undone. If the thread in one stitch broke, a tug on the thread caused the entire seam to unravel. Hunt used two spools of thread, one above the material and one below it, to produce the lock stitch. A shuttle pushed the thread below the fabric through the loop made by the upper spool as it was extended through the material by a needle with an eye near the tip.

Only short seams could be sewed with the Hunt design, and the vertical positioning of the material was awkward. The machine, which had to be reset frequently, wasn't capable of sewing a long, continuous seam. Bradshaw later refined the Hunt design with an improved method of providing loops in the thread that made forming the stitch easier. Hunt didn't patent the sewing machine that he invented in 1834.

Howe struggled to convince the public of the value of his sewing machine. He arranged a sewing contest at the Quincy Hall clothing factory featuring five of their fastest seam-stresses vs. his machine. A straight seam was given to each of the five seamstresses, and five straight seams were given to Howe. Not only did he finish first, but his seams were judged to be the straightest and the strongest. Howe's machine could sew 250 stitches a minute, approximately seven times faster than a seamstress. If the contest had involved any seam other than a straight one, his machine couldn't have done it.

Winning the contest should have helped to promote sales of his machine, but the mill owners thought that it was too expensive. At that time, a machine cost at least $300 to build.

Also, the public thought that sewing machines would put many people out of work. Sales of Howe's machine were disappointing. He constructed a second machine with a few improvements, submitted it to the patent office with his patent request, and was granted a patent on September 10, 1846.

Fisher spent $2,000 of his inheritance on Howe's development effort. He became discouraged when no orders were received and refused to provide further financial support. Howe obtained a loan from his father and constructed a third sewing machine that his brother, Amasa, took to England to promote sales there.

The only offer Amasa received was from William Thomas, who employed 5,000 workers manufacturing corsets, carpet bags, umbrellas, valises, and leather products. Thomas offered Howe £250, approximately $1,250, for the machine with an offer of £3 a week in wages to adapt it for use in corset manufacturing.

On February 5, 1847, Howe sailed for England. Thomas advanced the money for the passage to London for Howe's wife and three children. Over a period of eight months, Howe redesigned his sewing machine for use in manufacturing corsets.

Thomas made a verbal agreement with Howe to patent the machine in England and to pay him three pounds for each machine that he sold. However, he didn't pay Howe, even though Thomas received ten pounds on each machine sold in England. By the time that he died, Thomas had earned $1 million on his $1,250 investment.

Thomas became overbearing with Howe and assigned him to menial tasks. Howe quit his job with Thomas and found himself unemployed with three children and a sick wife, thousands of miles from his friends at home. He spent his meager savings to send his family home, but he couldn't afford to join them.

Howe was befriended by a coach maker, Charles Inglis, who rented him a room for a workshop and lent him money for living expenses. Howe built another sewing machine, hoping to sell it to earn passage home. After working four months to construct a sewing machine, the only buyer he could find offered five pounds for a machine worth fifty pounds. Howe pawned his first machine and his patent documentation to obtain money for his fare home.

Howe helped pay his passage by cooking for the steerage passengers. He arrived in New York with a half crown in his pocket and found a job in a machine shop. He was told that his wife was dying of tuberculosis in Cambridge, Massachusetts; his father loaned him ten dollars to be with his wife during her last days. Soon after the death of his wife, Howe lost all of his possessions when the ship bringing his household goods from England was wrecked off Cape Cod.

When Howe returned to New York in April 1849, after spending two years in England, he found that interest in sewing machines had increased considerably. He was surprised to see that many of the machines on the market infringed on his patent. The half crown in his pocket upon his return to New York was all he had to show for four years of work, and he needed money to support his children. He contacted all of the sewing machine manufacturers, informed them of his patent, and asked them for payment for licenses and royalties.

However, before he could sue to obtain satisfaction from those manufacturers who contested his patent, he had to reclaim his patent documents from the pawnbroker in Surrey, England. During the summer of 1849, he raised the necessary $100 to retrieve them, and an acquaintance who had gone to England on other business brought the documents back with him that autumn. Some manufacturers were willing to pay for the use of Howe's patent initially, but others who weren't willing talked those who were out of paying Howe what they owed him.

Howe had no alternative but to sue, but he couldn't afford to pursue cases in the courts. His friend, George Fisher, wouldn't lend him any more money; however, he was willing to sell his half interest in the patent. George Bliss of Massachusetts purchased Fisher's fifty percent interest. Bliss required a mortgage on Howe's father's farm before he would advance the money, but, at last, redress could begin.

The main obstacle in the litigation initiated by Howe was Isaac Merritt Singer, inventor of a sewing machine different from previous designs—it worked. Singer had borrowed many ideas from previous machines, including Howe's machine. He was more aggressive than the other manufacturers and was determined to fight Howe in court. The issue of originality was cloudy because so many individuals had contributed to the present configurations of sewing machines. The elements of the current successful designs were:

- ability to sew curved as well as straight seams—first done by Singer
- continuous thread from spools—first used by Howe
- the eye-pointed straight needle—Hunt was an early user
- the foot pedal (treadle) to control the speed of the machine—first used by Singer
- a horizontal table to hold the material—Howe was an early user
- the lock stitch—first used by Hunt
- an overhanging arm—first used by Thimonnier
- a shuttle used with the second spool of thread—Hunt was an early user
- thread tension devices that release thread as needed— Howe was an early user
- use of the carrying case as a table on which the machine was operated and as a treadle base—first used by Singer

In late 1850, Howe went to New York to supervise the manufacture of fourteen sewing machines made to his design. In October 1851, one of these machines was demonstrated at the Castle Garden Fair. In 1853, Howe's brother, Amasa, started to manufacture sewing machines. When Elias Howe began manufacturing machines in 1867, he used the same name that Amasa had been using, "Howe Sewing Machine Company." Amasa sued his brother, who had to change the name of his company to the "Howe Machine Company."

Howe's principal source of income was from licensing his patent to other manufacturers, not from profits received from the manufacture of sewing machines. Litigation, not manufacturing, had been his strength so far.

Singer didn't claim to be the inventor of the sewing machine. His main defense in the lawsuit with Howe was that Howe wasn't the inventor either, and that earlier inventors, such as Hunt, had prior claim to most of Howe's design. However, Hunt had never filed a patent. Without attempting to promote sales of the machine, Hunt had sold the one machine that he built, along with the rights to patent the design, to a businessman, George Arrowsmith. Hunt's machine used a shuttle to form a lock stitch, and, although it sewed, it didn't sew well.

To combat Howe's claim, Singer's supporters found some broken and rusty parts from Hunt's machine and asked Hunt if he could assemble them into a working machine. Singer provided the money, and Hunt went to work. Hunt was unsuccessful, even with the help of a skilled mechanic. Singer could show that Hunt was on the track of an important step in the design of a practical sewing machine, but he couldn't prove that Hunt had a prior claim to portions of Howe's design. Singer lost his lawsuit with Howe in 1854. In February 1855, Howe also won the Hunt vs. Howe suit.

After the settlement, all manufacturers were required to pay a twenty-five-dollar royalty to Howe for each machine they sold, but it wasn't that straightforward. All major manufacturers, including Singer and Company, Wheeler and Wilson, and Grover and Baker, claimed that the others were infringing on their patents. No single inventor, including Howe, could build sewing machines without claims of infringement from the others. In 1856, they were all headed for more litigation in Albany, New York.

Orlando Potter, president of Grover and Baker Company, suggested forming a "combination" of sewing machine manufacturers to eliminate the ongoing litigation. All of the major manufacturers formed a patent pool to allow each of them to produce machines with all of the current features. Grover and Baker contributed several patents to the combination, but its principal contribution was Potter's idea to form a combination.

Wheeler and Wilson contributed the A. B. Wilson patent for the four-motion feeding mechanism. Howe contributed his patent to use a curved, eye-pointed needle and a shuttle to form a lock stitch. The Singer Company provided the I. M. Singer patent for a heart-shaped cam to move the needle-bar and a patent purchased from Morey and Johnson for a spring or curved arm to apply pressure to material being sewed. The Singer Company also provided three patents purchased from Bachelder that included:

- Vertical needle motion in conjunction with a horizontal work-plate
- A mechanism to continuously feed material using a belt or wheel
- A device which pressed on the material, yielding it to the machine as needed

Initially, Howe objected to the combination, but he joined after his conditions were met: licensing of a minimum of twenty-four manufacturers (this wasn't a problem since there were scores of sewing machine manufacturers in the mid-1800s), payment of a royalty of five dollars on each machine sold in the United States, and a royalty of one dollar for each machine sold outside the United States. This agreement made Howe a wealthy man. He earned $2 million in royalties from 1856 to 1867, when the term of his patent expired.

The combination charged a fifteen-dollar license fee on each machine to all manufacturers, including themselves. The license fee was used to pay for litigation against infringers and to pay Howe his royalty; any remainder was split among the members of the combination. Howe's patent was renewed in 1860, and the license fee was lowered from fifteen dollars to seven dollars. At that time, Howe's royalty was reduced to one dollar per machine, which remained in effect until his patent expired in 1867. The combination survived until 1877, when the twice-extended Bachelder patents ran out. Most of the commonly-used features of the machine became public property, motivating many additional manufacturers to enter the field.

Howe could have been exempted from serving in the army during the Civil War, but he formed a Connecticut regiment and paid to equip it. He was offered the colonelcy of the regiment; he demurred because of his lack of military training and experience. He served as a private until he resigned due to poor health.

In a story told about his army experience, Howe asked the paymaster when the 17th Connecticut was going to be paid and was told that they would be paid when the government sent the money and no sooner. Howe asked how much was needed to pay the men and was told $31,000. He signed a draft for the full amount, received a receipt from the paymaster, and several days later received $28.60 in back pay, the same amount received by the other privates in the regiment.

Howe was a good-looking, outgoing man with considerable personal charm. However, after living in poverty in his early years and enduring the experience of having to fight to protect his patents, he became less outgoing and more quiet and reserved. He was known for his gifts to charity in his later years. He won a gold medal in Paris at the 1867 World's Fair for one of the Howe Machine Company sewing machines and was awarded the Cross of the Legion of Honor by France. On October 3, 1867, he died of pneumonia in Brooklyn, New York.

CHAPTER 26

ISAAC MERRITT SINGER

Sewing Machine Inventor and Promoter

"People are always blaming their circumstances for what they are. I don't believe in circumstances. The people who get on in this world are the people who get up and look for the circumstances they want, and, if they don't find them, make them."

George Bernard Shaw, *Mrs. Warren's Profession,* Act II

Isaac Merritt Singer was born near Troy, New York, on October 27, 1811. He was the eighth and youngest child of Adam and Ruth Singer. Adam Singer, a cooper and mill-wright, moved his family to Oswego, New York, shortly after Isaac's birth. Singer's childhood wasn't a happy one; his parents were divorced in 1821 when he was ten years old. Adam Singer remarried, and young Isaac didn't get along with his stepmother. He left home at the age of twelve, in his words, "without money, without friends, without education, and possessed of nothing but a strong constitution and a prolific brain" [and without humility, for that matter].

In 1822, Singer lived with an older brother in Rochester, a boom town during the construction of the Erie Canal. The canal was completed in 1825, and the towns along the canal between Albany and Buffalo experienced a further economic uplift. While living in Rochester, Singer worked as a laborer during the summer and attended school during the academic year.

In 1830, Singer married Catherine Haley of Palmyra. He was a woodworker and also worked as a dry goods clerk in Port Gibson. Next, he was an apprentice in a machine shop, but he stayed for only four months, until, in his opinion, he had learned the equivalent of a full apprenticeship.

Singer was restless. He moved to Auburn, where he constructed lathe-making equipment. This restlessness was a life-time pattern; he never stayed in one location for long. His longest stay in one city was the thirteen-year span from 1850 to 1863 when he lived in four different houses in New York. The unsettled conditions in his early childhood established a way of life that included few lasting personal relationships, particularly with business partners.

Singer was, inherently, an actor, and he frequently talked about his lifelong ambition to perform on the stage. However, the life of an actor wasn't considered respectable in the early 1800s. The profession was denounced from the pulpit; many actors who performed in the United States were from Europe.

Despite this, he wanted to act. His acting ability served him well in promoting the sewing machine in later years.

In 1830, a troupe of players directed by Edwin Dean performed in Rochester. Singer asked Dean if he could join the troupe and expressed an interest in King Richard III, Macbeth, and Othello roles. He was hired on the strength of an audition during which he recited lines from *King Richard III*.

Singer was good-looking, over six feet tall, blond, and outgoing. He possessed considerable assertiveness and charisma, and he had a knack for winning people over to his viewpoint. Women were charmed by him; he instilled trust in people.

In 1835, Singer moved to New York City where he worked at Hoe's Press. In the spring of 1836, he joined a troupe of traveling players as their advance man and later as an actor. Singer traveled and did odd jobs over the next two years. In 1839, he conceived his first invention, a rock-drilling machine powered by horses walking in a circle turning a crank supported by a wooden framework. He patented the invention and sold the patent for $2,000. This windfall allowed him to return to his first love, acting. As Isaac Merritt, he founded the Merritt Players in Chicago.

The troupe stayed together until 1844, when they disbanded in Fredericksburg, Ohio. Singer worked for a press in Fredricksburg, where he developed a machine for carving wooden type for printers. After experiencing success with his first invention, the rock-drilling machine, he hoped to generate income by selling his carving machine for wooden type. In 1846, he moved to Pittsburgh to take advantage of a larger market. On April 10, 1849, he patented his carving machine and moved to New York, an even larger market than Pittsburgh.

The design of his machine was ingenious. A parallelogram device, or pantograph, was used to move the cutter and follow the letter or number being drawn or traced. However, Singer's timing was off; wooden type was being replaced by lead type. At this time, Singer was thirty-eight years old, and, by any criteria, couldn't be considered a success. However, his personal qualities of motivation and boundless optimism wouldn't let him settle into a secure but quiet existence. He was a driven man.

George Zieber, a Philadelphia book publisher and jobber, financed the manufacture of a type-carving machine based on Singer's design that was completed in June 1850 and transported to Boston by Singer and Zieber in search of sales. In 1850, Boston wasn't only the center of the publishing trade, but also the largest city in a manufacturing region whose population was growing rapidly from immigration. Zieber and Singer rented a room on the first floor of Orson Phelps's shop in Boston next door to the main factory area, where Phelps constructed sewing machines designed by J. H. Lerow and S. C. Blodgett.

The Lerow and Blodgett machine used a lock stitch formed by a curved eye-pointed needle and two spools of thread. A shuttle was used on the lower spool of thread beneath the cloth, but the shuttle moved in a circular motion instead of back and forth as on other designs. The machine didn't work well and required frequent maintenance. Only eight or nine machines out of 120 were sufficiently reliable to be used by the tailor's shop on the top floor of the building.

Phelps asked Singer whether he and Zieber could redesign the machine at their own expense and make it more reliable. Singer assured Phelps that he could do the redesign, and that Zieber had $80,000 available to finance the development work. That was a stretch of the imagination; Zieber had to borrow most of the $3,000 he had advanced to Singer to build the type-carving machine. Singer told Zieber in private that he hesitated becoming involved with such a "paltry business." Singer observed, "What a devilish machine!" and "You want to do away with the only thing that keeps a woman quiet, their sewing!"

However, Phelps convinced Singer that more money could be made from sewing machines than from type-carving machines, which had a very limited market. Singer developed a credo that helped to establish his fortune: "I don't give a damn for the invention, the dimes are what I am after." That statement distinguished Singer, the entrepreneur, from Singer, the inventor. Inventors tend to be very protective of their invention and resist changes to it, even if the changes will improve sales. Clearly, Singer was primarily an entrepreneur. In convincing Zieber to raise the money for the improvement of the machine, Singer reminded him that this was their chance to be millionaires.

Singer redesigned the Lerow and Blodgett machine by replacing the circular motion of the shuttle with a back and forth motion. The circular motion had tended to unwind the thread, causing it to break. He also replaced the curved needle, which was brittle and had a tendency to snap, with a straight needle that was much stronger. Singer overcame a major shortcoming of the Howe machine by eliminating the baster plate. The material to be sewed was attached to the baster plate with pins. After a short seam was sewn on Howe's machine, the material had to be unpinned from the baster plate and moved down.

Phelps, Singer, and Zieber signed an agreement in which Phelps and Zieber each put up forty dollars to build a model of the machine to obtain a patent, and Singer contributed his ability as an inventor. The patent was applied for in the names of Phelps and Singer, but all three partners were equal owners of the patent.

Singer worked twenty-hours a day and skipped many meals to complete the machine in eleven straight days. Beginning at nine p.m. on the eleventh day, Singer and Zieber repeatedly tried using the machine without success. They returned, discouraged, to their hotel at midnight. At the hotel, Zieber asked Singer if he had noticed that the loops of thread above the material were loose. Singer realized that he had forgotten to adjust the tension on the thread. He hurried back to the shop, adjusted the thread tension, and sewed five success-ful stitches before the thread broke. Singer got a good night's sleep and had the machine working by three o'clock the next day.

Singer took the machine to New York to begin the patent application process. The application was one of the early steps in revolutionizing the clothing industry, the shoe indus-try, and many other businesses that involved sewing.

Working conditions in the clothing industry were notori-ously bad; the industry had a reputation for burning out young women seamstresses at an early age. Thomas Hood captured the conditions that prevailed at the time in his "Song of the Shirt:"

> With fingers weary and worn,
> With eyelids heavy and red,
> A woman sat, in unwomanly rags,
> Plying her needle and thread,
> Stitch! Stitch! Stitch!
> In poverty, hunger and dirt;
> And still with a voice of dolorous pitch—
> Would that its tone could reach the rich!—
> She sang this "Song of the Shirt!"[64]

When Singer and Zieber began to market their machine, they encountered considerable resistance from those who had tried earlier sewing machines and had been dissatisfied with them. People were concerned that sewing machines would displace thousands of tailors and seamstresses. Also, the price of the machines was more than shops in the clothing industry could afford to pay. Initially, sewing machines couldn't be sold to housewives for use in the home because of their high price.

Singer was in his element in promoting sales of his sewing machine. The actor in him came out as he demonstrated his

"Jenny Lind" sewing machine at carnivals and circuses, in rented halls, and wherever people would listen to his pitch. He even recited moving renditions of the "Song of the Shirt" at these gatherings. He wrote articles promoting the machines, advertised heavily, and sent out agents to tout the advantages of the sewing machine. Singer was an actor, an inventor, and an entrepreneur, but he demonstrated strongly in this phase of his life that he was above all—a promoter.

In late 1850, Singer rented space in the window of the Smith and Conant clothing store to demonstrate his sewing machine. Two machines were set up in the window, and Miss King, a seamstress from Boston, demonstrated complicated sewing, and Singer's son, Gus, demonstrated straightforward sewing.

Elias Howe saw the demonstration at the Smith and Conant store and realized that Singer had infringed upon his patents. Howe approached Singer at the machine shop and offered to sell the rights to his patent for $2,000. Singer argued with him and threatened to kick him down the stairs. Singer was frustrated because he and Zieber couldn't raise that amount, even if they wanted to. It was the best offer they ever received from Howe; in fact, they ultimately paid Howe considerably more for the use of his patent.

Zieber borrowed money from friends to keep the enterprise going, and Singer borrowed $500 from his brother John, a sea captain. Forty years later, John commented that not only hadn't his brother paid interest on the loan, he hadn't paid back the principal either. Singer and Zieber advertised unsuccessfully in the Boston *Daily Times* for a partner interested in purchasing twenty-five percent of the venture for $1,000. Singer was so discouraged that he offered to sell out his interest in the business for $1,500. Zieber talked him out of it.

Meanwhile, Phelps had ten to twenty machines under construction in Boston. Singer visited him and told him to stop production because there was no money to continue. Phelps asked what had become of Zieber's $80,000 and was told that it was tied up in land holdings; Zieber had a liquidity problem. The business was saved when orders were received, including a $1,200 advance on a $3,000 order from a New Haven shirtmaker. Singer kept $1,000 and gave $200 to Zieber to use in making more machines. Singer planned to use the $1,000 to buy out Phelps. He picked quarrels with Phelps and treated him in a condescending manner.

Singer promised Phelps $1,000 down and $3,000 additional in three installments, along with a verbal agreement to keep his shop busy for five years, the duration of the partnership. Phelps, who wasn't strong enough to contest Singer's aggressive pitch, signed the contract on December 24, 1850.

Singer immediately told Phelps that he would have to go on the road selling machines, which Phelps didn't want to do. Singer then sold Phelps' one-third interest to Barzillan Ransom, a manufacturer of cloth bags, for $10,000. Ransom sold machines in Philadelphia and Baltimore, but became ill and couldn't work regularly. Furthermore, he was unable to come up with all of the $10,000 for his one-third share. Singer began to treat Ransom as he had treated Phelps. Singer's abusive treatment aggravated Ransom's illness. In May 1851, Singer and Zieber gave Ransom forty machines in return for his interest in the venture. Ransom died several months later.

Zieber thought that he had a verbal agreement with Singer for half of Phelps' share of the business. Several of the individuals from whom Zieber had borrowed money were pressing for payment. Zieber asked Singer for part of Phelps' share to pay these debts and was roughly greeted with, "What do you mean? By God, you've got enough! You shan't have any more!" Having come to Singer as a friend requesting only what was due him, Zieber finally realized that his partner was a blatant opportunist.

Zieber visited Edward Clark, a partner in the law firm of Jordan, Clark, and Company who had drawn up contracts for the partnership, to ask for advice on dealing with Singer. Clark told him that since the agreement about Phelp's one-third interest wasn't in writing, he couldn't do anything about it. Zieber speculated that maybe he should sell out, and Clark agreed that that might be a good idea. Zieber didn't know it at the time, but Singer had invited Clark to join the business.

Singer was aware that neither he nor Zieber had the necessary financial or legal background to deal with the venture as it grew. Singer offered Clark a one-third share of the business for his services. Clark was the one partner whom Singer couldn't bully. He seemed to have a hold on Singer. Clark told Zieber that, "Singer will not break the agreement I shall make with him." Clark was a vital addition to the enterprise and the source of many innovations that generated profits for the business.

In December 1851, Zieber became ill, and his doctor confined him to bed. Singer visited him and told him, "The doctor thinks you won't get over this. Don't you want to give up your interest in the business altogether?"[65] Zieber was alarmed; he didn't realize he was that ill. He became concerned that if anything happened to him, the friends from whom he had borrowed wouldn't be paid. Singer offered him $6,000 for his share of the business (annual profits at that time were $25,000). Clark drew up the agreement; Zieber signed it in bed the next morning.

Zieber learned that Singer hadn't talked with his doctor, who had made no such diagnosis. Zieber recovered within a short time and realized his mistake. He had given up all claim to Singer's patents and had been replaced as a fifty percent patent holder by Clark. Singer and Zieber had operated as friends (most of the time) as well as partners. Clark and Singer didn't have the same relationship; they were antagonists from their first meeting.

In 1851, Howe visited the Singer and Clark venture to request $25,000 for a license to use his patent and was thrown out again. Clark underestimated the validity of Howe's claim and made a poor business decision, a rarity for him. As before, the Singer partnership would pay much more than the amount Howe had requested. During the next three years, almost all of the partnership's profits and most of Clark's energy were spent on legal battles. The litigation became known as "the sewing machine war." By 1853, other major sewing machine manufacturers, including Grover and Baker as well as Wheeler and Wilson, had signed licenses with Howe to use his patent.

In July 1854, Howe won his suit against Singer and threatened to sue him in New Jersey as well as New York. Singer was directed to pay Howe $15,000 and a royalty of twenty-five dollars per machine. Litigation among the manufacturers of sewing machines didn't settle down until October 1865, when Orlando Potter, president of Grover and Baker, suggested the "combination," a patent pool in which all companies in the combination had the use of the other company's patents for a fee.

In 1855, the United States was in an economic slump—the worst since 1837. Singer sold only 883 machines and was struggling after making payments to Howe. Also that year, Singer designed the "turtleback," a smaller, lighter machine for use in the home. The cost of the machine was $125 at a time when the average annual family income was $500. Clearly, housewives needed help in purchasing their first sewing machine. Clark had the idea of leasing the sewing machine to the housewife and applying the lease payments toward the purchase of the machine. Clark's installment plan idea boosted sales to 2,564 machines in 1856; sales tripled in one year.

Clark also suggested selling sewing machines for half price to church ministers to use in establishing sewing societies associated with their churches to show that respectable women sewed. This also introduced the sewing machine to groups and familiarized individual housewives with it. Clark admitted frankly in his proposals that his offer was motivated by the desire to make a profit, not by humanitarian concerns.

As sales increased, Singer acted to prevent sales of used

machines, which reduced the sales of new machines. Singer offered fifty dollars for an old machine, which was destroyed to prevent its resale, and the amount was applied toward the purchase of a new machine. In 1857, sales increased to 3,630 machines.

The production of sewing machines grew rapidly in the years following 1858. I. M. Singer and Company produced 10,038 in 1859, but the company didn't overtake Wheeler and Wilson as the largest manufacturer until 1867. By 1870, Singer had produced 127,833 machines using mass production techniques, such as the use of interchangeable parts—a concept devised by Eli Whitney.

European sales were a principal reason for the rapid growth of I. M. Singer and Company; Singer's competitors didn't exploit foreign markets nearly as aggressively as he did. By 1861, Singer had sold more machines in Europe than in the United States. In 1867, the company opened a factory near Glasgow that was controlled by the parent company in New york. I. M. Singer and Company was one of the earliest multinational corporations.

In 1863, Clark and Singer agreed to dissolve their partnership and form a joint stock company. Each received forty percent of the stock in the company plus an equal share of the bond holdings, and both men agreed to step down from active management of the company. Neither wanted the other in charge; if Clark wanted Singer to give up his control, he would have to give up control also.

Singer moved to England and built a mansion called the Wigwam at Paignton, near Torquay. The Wigwam had a private theater; Singer never stopped being an actor. Unfortunately, he didn't live to see the Wigwam completed. He developed a heart condition, and the combination of a chill and heart problems caused his death on July 23, 1875. He was buried in Torquay cemetery.

Isaac Merritt Singer's life was certainly a Horatio Alger story. He made significant contributions as an inventor. His drive and aggressiveness contributed significantly to his success. However, his ability to promote the sewing machine, using skills developed as an actor, was his most important accomplishment.

Note: This profile of Isaac Singer, with additions, is reprinted from *People of the Finger Lakes Region.*

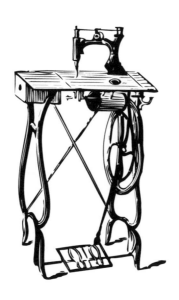

CHAPTER 27

INVENTION OF THE SEWING MACHINE

SUCCESS VS. FAILURE—SUMMARY AND ANALYSIS

"Firmness of purpose is one of the most necessary sinews of character, and one of the best instruments of success. Without it, genius wastes its efforts in a maze of inconsistencies."

Philip Dormer Stanhope

A comparison of Elias Howe and Isaac Merritt Singer is a comparison of two entrepreneur / inventors. Both men were extroverts who possessed creative mechanical ability. With their outgoing nature, they made friends easily. Singer was the more aggressive and strong-willed of the two and was less affected by the setbacks that he encountered. Howe was changed in contending with many obstacles in his path to success. Later in life, he was a more subdued and a less outgoing individual than he had been as a young man.

Howe and Singer were endowed with perseverance and determination. They were highly motivated, and both knew poverty early in their lives. Howe was, without question, the more ethical of the two. Howe was a businessman as well as an inventor; he didn't indulge in dubious business practices.

In contrast, Singer was self-centered and had questionable business ethics, particularly in his treatment of his partners. He treated Phelps and Ranson unfairly, but his treatment of his friend and partner, Zieber, was particularly detestable.

Singer had few peers on the subject of immorality. With five wives, three of them concurrent, and over twenty children, he couldn't be mistaken for a misogynist. However, to his credit, he acknowledged being the father of all of his children and provided for their support. Before I. M. Singer & Company became economically successful, this support was provided at the expense of his partners' shares.

Determining whether Howe or Singer was stronger in the financial arena is difficult. In their early development efforts, both were able to obtain minimum financing for their development work. However, Singer realized that he lacked skill in raising money, knowledge of legal matters, and experience in organizational tasks. He brought in Clark to deal with those issues. Once Clark overcame the early patent problems, he contributed heavily to the growth of the venture. Singer knew that he needed Clark, but couldn't control him once he had him.

Singer was, by far, a better marketer and promoter than

Howe. As a promoter, with the possible exception of Barnum of Barnum & Bailey, Singer had no equal. The ham in him, developed during his many formative years as an actor, created a promoter of the highest order. Howe didn't have to function as a marketer or a promoter until late in life when he began to manufacture sewing machines.

Howe's organizational ability is difficult to evaluate because of his late entry into manufacturing. Singer had a reasonably strong organizational ability, but increasingly left business decisions to Clark, a stronger organizer. In terms of strategic ability, Howe was intelligent enough to comprehend the economic benefits of litigation. Clark made many of the strategic decisions for I. M. Singer & Company, such as instituting the installment plan and the expansion into Europe.

Today, most people think of Singer, not Howe, when they think of the sewing machine. However, the success if the sewing machine was primarily because of the accomplishments of another inventor, neither Singer nor Howe. Production and sales of sewing machines grew at an exponential rate in the late 1850s and throughout the 1860s because of the dramatic lowering of the cost of its manufacture due to the contributions of Eli Whitney.

Whitney implemented his concept of interchangeable parts in fulfilling contracts for rifles for the U.S. government, and he invented the milling machine to reduce the cost of making rifle parts. His efforts significantly improved manufacturing processes, initially in the United States and later abroad.

The results of an evaluation of success vs. failure with respect to the sewing machine are mixed. Again, Howe was more successful as a litigant; Singer was more successful as a promoter. Singer knew how to chose a business partner; however, Howe knew how to select a patent attorney. Financially, both were successful. As human beings, Howe's gifts to charitable institutions late in life place him ahead of Singer.

However, if success is measured by the accomplishment of the organizations that they left behind, there is no contest.

I. M. Singer & Company, later the Singer Company, significantly outdistanced the accomplishments of the Howe Machine Company.

EARLY FAILURE / LATE SUCCESS

Evaporated Milk Development

CHAPTER 28

GAIL BORDEN

Developer of Evaporated Milk

"I tried and failed, I tried again and again, and succeeded."

Gail Borden

Gail Borden was born on November 9, 1801, in Norwich, New York, the oldest of four sons of Gail and Philadelphia Borden. Gail Borden, Sr., sold his farm and his half-interest in a sawmill in 1812 to participate in the westward movement. He transported his family to Pittsburgh and down the Ohio River to Cincinnati. The family lived across the Ohio River in Covington, Kentucky, just long enough for their only daughter, Esther, to be born and then moved to New London, Indiana.

Young Gail completed his schooling in New London. At the age of twenty-one, he had three alternatives for earning a living: farming, surveying, and teaching. His first job was teaching school in Amite County, Mississippi, on the Louisiana border. Borden supplemented his income by working as the county surveyor.

Borden met and fell in love with Penelope Mercer, whose family were farmers and storekeepers. They were married in Amite County in February 1828.

Borden had heard about Texas from his brother, Tom, one of Stephen Austin's "Old Three Hundred," who had lived there since 1824. Tom convinced his parents to move to Texas in 1828; Borden decided to join them. He and Penelope took the schooner *Hope* to New Orleans and continued onward by boat to Texas. Borden was reunited with his father and brothers in Texas, but his mother and his sister, Esther, died during the journey.

Availability of land was a principal attraction of Texas. Mexico generously granted Borden a sitio (4,428 acres) of land in Fort Bend County. Initially, Borden farmed and raised cattle; he performed his brother's surveying duties for Stephen Austin when Tom was on extended trips.

In October 1835, Borden, Tom, and Joseph Baker began publishing a newspaper in San Felipe. The *Telegraph and Texas Register*, the first Texas newspaper to stay in business for more than two years, had a forty-year run. Eventually, publication was moved to Houston, where Borden sold his share before moving to Galveston.

In 1837, Borden was appointed collector for the port of Galveston by Sam Houston, President of independent Texas. Borden established the first customs office; his attention to detail served him well in his new duties. According to the Texas Constitution, a President could serve only one term, and, in 1838, Mirabeau Lamar succeeded Houston as President of Texas. Borden was a hard-working, conscientious collector, but the job was a political appointment. He was replaced by one of Lamar's men.

For twelve years, Borden served as the agent for the Galveston City Company, the organization that promoted and controlled Galveston's growth during its first seventy-five years. Galveston's population more than tripled during that time; it became the largest city in Texas. In 1844, an epidemic of yellow fever struck Galveston. It took Penelope Borden's life and left Borden with five young children.

Borden had great quantities of nervous energy, and he didn't need as much sleep as most people. As he approached his fiftieth year, he was always in a hurry and frequently preoccupied. He was full of ideas; many considered him eccentric. While showing a friend, William Baker, around his home and yard, they walked by cast-iron kettles, empty barrels, and pieces of machinery. Borden explained:

> That was one of my ideas, just then I was full of hydraulic pressure. I would put in water, half a hogshead of sugar, and a cartload of fruit, figs say, into the kettle. Then, while hot, I would press the preserves into ten-pound canisters.... But I learned better. I never drop an idea except for a better one—never! You can do almost anything with everything. If you plan and think, and, as fast as you drop one thing, seize upon another.... The world is changing. In the direction of condensing.[66]

He used the word "condensing" in a general sense. To him, condensing meant giving short quotations to his son from the Bible instead of long lectures and eating a meal in fifteen minutes instead of an hour or more.

Borden invented an amphibious prairie-schooner that he called a "terraqueous machine" intended for use in crossing rivers without a ferry. He invited his neighbors to a midnight meal and some unspecified "entertainment." Borden described the food: "There are articles on this table from which, if you knew what they were in their original condition, you would turn with loathing and horror. I have passed them, however, through certain processes by virtue of which they are delicious. Out of the offal of the kitchens and the streets, I have created ... a food for the poor which will cost almost nothing. I have transmuted the dirt itself into delicacies." The feast included butter made by churning lard in milk, bread made from ground bones, and jelly made from the hoofs and horns of oxen.

The "entertainment" was a ride in his terraqueous machine. As his neighbors boarded the floating wagon, the owner of the livery stable where it was housed commented that "we may all end up in eternity." Borden steered the vehicle toward the Gulf of Mexico; the women on board began to scream before he was near the water. He braked the wagon and returned home.

Borden attempted a daylight run. He mounted a mast with a square sail on the front of the wagon to propel it, assisted by the wheels that operated as propellers when the vehicle was in the water. With a sail full of wind, he steered the wagon into the bay at high speed. When the sail dropped, all of the passengers moved to the landward side of the vehicle. The wagon capsized, dumping its passengers into fifty feet of water. His invention was a failure. However, his credo was, "If I miss it in one thing, I will hit it in another."[67] Resilience was one of Borden's personal characteristics.

Next, Borden developed the "meat biscuit," similar to

Comanche food called pinole. It was compact, easy to transport, and travelers could subsist on it. The Indians prepared it pinole by crushing dried buffalo meat and mixing it with crushed, dried hominy and mesquite beans. They ate pinole dry or added water and baked it into a cake. On the trail, they stuffed the mixture into a section of buffalo intestine and wore it as a belt.

In 1849, Borden began experimenting with meat biscuits, which he hoped to market to armies and navies. In early 1850, the U.S. Army expressed interest in his new product. Also, he provided Dr. Elisha Kane with biscuits packed into canisters for his Arctic search for the lost English explorer, Sir John Franklin. On February 5, 1850, Borden was granted a U.S. patent for his product.

Borden made meat biscuits by boiling eleven pounds of meat, usually beef, into one pound of extract and filtering the broth from the "solid nutritive portions." He boiled the broth until much of the water had evaporated; this formed a liquid of the consistency of "sugar-house syrup." He used a liquid gauge to ensure a consistent density and then added flour in the ratio of three pounds of flour to two pounds of extract. The five-pound mixture was kneaded, baked (resulting in a biscuit that weighed four pounds), and then prepared in a number of ways, including frying, further baking, or mixing into a pudding. Borden's main claim to originality was the addition of flour.

The meat biscuit was Borden's focus for two years. He managed production of the biscuits, so he asked Dr. Ashbel Smith, an old friend, to promote the biscuit to the public and to potential customers. The first test results of the meat biscuit by the U.S. Army were favorable. Brevet Colonel E. V. Sumner, Fort Leavenworth, Kansas, wrote a glowing report to the War Department in Washington, D.C.

About $10,000 was required to buy production equipment, such as boilers, caldrons, pipe, and tubs. Borden raised capital by mortgaging his property. He went another $5,000 into debt in 1851, the year of the Great Council Exhibition at the London world's fair. To promote the product, Borden and Smith traveled to the fair, where they received a Gold Medal award for their entry. About this time, *Scientific American* reported the meat biscuit as "one of the most valuable inventions that has ever been brought forward."

In June 1851, the results of the Army's extended trial were published. The board of six army officers was unanimous in rejecting the product in a report known as the Waco Report:

> The biscuit could not replace the ordinary army ration, it did not have the food value "to sustain life and vigor, whilst on active duty ... even when increased to ... 12 ounces per ration" [Borden recommended six ounces]; it was "not only unpalatable, but fails to appease the craving of hunger—producing headache, nausea, and great muscular depression;" and it "impairs the capacity of the healthy human-system to sustain much mental or bodily labor as it can be legitimately called upon to perform; ... it diminishes the power of resisting the extremes of heat & cold."[68]

Borden's prospects of selling his meat biscuit to the U.S. Army didn't recover from this critical report. By 1851, Borden had spent $30,000, most of it from sales of property, on the business. Ultimately, he lost $60,000 on the meat biscuit venture.

Dr. Elisha Kane thought that the biscuits contained too much gelatin. Kane and the doctors that accompanied his expedition decided to take pemmican on their next Arctic trip. Borden tried to break into other markets, such as hospitals and ships, without success. In 1853, Dr. Ashbel Smith backed out of his agreement to market the biscuit in Europe. The last order for meat biscuits was filled in 1855.

Borden's next effort occupied him for the remainder of his life. The development and sale of condensed milk began when he gave up on the meat biscuit. ("I never drop an idea except for a better one.")

Borden became aware of the need for condensed milk on his return home from the Great Council Exhibition in London. The voyage across the North Atlantic was rough. Cows in the hold of the sailing vessel were seasick and couldn't be milked to feed the large number of immigrant children on board. The crying of hungry babies disturbed Borden; he was determined to do something about it. His goal was to treat milk so that it would keep for several weeks or longer, while retaining its nutritional qualities and purity.

The preservation of milk wasn't a problem; retaining its purity and palatability was. Previous attempts to preserve milk used brown sugar, which gave the resulting product an off color and an unappealing odor. Borden borrowed a vacuum pan from Mother Ann Lee's Shaker Colony at New Lebanon, New York, in an early experiment to retain the taste of the milk. When he had modest success with its use, he ordered his own vacuum pan.

The albumin in the milk that he boiled stuck to the vacuum pan, causing foam and boiled-over milk. A local sugar-boiler told Borden that condensing milk using a vacuum pan wouldn't work. However, Borden solved the problem easily; he greased the pan like the housewife does when she bakes.

In May 1853, Borden applied for patents in the U.S. and England for his process of condensing milk. In 1851, an inventor had been awarded a patent for condensing milk "in any known mode," including the use of a vacuum pan. Borden's London patent attorney, C. Barlow, told him that no previous inventor had actually used a vacuum pan to evaporate milk. Borden thought that this answered the complaint of the Patent Office that his process lacked novelty. Two of the most important criteria for patent applications in the U.S. were that the inventions were "new" and "useful."

Patent office authorities weren't convinced that condensing milk in a partial vacuum distinguished Borden's process from earlier patents. His patent application was denied. He immediately began collecting testimonials to support his next patent application. An early testimonial was from Robert McFarlane, editor of *Scientific American*, who reported that he had stored Borden's condensed milk in a warm room for three months, and the milk had stayed sweet.

Borden experimented with the condensation of coffee, tea, and apple juice, but his principal studies were with milk. He wrote frequent letters to the Patent Office and visited Washington, D.C., again to plead his case. He persisted; he sought testimonials from additional scientists to support his claim. The acting Commissioner of the Patent Office failed to see the importance of the partial vacuum in the process and rejected his second patent application.

Borden continued to lobby for his patent. In May 1856, his third application for a patent was rejected, but the Commissioner of the Patent Office, Charles Mason, left the door to approval open. He wrote:

> Borden claims evaporation in vacuo to be a valuable feature of his discovery, and necessary. The Commissioner sees no reason to believe this. If it were really a discovery, Borden would be entitled to a patent. If Borden could prove that the removal of air in contact with the milk was important and that milk, taken fresh from the cow, and evaporated in the open air ... would not answer substantially the same purpose as when evaporated in vacuo, I would certainly grant to Mr. Borden the patent he is asking.[69]

Borden consulted again with scientists, including Dr. John Currie of New York. They studied all known methods of con-

densing milk and documented the results. Then they conducted more tests, prepared numerous charts, and wrote many
affidavits. The results indicated that condensing milk in vacuo
over low heat was superior to all other known methods; the
exclusion of air was critical to its preparation.

The documentation was forwarded to London and
Washington, D.C. Borden's U.S. patent application was
granted on August 19, 1856, and his English patent application received final approval on August 26, 1856. It had taken
three years and three months and four patent applications for
Borden to receive U.S. patent no. 15,553. He was now almost
fifty-six years old and was considered a failure by many of his
acquaintances and friends.

Borden didn't have the necessary financing to establish
manufacturing facilities for the production of condensed
milk. He recruited two partners, Thomas Green and James
Bridge, to obtain financial backing; Borden retained three-
eights of the ownership for himself. He built his first factory
in Wolcottville, Connecticut, west of Hartford. He sold his
first output to stores in the region; however, he realized that
he needed a substantially larger market. A milk depot in New
York provided the means of reaching that expanded market.

New Yorkers weren't interested in his product, and his
partner, Bridge, refused to contribute more than $1,900 to the
venture. Borden needed money to pay farmers for their milk;
he couldn't convince these frugal New England farmers to
wait for their money. If Borden couldn't pay them, other customers could. Borden was forced to close his factory at
Wolcottville.

Borden signed over fifty percent of his milk patent and his
further developments to reach an agreement with Green.
Green convinced Bridge to reinvest in the venture with the
three partners sharing expenses, profits (and losses), in the
same proportion as their ownership of the patent. A second
factory was established at Burrville, five miles north of
Wolcottville. The country was in the middle of the Panic of

1857—not a good time to start a business or to expand one. Banks were failing and many companies were going out of business. Borden's partners were reluctant to advance any more money; the outlook for the enterprise was bleak.

Borden shut down operations at his factory and boarded a train for New York to negotiate with his creditors. A serendipitous event happened. Timing, being at the right place at the right time, can be a critical element of success. On the train to New York, Borden had the good fortune to sit next to Jeremiah Milbank, owner of a wholesale grocery business.

Thirty-nine-year-old Milbank became a successful banker, broker, and railroad director. According to *Harper's Weekly,* Milbank "was one of those merchants whose careers are the true glory of the metropolis ... farseeing, conservative, and enterprising, a conceiver of large schemes, a financier who did not fail, a friend to wise charities."[70]

While they traveled to New York, Borden told his young companion of his development effort and of the importance of continuing with it. Borden spoke with conviction, sincerity, and with very little break in his monologue. He was animated and enthusiastic, and he impressed Milbank as being an honest man possessing considerable drive and motivation. Backing Borden was a substantial risk. The country was in the middle of a financial panic, and Borden's relationship with his partners was complicated. All of Milbank's instincts told him to go for it, however. Back the old man with the stooped shoulders and the fire in his eye.

In Milbank, Borden had a partner who knew that it took money to make money. Milbank realized that few economic shortcuts exist, and that you must be prepared to absorb short-term losses in order to be around for the long-term gains. Above all, you must be aggressive, persevering, and strong enough to overcome the inevitable setbacks. Venture capitalists didn't exist in the mid-1800s, but Milbank came close to fitting the definition. In fact, he probably had a stronger interest and a longer term commitment in the venture than many of today's venture capitalists.

Milbank paid off Borden's $6,000 debt incurred at Burrville and negotiated with Green and Bridge to settle their patent claims. The company was renamed the New York Condensed Milk Company to reflect its largest market. Borden imposed strict rules on the dairy farmers who sold milk to him, including:

- Barns must be kept clean; manure must be kept out of the milking stalls.
- Cow udders must be washed in warm water before milking.
- Milk strainers must be cleaned with boiling water and dried twice a day.
- No milk should be provided from cows who have calved within twelve days.
- No milk should be provided from cows that have been fed silage or turnips, which affect the taste of the milk.

In 1858, conditions in New York were a boon to Borden's sales of condensed milk. Thousands of babies and infants died each year due to unsanitary conditions in dairies and milk delivery wagons. Occasionally, manure and milk were hauled in the same wagon. New York's infant mortality rate was higher than Glasgow's and Liverpool's and was increasing.

By 1860, the business had grown sufficiently for John Burr, owner of the Burrville factory site, to ask for additional remuneration for water use. Borden moved his factory across the New York-Connecticut state line to Wassaic, New York, in dairy farm country on a branch of the New York Central Railroad.

Noah Gridley, one of Wassaic's town fathers, agreed to build the factory for Borden; then he pressed Borden for payment. Milbank reentered the scene, paid off Gridley, Green, and Bridge and pushed for an aggressive sales campaign. When the business expanded and Gridley realized the opportunity he had lost, he shut off the supply of water to the factory. Borden built a reservoir with water lines to the plant.

With the outbreak of the Civil War, the New York Condensed Milk Company switched emphasis from expanding consumer demand to filling the demand from its largest customer, the Union Army. In 1860, the daily output of the Wassaic factory reached 5,000 quarts and grew to 14,000 quarts by 1863.

Borden continued to improve his process and to apply for patents. He was granted additional patents in 1862, 1863, 1865, and 1866. Borden was personally involved in the details of running the factory, including routine maintenance and repair. Much of his redesign involved trial and error. He didn't have an engineering background, but he persisted in working on a design problem until he solved it.

Plants were established in other regions when orders for milk outstripped the plant's capacity, including one in Elgin, Illinois, forty miles west of Chicago; the business expanded until, in 1866, the Elgin Milk Company bought over 300,000 gallons of milk per year.

By 1867, Borden had overexpansion problems. Sales had tapered off dramatically in the years following the Civil War. The Elgin facility was closed in mid-1867. Overcapacity was addressed successfully, and Borden turned the business over to his sons.

In late 1867, Borden retired from active management of the business. He died on January 11, 1874, in Texas. His funeral service was held in White Plains, New York, where he was buried in Woodlawn Cemetery. Gail Borden's monument is a granite milk can inscribed with: "I tried and failed, I tried again and again, and succeeded."[71]

URBAN DEPARTMENT STORE EVOLUTION

CHAPTER 29

R. H. MACY

Founder of Macy's Department Store

"Those who would attain to any marked degree of excellence in a chosen pursuit must work, and work hard for it, prince or peasant."

Bayard Taylor

Rowland Hussey Macy was born on August 30, 1822, on Nantucket Island to John Macy and Eliza Myrick Macy, who were Quakers. John Macy, captain of a sailing ship, was a descendent of Thomas Macy, the first white man to settle on the island. R. H. Macy was the fourth of six children; he had three older brothers and two younger sisters. Many of the personal characteristics displayed by Macy in later years were nurtured in Nantucket, including drive, frugality, originality, and perseverance.

Macy's first job was crew member on the three-masted, 368-ton whaler, *Emily Morgan*, of New Bedford, Massachusetts. The ship visited Pernambuco, Brazil, sailed around Cape Horn, and put in at Samoa, the Gilbert Islands, Ascension Island, and New Zealand.

In September 1841, the *Emily Morgan* returned to New Bedford loaded with 3,000 barrels of sperm oil, over 100 barrels of whale oil, 1,000 pounds of whale bone, and a cask of ambergris, which was used in making perfume. Nineteen-year-old Macy returned home with his earnings for four years, one 175th share ($500), which he used later to begin his first retail venture.

Macy moved to Boston and worked in several jobs, including as an apprentice in a printing shop, before deciding to go into business for himself. In 1844, he established his first retail store, a small thread and needle store at 78 1/2 Hanover Street in Boston. It failed in its first year.

His second attempt in the retail business, a dry goods store at 357 Washington Street, Boston, opened in 1846. Macy sold mainly European-made items purchased at public auction. However, this venture wasn't successful either, and he had to close this store in late 1847. On the last page of his account book, he made the following entry:

I have worked two years for nothing

Damn

Damn
Damn
Damn[72]

In 1848, Macy teamed with his brother-in-law, Samuel S. Houghton, in a store at 175 Tremont Street in Boston. Houghton, who later founded the Boston department store Houghton & Dutton, specialized in embroidery and lace. Macy learned many of his principles of retailing from this early experience. He formed definite opinions about doing business on credit and the value of intensive advertising. He learned from his failures.

Macy's next opportunity was in California during the gold rush. In 1849, he left his wife and child behind in Massachusetts and traveled to California with his brother, Charles. In July 1850, Macy and his brother formed a partnership with two other men in Marysville, California, forty miles north of Sacramento. Macy and Company sold clothing, dry goods, and provisions.

Macy and Company competed with at least thirty other general stores in the area. Most of their customers were miners. When the gold ran out in the Marysville area, the miners moved on to the next find; Macy and Company's business declined dramatically.

In September 1850, they sold out, and Macy returned to Massachusetts with earnings of three to four thousand dollars. He had gained from this experience, since he had become familiar with dealing with customers from all over the world. He also learned about doing business on a large scale in an environment of inflated prices.

In April 1851, Macy began his fifth endeavor in the retail business, a dry goods store on Merrimack Street in Haverhill, Massachusetts. By this time, Macy was experienced in the retail business. Some of that experience was in what not to do.

Many of the ideas and operating methods that served him well in his New York store in later years were first implemented at the Haverhill store: selling at a fixed price (which wasn't common in the mid-nineteenth century), buying for cash, selling for cash, and advertising at about three times the rate of his competition. Macy did his own copywriting of advertisements, and he was good at it. Not only was his advertising cleverly done, it was innovative, such as using considerable white space around his words to draw attention to them.

However, Haverhill had too many dry goods stores to serve that small market. Macy went out of business just before Christmas in 1851. If imitation is the sincerest form of flattery, he should have been flattered. His competitors copied many of his techniques. Macy did most of the buying for his store personally. He bought from manufacturers and importers, not from wholesalers and jobbers. He eliminated one layer of middlemen.

In November 1852, he reopened at a new location in Haverhill, in the New Granite Store at 68-74 Merrimack Street. He sold his goods for the lowest prices in town. However, by 1855, the combined population of Haverhill and nearby Bradford was just over 9,000, and the market he had chosen wasn't large enough to sustain another store. He sold out in July 1855.

After Macy's sixth failure in the retail business, he declared bankruptcy. He promised creditors fifty cents on the dollar; he could pay only twenty-five cents. Macy salvaged two to three thousand dollars for living expenses, but this black mark stayed on his credit record for ten years. He had to contend with it three years later when he founded his New York store.

Macy decided to try a different line of work than retailing, hopefully one with fewer disappointments. He became a stockbroker and exchange broker in Boston, while continuing to live in Haverhill. In early 1857, he moved to Superior City on Lake Superior in Wisconsin to work as a real estate broker and money broker. Heavy ship traffic was anticipated for the new Soo Locks, and substantial growth was predicted for Superior City. The financial panic of 1857 dashed all of that optimism. In 1858, Macy returned to the East.

Macy was now thirty-six years old. He had been a whaler, retailer, gold miner, stockbroker, and real estate broker. He didn't have much to show for his efforts. A potential employer might look at his frequent job changes and not rate his prospects very high. However, that employer would have overlooked the overwhelming perseverance of the man. Macy also had good business sense; he knew value when he saw it, and he exuded persuasiveness.

Macy used this quality of persuasiveness in financing his next venture in the retail business, a small dry goods store at Sixth Avenue near 14th Street in Manhattan. The store, which had a twenty-foot front and was sixty feet deep, was financed by long-term credit from his suppliers. Considering his lack of cash and his previous track record, his success in obtaining credit was a tribute to his ability to sell himself.

Finally, Macy served a market in which he could be successful. New York had a total population of 950,000 in 1858, including 200,000 in Brooklyn across the East River. New York was the largest city in the United States and was growing rapidly. Approximately two-thirds of U.S. imports came in through the Port of New York, and about one-third of exports left from there. New York was dominant in banking, finance, clothing manufacturing, and the wholesale dry goods market.

Macy employed his established methods of operation and was successful beyond his dreams. He used techniques that he had developed over the years, including selling for cash only, offering only one selling price, selling at low prices based on high volume, and using bold advertising.

His offer of returning customers' money within a week if they were not satisfied with their purchase also contributed to his success. Macy's discontinued his "cash only" policy in 1939 because of the popularity of installment buying.

A story told about Macy's relationship with its customers involved store manager Percy Straus, who promised one Christmas season that all purchases from Macy's would be delivered by Christmas day. Straus went to bed at midnight on Christmas Eve and was awakened at 2:00 a.m. by the sweet, feminine voice of a customer who told him that she was very satisfied with the dancing bear that she had bought for her granddaughter for Christmas. Straus said that he was happy to hear that, but asked why she called him at home at 2:00 a.m. to tell him. She explained that she was calling because his @#*&% truck had just awakened her delivering it.

Another story involved a regular Macy's customer who had ordered a flagpole to fly the stars and stripes on the Fourth of July. He had the flagpole installed in his front yard at his home in Connecticut, but it was shorter than the length he had ordered. He called Macy's, described his problem, and insisted that one the correct length be delivered. Macy's immediately sent a truck to Connecticut to deliver the second flagpole and to return the original one to the store. The customer had the second flagpole installed and found that this one was too long.

Frustrated, he went to a local store, bought one the desired length, and had this third pole installed on his lawn; he placed the pole from Macy's in his garage. He called Macy's to tell them to retrieve their flagpole and not to bother bringing a third one. Macy's truck came on July 3rd while the customer was out, dug up the flagpole from his front yard, and took it back to New York. The patriot from Connecticut flew the flag from the roof of his house that Fourth of July, but remained a loyal Macy's customer.

Macy credited much of the success of his New York store to Margaret Getchell La Forge, Macy's first woman executive. A distant Macy relative, Margaret Getchell started working at the store as a cashier in late 1860. She advanced rapidly to a bookkeeping position and then to superintendent of the store.

Getchell was fair, tactful, and attentive to detail in supervising day-to-day operations. She was known for her executive ability and was a strong influence on Macy in establishing policies for the operation of the store.

Her motto was "Be Everywhere, Do Everything, and Never Forget to Astonish the Customer."[73] She knew how to display items, and she had a knack for publicity. She dressed two live cats in dolls' clothes and placed them in twin cribs in the toy department to attract customers. A salesclerk once dropped an expensive imported toy bird on the floor, breaking its singing mechanism. Getchell picked it up, removed a hairpin from her hair, and fixed it on the spot. She was a take-charge person.

In 1869, she married Abiel T. LaForge, Macy's lace buyer and a trusted employee, who had been a fellow Union officer of Macy's son in the Civil War. In 1872, Abiel LaForge became a partner of R. H. Macy & Company. Robert Macy Valentine, Macy's nephew, became a partner in 1875.

On March 29, 1877, Rowland Hussey Macy died on a buying trip to Paris. Abiel LaForge and Valentine managed the store, but, shortly afterward, LaForge died of tuberculosis contracted during the war. Shortly afterward, both Mrs. LaForge and Valentine passed away. Within a short period of time, Macy's had lost its entire management staff.

Charles B. Webster, a former floorwalker who had been made a partner after the deaths of Macy and LaForge, became store manager. In 1887, Webster invited Isador and Nathan Straus, sellers of imported china and glassware in rented space at Macy's since 1874, to become partners. In 1898, Webster sold his interest in the store to the Straus family for $1.2 million. More than five generations of the Straus family have been involved with the store.

Without perseverance, Macy would have been an unknown. By persevering, Macy's efforts resulted in the largest store in the world under one roof, spread over an entire city block. R. H. Macy's is known for the Macy's

Thanksgiving Day Parade and as the location for the original version of the movie, *Miracle on 34th Street*. To many people, Macy's Department Store is an institution.

CHAPTER 30

EARLY FAILURE / LATE SUCCESS

SUMMARY AND ANALYSIS

"Few things are impractical in themselves; and it is for want of application, rather than of means, that men fail of success."

La Rochefoucauld

Gail Borden and Rowland Hussey Macy are good examples of individuals who suffered failures early in their lives but were later successful. Borden, the entrepreneur / inventor, and Macy, the entrepreneur, displayed strong qualities of perseverance and determination. Both had to overcome major setbacks and were sufficiently resilient to try again.

Macy, in particular, exhibited enviable resilience in rebounding from six failed ventures in dry goods stores. With six failures and a success on the seventh attempt, Macy's experience is reminiscent of that of Robert Bruce, King Robert I of Scotland, in his twenty-two year struggle with England, resulting in Scotland's independence in 1328. Sir Walter Scott captured Bruce's thoughts after six successive defeats by the English in the story of the spider in the "History of Scotland" from *Tales of a Grandfather*:

> While he was divided twixt these reflections, and doubtful of what he would do, Bruce was looking upward toward the roof of the cabin in which he lay; and his eye was attracted by a spider which, hanging at the end of a long thread of its own spinning, was endeavoring, in the fashion of that creature, to swing itself from one beam in the roof to another, for the purpose of fixing the line on which it meant to stretch its web. The insect made the attempt again and again without success, and at length Bruce counted that it had tried to carry its point six times, and been as often unable to do so.

> It came to his head that he had himself fought just six battles against the English and their allies and that the poor persevering spider was in the same situation as himself, having made as many trials, and had been as often disap-

pointed in what he had aimed at. "Now," thought Bruce, "as I have no means of knowing what is best to be done, I shall be guided by the luck which guides this spider. If the spider shall make another effort to fix its thread and shall be successful, I will venture a seventh time to try my fortune in Scotland; but if the spider shall fail, I will go to the wars in Palestine [the Crusades], and never return to my home country more."

While Bruce was forming this resolution, the spider made another exertion with all the force it could muster, and fairly succeeded in fastening its thread to the beam which it had so often in vain attempted to reach. Bruce, seeing the success of the spider, resolved to try his own fortune; and as he had never before gained a victory, so he never afterward sustained any considerable or decisive check or defeat.[74]

Bruce's seventh battle against the English was at Bannockburn in June, 1314, where he won a decisive victory against the army of King Edward II. Macy didn't have the benefit of the symbolism of the spider; nevertheless, he was also successful on his seventh try.

Borden had fewer setbacks than Macy, but he lost more money on fewer failures. Loss of $60,000 on his meat biscuit venture was an example. He also had a wider range of failures than Macy, from floating prairie schooners to unappetizing meat biscuits to condensed apple juice. Borden was a religious man who was tireless and resourceful in his business pursuits.

Both Macy and Borden were successful in raising funds for their ventures. Macy required less financing in establishing his seventh store than Borden needed to establish factories to produce condensed milk. However, Macy's ability to raise this money with a poor credit rating was notable, particularly since he obtained it from his suppliers.

Fortunately, Borden owned large blocks of Texas real estate to use in financing his early development efforts. However, when additional money to manufacture and market condensed milk was needed, he wasn't able to provide it. He was extremely fortunate to sit next to Jeremiah Milbank on a train and to be able to convince him of the potential of his enterprise. Borden was also successful in convincing Milbank that he was an individual worth investing in.

Milbank was the 1850s version of a venture capitalist. However, today's venture capitalists usually look for a return of twenty to fifty percent over a short period of time, such as five years. They infrequently take a personal interest in the venture or become directly involved in running the business. Milbank took a personal interest in Borden's business, but it is unlikely that he received anything close to a return of twenty to fifty percent.

Macy was a stronger marketer than Borden. His early efforts in running dry goods stores taught him the importance of marketing. He was an innovator in advertising, and his copywriting techniques were widely imitated. Macy excelled at promoting his wares; he was a better promoter than Borden.

Both Macy and Borden had strong organizational ability. Each knew how to pick capable lieutenants. Borden was blessed with sons with business sense; however, Macy was disappointed with his "ne'er-do-well" son, Rowland, Jr., whom he couldn't trust to manage the business. Macy's promotion of Margaret Getchell to store management was an outstanding choice.

Many factors contributed to the success of Macy and Borden, but the main factors were strategic ones. The principal factor in Macy's ultimate success was his decision to serve the New York market. Finally, he had a market large enough to permit him to succeed. The techniques learned in his earlier experiences applied to a market of almost a million potential customers virtually guaranteed success.

In Borden's case, the time for a nutritious milk product with keeping qualities had come. The public's desire to reduce the high infant mortality rate in New York City and the need to improve the unsanitary conditions in the production and delivery of milk led to widespread use of Borden's condensed milk. The demand for condensed milk for the Union Army provided a huge market and contributed significantly to the early growth and profitability of Borden's enterprise.

Gail Borden is an excellent example of an individual who achieved success late in life. He was fifty-three when he developed his process for condensed milk, and almost fifty-six when he was granted the patent for it. Many become successful entrepreneurs between the ages of twenty-two and fifty-five. Borden is an exception, since much of the growth and success of his enterprise occurred when he was in his late fifties and his sixties.

Macy was known for his uncontrollable temper, over which he eventually gained control. Late in life, he suffered with ulcers but so did his peers, Frank Woolworth and Justin Strawbridge of Strawbridge & Clothier. Macy was a frugal man, some called him stingy, all of his life.

Macy's buyers had a reputation of obtaining the lowest possible prices from suppliers. In one story, a circus strongman who had just squeezed a coconut dry was challenged by a spectator. The spectator proceeded to squeeze out more drops of coconut milk. The strongman asked, "Who are you?" The spectator replied, "I am a Macy's buyer."[75] Holding costs down to generate profits fueled Macy's growth.

Eventually, through additions, Macy's department store filled the entire block from Thirty-fourth Street to Thirty-fifth Street and from Broadway to Seventh Avenue. It contained 2,200,00 square feet of floor space.

Macy and Borden are examples of individuals who were

failures early in their lives, but had the drive and will power to become successful later in life. Both were sufficiently resilient to persevere until they achieved success.

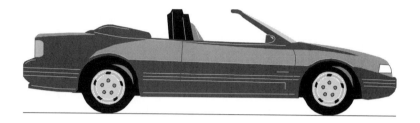

CONVERTING FAILURE INTO SUCCESS

Rescuing a Failing Company

CHAPTER 31

LEE IACOCCA

Rescuer of Chrysler Corporation

"It is not enough to begin; continuance is necessary. Mere enrollment will not make one a scholar; the pupil must continue in the school through the long course.... Success depends on staying power. The reason for failure in most cases is the lack of perseverance."

J. R. Miller

Lido "Lee" Iacocca was born on October 15, 1924, in Allentown, Pennsylvania, the older of two children of Nicola and Antoinette Iacocca, who immigrated to the United States from Italy. The Iacoccas were a close-knit family and young Lee and his sister, Delma, were encouraged to excel in school. Iacocca's interest in cars began in his teens. His first car was a 1938 Ford. In 1942, Iacocca enrolled at Lehigh University, where he completed the engineering program in three years.

When he graduated, he was one of fifty college graduates who received an offer to work for the Ford Motor Company at Dearborn, Michigan. Because he also received a fellowship to study for a master's degree at Princeton University, he delayed starting his job at Ford until August 1946. Halfway through Ford's eighteen-month training program, he realized he didn't want to be in engineering; he wanted to work in sales. He was told that he could switch if he could find his own sales job within the Company.

Iacocca found a position in fleet sales in Chester, Pennsylvania. By 1949, he was a zone manager in Wilkes-Barre, working with eighteen dealers. He advanced rapidly and, at the age of thirty-six, was promoted to general manager of the Ford Division, the Company's largest division. His greatest success with the Ford Division was the introduction of the Mustang in 1964. In January 1965, he was promoted to group vice president of the Ford and Lincoln-Mercury Divisions. In December 1970, Iacocca became president of the Ford Motor Company.

By 1975, the working relationship between Iacocca and Henry "my name is on the building" Ford II began to deteriorate. In July 1978, Henry Ford II fired Iacocca. When he asked why, Iacocca was told, "It's personal, and I can't tell you any more. It's just one of those things." Iacocca pressed further and was told, "Well, sometimes you just don't like somebody."[76]

Iacocca received offers from many companies, including International Paper, Lockheed, and Tandy Corporation. He also received an offer to be the dean of the New York University business school as well as several other business schools. However, he had been a car man for thirty-two years, and he didn't want to make a career change at the age of fifty-four. He was courted by Chrysler Corporation, initially by directors on the board and then by John Riccardo, the chief executive officer.

Riccardo knew that Chrysler had problems that he couldn't fix; however, he was willing to give up his job to someone who could. Iacocca realized that he wouldn't be happy for long as the number two man at Chrysler; he had to be CEO. Riccardo promised Iacocca that he would become the Chairman of the Board and CEO of Chrysler within a year.

Iacocca knew that Chrysler had aging plants, low employee morale, high inventory, and reliability problems with its cars, but he was unaware how severe their problems were. He admitted: "If I had the slightest idea of what lay ahead for me when I joined Chrysler, I wouldn't have gone over there for all the money in the world."[77] Nevertheless, he observed: "I had to do it. I had to prove to myself that I've still got it."[78] He was astounded to find that the design and manufacturing departments didn't talk with each other, neither did manufacturing and marketing.

Iacocca noticed the lack of discipline at Chrysler in his first week on the job. An example of the looseness in discipline was use of the office of Gene Cafiero, president of Chrysler, as a thoroughfare. Managers carrying cups of coffee walked through Cafiero's office to get to other offices. Cafiero was unable to conduct a confidential conversation unless he left his office to do it. Iacocca also noticed that Chrysler employees made many more personal calls during working hours than Ford people did.

Iacocca's biggest surprise at Chrysler was the virtual absence of financial controls. The previous CEO, Lynn Townsend, and the present CEO, Riccardo, had come to Chrysler from the Detroit office of Touche Ross, the public accounting firm. However, instead of implementing financial controls, both Riccardo and his predecessor spent inordinate amounts of time renegotiating loans with Chrysler's bankers to prevent cash flow problems.

Iacocca knew that Chrysler had lost almost $160 million in the third quarter of 1978, the quarter before he joined the company. One year after retired Ford executive Paul Bergmoser started at Chrysler, he showed Iacocca an internal financial report noting that the company had lost a billion dollars in the previous year. Unfortunately, the report provided no analysis of how the money was lost.

Engineering had always been considered Chrysler's strength. But when earnings sagged, Townsend had cut funding to engineering and product development. Instead of supporting future development in the United States, he expanded overseas by purchasing Rootes Motors of England and Simca of France. Neither was a good investment.

Shortly after joining Chrysler, Iacocca requested a list of all the plants with their rate of return on investment. The information wasn't available. He was astounded that "I couldn't find out anything."[79] When Iacocca attended his first board meeting at Chrysler, he was surprised to find how poorly informed the directors were. He had always thought that the Ford directors weren't as well informed about company activities as they should have been. However, Ford's directors knew orders of magnitude more about company operations than Chrysler's directors did.

Chrysler had many managers in positions in which they had no experience. Apparently, managers were considered universal at Chrysler; they could be moved to areas other than those in which they had experience. The large number of managers out of place was reflected in the company's performance. Many managers were uncomfortable with their assignments.

In order to survive, Chrysler had to solve many problems, including those listed by Iacocca in his book, *Iacocca: An*

Autobiography:
- A sound system of financial planning and financial control didn't exist.
- All thirty-five vice presidents ran their area of responsibility as a fiefdom with little communication among the functional areas.
- The actual quality and perceived quality of Chrysler products were low because of the shortcomings of the Plymouth Volare and the Dodge Aspen.
- Cars weren't built to customer and dealer orders. The Manufacturing Division decided how many cars to build and what options they would have, and the Sales Division had to sell those particular cars.
- Managers were reassigned frequently; many managers were responsible for functions for which they had no experience and little aptitude.
- Chrysler leased cars to car leasing companies such as Hertz and Avis instead of selling them. The rental companies leased new cars for six months and then returned them to Chrysler as used cars.
- The company's manufacturing facilities were old.

Iacocca assembled a capable, experienced team of automotive executives. He brought in managers he had known at Ford, such as Gerald Greenwald, and other former Ford managers, including Steve Miller from Ford Venezuela. Iacocca named Hal Sperlich, who had moved to Chrysler from Ford two years previously, vice president of product planning and later head of North American Operations. Also, Iacocca persuaded retired Ford executives, such as marketer Gar Laux and quality control guru Hans Matthias, to come out of retirement and help him at Chrysler. Layoffs at Chrysler were unavoidable. In less than three years, Iacocca had replaced thirty-three of the thirty-five vice presidents that he had inherited.

Upon joining Chrysler, Iacocca noted that: "I was ... confident of my own abilities. I knew the car business, and I knew I was good at it. In my heart I honestly believed that the place would be humming within a couple of years."[80]

However, his timing in joining Chrysler couldn't have been worse. In January 1979, less than three months after he joined the company, the Shah was exiled from Iran. The price of gasoline doubled within three weeks. Chrysler shifted production from the large gas-guzzling cars to small economy cars, such as the Plymouth Horizon and Dodge Omni. As this shift was occurring, the country went into a recession. Car sales dropped by half.

Chrysler was in a precarious position. Bankruptcy wasn't a good alternative because, among other reasons, few customers would buy a car from a bankrupt company; the buyer couldn't be sure that the company would remain in business to provide parts, service, and warranty work. Many Chrysler assets had already been sold, including the division that made tanks for the U.S. Army, and much of the company's real estate had also been sold. In addition, Chrysler had pursued every lead for a prospective purchaser of the company as well as many merger opportunities, including one with Volkswagen. The only remaining alternative was to seek a loan from the U.S. Government.

Opposition to a bailout, a government loan to a manufacturer, was prevalent, particularly among businessmen. Their motto was "make it on your own or go under." The National Association of Manufacturers came out against federal loan guarantees. However, precedent existed for a federal loan guarantee: $250 million to Lockheed in 1971, $111 million to Jones & Laughlin Steel company in 1974, and $150 million to the Wheeling-Pittsburgh Steel Corporation. One of the largest loan guarantees was to the Washington, D.C., Metro, which had received $1 billion.

The Treasury Department estimated that it would cost the government $2.7 billion for unemployment insurance and welfare payments in the first year if Chrysler went under. Iacocca asked the federal government to make a choice; pay out $2.7 billion now or guarantee loans for half that amount with a reasonable chance of being paid back. Congress made Iacocca sweat to obtain the loan.

Eventually, Chrysler was in debt to over 400 banks and insurance companies for $4.75 billion. The banks were located all over the world, including Frankfort, London, Ottawa, Paris, Tehran, and Tokyo. The smallest U.S. bank involved was the Twin City Bank of Little Rock with a loan of $78,000, and one of the largest was Manufacturers Hanover that Chrysler owed $200 million.

As a sweetener to prospective lenders, Chrysler issued 26.4 million stock warrants that were valid until 1990. The stock warrants could be exercised when the price of Chrysler's stock reached $13.00, which represented a sizable dilution of Chrysler's equity.

The risk taken by the federal government was less than most people realized. The government took all of Chrysler's $6 billion worth of assets as collateral, including cars, plants, real estate, and tooling. The liquidation value of Chrysler's assets had been appraised at $2.5 billion. The government had the first lien. If Chrysler didn't survive, the federal government would recover $1.2 billion in loans before other creditors' claims were satisfied.

Iacocca negotiated concessions with the United Automobile Workers Union. Initially, union workers gave up $1.15 an hour from their paychecks. Within the first year and a half, that concession grew to $2.00 an hour less pay. On the average, each Chrysler union member gave up $10,000 in pay while the concessions were in effect.

Chrysler's survival was dependent on the success of the K-cars, the Plymouth Reliant and the Dodge Aries. The company couldn't afford to build more cars like the Plymouth Volare and Dodge Aspen, whose engines stalled and whose hoods flew open unexpectedly. Repair of the Volare's rusty fenders had cost the company $109 million. Fortunately, Reliant and Aries were cars that consumers wanted.

In 1983, Chrysler made an operating profit of $925 million. On July 13, 1983, Iacocca announced his decision to pay off the loan, in its entirety, seven years before it was due. In his autobiography, *Iacocca*, he commented:

> For a variety of reasons, Chrysler turned out to be a hell of a lot worse than I bargained for. But once I was in, once I decided it was what I wanted to do, I never thought seriously of leaving. Of course, that's not always the best policy. People sometimes die with that attitude. They get swamped and overtaken by events, and they're still holding on as the waters rise up above them. When I signed on for my new job, I couldn't imagine anything in the automobile business could be that bad. I was wrong. In retrospect, I have to admit that there were several times at Chrysler when I came close to drowning.[81]

However, Iacocca didn't drown at Chrysler—he persevered—and brought a major automobile manufacturer back from the brink.

SAVING A FAILING PROJECT

CHAPTER 32

AL NEUHARTH

Creator of *USA Today*

"Success is the sum of detail. It might perhaps be pleasing to imagine oneself beyond detail and employed in only great things, but as I have often observed, if one attends to only the great things and lets the little things pass the great things become little."

Harvey Firestone

Al Neuharth, the younger of two sons of Daniel and Christina Neuharth, was born in Eureka, South Dakota, in 1924. Daniel farmed eighty acres until he injured his leg in a farm accident. He died of tuberculosis in 1926. Christina took in laundry and sewing and waited on tables to support the family. Her motto was "do a little bit more tomorrow than you did today, a little better next year than you did this year."[82]

At the age of eleven, Al Neuharth delivered the Minneapolis *Tribune*; at thirteen, he worked after school in the composing room of the Alpena *Journal*. In 1942, he graduated from high school and enrolled briefly at Northern State Teachers' College before enlisting in the U.S. Army. He won a bronze star as a combat infantryman. By the end of the war, he had earned sergeant's stripes.

In 1946, Neuharth returned home to enroll at the University of South Dakota on the G. I. Bill. He announced sports events for the college radio station before shifting his interest to the college newspaper, the *Volante*, and becoming its editor. In 1950, he was elected to Phi Beta Kappa. After he graduated, he accepted a job as reporter for the Associated Press.

In 1952, with $50,000 from the sale of shares, Neuharth and a friend started *SoDak Sports*, a statewide sports weekly modeled on the national *Sporting News*. Within a year, circulation had increased to 18,000, but sales of advertising space were sluggish. Their few advertisers began to shift to television commercials.

In 1954, Neuharth and his partner tried unsuccessfully to sell their weekly. Finally, they declared bankruptcy; their creditors received less than thirty-five cents on the dollar. Neuharth looked upon it as a learning experience. No plan had been prepared for projected sales revenue, expected advertising revenue, or anticipated profit and loss. Lack of a business plan was their worst mistake, a mistake Neuharth wouldn't make again.

Neuharth accepted a position as a reporter for the Miami

Herald. He wrote a series of articles about mail order scams and was at the right place at the right time on some fast-breaking stories. His career took off, and he was given an assignment with the *Herald's* Washington bureau. In 1959, he was promoted to assistant managing editor of the *Herald* and was chosen to open its Brevard County, Florida, bureau to handle the news from the Cape Canaveral Space Center.

The following year, Neuharth was appointed assistant to the executive editor of the Detroit *Free Press.* He worked in both the news and business operations; his performance was noticed both inside Knight Newspapers and outside. In 1963, he accepted a position with Gannett Newspapers as general manager of their Rochester, New York, newspapers: the *Democrat & Chronicle* and the *Times-Union.* He was considered heir apparent to Paul Miller, chief executive officer of Gannett Newspapers.

Neuharth suggested to Miller that Gannett start a daily newspaper in Brevard County, serving the Cape Canaveral area. Miller had tried unsuccessfully to buy a small Florida daily as a nucleus for expansion; he was receptive to Neuharth's suggestion even though it was counter to the national trend of fewer daily newspapers. Neuharth bought the Cocoa *Tribune* for $1.9 million; instead of revamping it, he started a new paper, *Today: Florida's Space Age Newspaper*, with a fresh format. He supplemented the small staff with "loaners" from other Gannett newspapers.

Neuharth avoided two mistakes he had made in starting *SoDak Sports.* First, he authorized the preparation of a comprehensive business plan; second, he ensured that he had sufficient funds to pay for the start-up. Neuharth was a hands-on manager. He was on-site in Cocoa functioning as the managing editor. He organized the new paper into three distinct sections: news, business, and sports. The comics section was printed in color, a *Today* innovation. *Today* was profitable in twenty-eight months, due mainly to the guts, innovation, and drive of Neuharth.

In 1973, Neuharth became chief executive officer of Gannett Newspapers. He was appointed chairman when Paul Miller retired in 1978. Neuharth had considered the idea of a national newspaper for ten years; finally, he proceeded with the idea for both professional and personal reasons. He knew that the profession of newspaper journalism could do a better job than it was doing, and, personally, he needed new worlds to conquer.

Improvements in satellite communications helped to make the idea achievable. Neuharth's lack of modesty was apparent in his goal: "We'll reinvent the newspaper." He wanted to create a newspaper so captivating that it would attract millions of readers, including many who currently didn't read a newspaper. He also wanted to innovate the design and content of the new paper to "pull the rest of the industry into the twenty-first century, albeit kicking and screaming."

By late 1979, Gannett had newspapers across the United States, including many in the major city markets. In areas where Gannett didn't own a printing plant, they could make contract printing arrangements. Neuharth considered three start-up possibilities that could use this network to Gannett's advantage:

- a national sports daily, similar to the *Sporting News* and *Sports Illustrated*
- a daily and / or Sunday supplement for the Gannett community newspapers with national news and advertising
- a national general-interest daily newspaper

He asked for the opinion of three key Gannett managers: John Quinn, the chief news executive; Jack Heselden, president of the newspaper division; and Douglas McCorkindale, the chief financial and legal officer. At the year-end board of directors' meeting, Neuharth announced that he was going to set aside $1 million in 1980 to "study what's new in newspapers and television. And especially whether we can harness the satellite to deliver more news to more people in more ways."

The research and development effort was called Project NN. NN meant "National Newspaper" but Neuharth promoted the idea outside of Gannett that it stood for "New Newspapers." Project NN soon became known outside the company as "Neuharth's Nonsense." The five-person project team that assembled in Florida included:

- Tom Curley, a newsman with an excellent record in news research
- Paul Kessinger, a research and marketing guru
- Larry Sacket, an expert in satellite communications technology
- Frank Vega, a savvy circulation specialist

Neuharth chose Vince Spezzano, the veteran publisher of *Today* in Florida, as coordinator of the team. The average age of the team's members, excluding Spezzano, was thirty.

Neuharth courted the board of directors' support for his project and kept them informed. In October 1980, the Project NN report was presented to the board, and an additional $3.5 million was budgeted for planning and prototypes in 1981.

In August 1981, research conducted by Lou Harris and Associates and Simmons Market Research Bureau was presented to the board, and the prototypes were reviewed. In December 1981, the board of directors voted to launch *USA Today* by a unanimous 12-0 vote, even though the Gannett financial organization counseled against going ahead.

The next phase was called GANSAT, Gannett Satellite Information Network. The team members were:

- Moe Hickey, president and supervisor of business planning
- Ronald Martin, planning editor responsible for prototype development
- Chuck Schmitt, finance director
- Frank Vega, director of circulation

Neuharth personally worked on the news product and circulation planning; he continued to be a hands-on manager. John Quinn worked virtually full-time with Martin on prototype plans.

The team decided that *USA Today* must be different from other newspapers, both in appearance and in content. Early goals were to have four highly organized sections, emphasis on color, easy-to-read stories, frequent use of charts and graphics, news from all fifty states, and a concentration on sports, TV, and weather.

Neuharth used "intrapreneurship" on *USA Today* by obtaining "loaners" from the other Gannett papers. "Loaners" were away from their parent newspapers for an average of four months and weren't replaced. Young newspaper journalists were provided with a broadening experience as well as an introduction to new techniques and technology.

On September 15, 1982, *USA Today* was launched at a party in Washington, D.C., attended by President and Mrs. Ronald Reagan, Speaker of the House "Tip" O'Neill, and Senate Majority Leader Howard Baker. Red, white, and blue *USA Today* banners waved from the 60-foot-wide by 140-foot-long tent erected on the National Mall. The 800 guests included cabinet members, representatives, senators, publishers, and executives. The party on the Mall was followed by dinner at *USA Today* headquarters across the Potomac River in Rosslyn, Virginia, where food from all fifty states was served.

By 1983, circulation of *USA Today* passed 1 million, which surpassed all other newspapers except the *Wall Street Journal*, the New York *Daily News*, and the Los Angeles *Times*. Attracting advertisers was difficult because the only official circulation numbers were those provided by the Audit Bureau of Circulations (ABC), and they wouldn't review circulation until after the first year of operation.

Neuharth commissioned a circulation survey by Price Waterhouse, the public accounting firm, who verified that circulation had surpassed 1 million. Madison Avenue didn't consider the results to be official. Finally, in late June 1984, ABC verified that circulation was 1.28 million.

In August 1984, Neuharth estimated that *USA Today's* losses would be $124 million in 1984, $81 million in 1985, and $25 million in 1986, but that the venture would break even in 1987. He also estimated that the cumulative losses since start-up would approach $400 million before taxes by the end of 1987. That evaluation of *USA Today's* finances was "as close as we ever came to folding ... " Advertising increased notably after Cathleen Black was brought in from *New York* magazine as president of *USA Today* and was assigned the responsibility for advertising.

Losses continued at $10 million a month during 1984, which translated into $339,726 per day, $14,155 per hour, and $236 per minute. Neuharth knew that serious steps would have to be taken to save the paper. On Sunday, November 11, 1984, he held a meeting of *USA Today's* management committee at his Florida home. He told the committee that the current mode couldn't continue; they had alternatives of quitting or making a concerted effort to implement crucial changes.

Neuharth observed that they must reduce their losses by substituting management for money, such as the following steps:

• We must produce and present even more news, with fewer people, in less space, at lower cost.
• We must sell and present even more advertising, at higher rates, with fewer people, at lower costs.
• We must produce and print more newspapers, with even better quality, with fewer people, at lower cost.
• We must circulate and sell even more newspapers, at higher prices, with fewer people, at lower cost....[83]

He directed a reduction of payroll costs by five percent by the end of 1985 and required new hires to have his or editor John Curley's approval. Also, he set a goal for losses of under $75 million in 1985.

USA Today wasn't considered to be a serious newspaper by many members of the journalism community, to whom it was "McPaper." *USA Today* staffers heard the name McPaper and commented that many papers were stealing their McNuggets. John Quinn quipped that if *USA Today* ever won a Pulitzer Prize, it would probably be for "the best investigative paragraph." In *The Making of McPaper*, Peter Prichard quoted Quinn's speech to the National Press Foundation, in which Quinn commented on differences in headlines about the end of the world:

Wall Street Journal
STOCK EXCHANGE HALTS TRADING AS WORLD
ENDS

New York *Times*
END OF WORLD HITS THIRD WORLD HARDEST

Washington *Post*
WORLD ENDS; MAY AFFECT ELECTIONS,
SOURCES SAY

USA Today
WE'RE GONE ... STATE-BY-STATE DEMISE ON 6A
FINAL SCORES ON 8C[84]

Quinn also observed: "Neuharth has an ability for histrionics, like in the old movies. But he also has the ability to massage people, to handle them in a way to get the best out of them."[85] Nevertheless, along with the ability to motivate people and to get the most of them, Neuharth had an abrasive side. Jimmy Thomas, Gannett treasurer, acknowledged: "There is a fear of Al. He strikes you as a person who has the capability and mind-set and sometimes willingness to fire you ... or demote you so low in the company you'll never be seen again."[86]

Earnings from Gannett's other eighty-eight papers were paying the bills for *USA Today*. By mid-1985, the "Nation's Newspaper" began to turn the corner financially. Gannett

288

reported a twenty percent earnings increase compared to the first half of 1984. Cathy Black had increased the advertising revenue 106 percent compared with the previous year. The price was increased from thirty-five cents to fifty cents when the volume of the paper went to sixty pages. However, the losses were still staggering: $102 million in 1985 and $70 million in 1986.

In May 1986, Neuharth stepped down as CEO of Gannett but retained the title of chairman. He recalled his difficult transition with Paul Miller and wanted to ensure that the transition with president John Curley was more orderly. He said that he intended to stay on as chairman until 1989, when he would be sixty-five.

In July 1986, Simmons Market Research conducted a survey noting that *USA Today* had 4,792,000 readers per day, the most readers of any U.S. daily. The *Wall Street Journal's* paid circulation was still much higher, but each *USA Today* was read by three readers while the *Journal* was read by only two readers on the average. Increases in *USA Today's* advertising followed the increases in readership.

On June 15, 1987, Curley sent a telegram to Neuharth, who was on a business trip: "McPaper has made it. *USA Today* broke into the black with a profit of $1,093,756 for the month of May, six months ahead of schedule."[87] The Nation's Newspaper had become profitable faster than many other media new ventures: *Sports Illustrated* required ten years to move into the black; *Newsweek* nine years; and *Money* magazine eight years.

Neuharth's vision, determination, and pure strength of will brought a daily national newspaper into existence when many said it couldn't be done. In his opinion:

The most satisfying victories are those where the odds against your winning are the greatest. But long odds don't necessarily make the job more difficult.

289

In fact, the more that people tell you that it can't be done, the more likely that you have a winner. That usually means that you know something that they don't know. Or that your idea is so different or so daring that they can't comprehend it.

If your sights are clearly set on a goal, the fact that others say it can't be done shouldn't slow you down. It should spur you on.

CHAPTER 33

CONVERTING FAILURE INTO SUCCESS

SUMMARY AND ANALYSIS

"When failure opens your luckless door,
And struts across the creaking floor;
When fortune flees and leaves you bare,
And former friends but coldly stare:
It's time for you to take a tack,
And show the world you're coming back!"

Lilburn Harwood Townsend

The circumstances that led to Lee Iacocca's rescue of the Chrysler Corporation in the late 1970s were more dire than those that confronted Al Neuharth at *USA Today*. Nevertheless, the severity of Neuharth's struggle shouldn't be downplayed; *USA Today* was losing $10 million a month during 1984. However, Neuharth had the cash flow from the rest of the Gannett Corporation to pay the bills. Iacocca, on the other hand, was dealing with a "you bet your company" situation that depended on customer acceptance of the K-cars, the Plymouth Reliant and the Dodge Aries.

Chrysler had lost almost $160 million in the quarter before Iacocca joined the Chrysler Corporation and lost hundreds of millions in his first year. When he became CEO of Chrysler, he inherited many organizational problems, which were sufficiently challenging without changes in the automobile marketplace. In January 1979, the price of gasoline doubled within three weeks because of the political instability in the Middle East. Iacocca shifted production from large gas-guzzling cars to small economy cars as the country entered a recession. Sales of automobiles dropped by half.

Iacocca had years of experience in the automobile industry and understood the car business. He knew how to generate earnings by marketing and selling automobiles; he had done it successfully at the Ford Motor Company. He knew many people within the automotive industry, and they respected him.

When Iacocca needed managers to help him turn Chrysler around, he lured key people from Ford and also convinced a number of retired Ford executives to come out of retirement to help him. He was a winner, and his colleagues knew it.

Iacocca had to lay off many workers at Chrysler and had to replace many executives. He tried to find other positions for many of them; he didn't shrink from taking the necessary actions.

Iacocca was a good communicator in presenting Chrysler's case to the federal government for a loan guarantee. Many congressmen and senators were against the guarantee, and he had to fight to obtain the approval of Congress. Later, he became an effective pitchman in Chrysler's commercials on television.

Iacocca's managerial ability, self-confidence, and will to succeed served him well in his challenge to save Chrysler. He met Chrysler's problems head-on until they were solved, while providing a vision and making plans for the future of the company.

Al Neuharth learned from his mistakes; fortunately, he made very few of them. In particular, he benefitted from his early failure with *SoDak Sports*. From that time onward, start-up of a new venture was accompanied by a comprehensive business plan with advertising estimates, circulation estimates, and projected cash flow. Also, he ensured that the necessary funds were available to finance the venture before starting it.

Neuharth was an innovator who created new products. He had a sufficiently thick skin that allowed him to ignore criticism and to endure mockery. In fact, he used his detractor's statements to add humor to his presentations in meetings. He was an expert at judging the proper timing to reveal information and to take action. He restricted the release of project estimates, but, when he was cultivating support, he provided project planning information to bring others around to his point of view.

Neuharth paid great attention to detail. He was a hands-on manager who helped with the editing of a new newspaper and assisted with its layout, particularly the front page. He even arranged the seating at meetings to control the sequence of voting on controversial issues.

Neuharth knew how to pick capable managers from within Gannett, and he knew how to identify quality outsiders and persuade them to join Gannett. He insisted that everyone work hard and work long hours, as he did. When a manager struggled in an assignment, he reassigned the individual.

Neuharth was a strong promoter of his visions. He didn't spend promotion money recklessly; however, neither did he believe in lessening the company's image by scrimping on banquets and parties. He certainly didn't scrimp on the *USA Today* launch party held on the Mall between the Capitol and the Lincoln Memorial in Washington, D.C., or on the dinner after the party at Gannett headquarters across the Potomac River in Rosslyn.

When *USA Today* losses continued at $10 million a month, Neuharth implemented measures to reduce the losses. He convinced managers who were already working hard, working lean, and providing a quality paper at a low cost to work harder, work leaner, and to provide a higher-quality paper at a lower cost.

Neuharth's strongest qualities in creating a new national newspaper were his boldness, his determination to succeed, his vision, and his ability to implement the vision. His boldness was displayed in convincing the President of the United States, the Speaker of the House, and the Senate Majority Leader to attend a launch party for a commercial enterprise. The determination to win was evident in everything that he did. His visions ranged from starting a local weekly paper in Florida when local weeklies were dying to establishing "The Nation's Newspaper" when many of his peers said it couldn't be done. He showed them it could. He willed it done and implemented his vision.

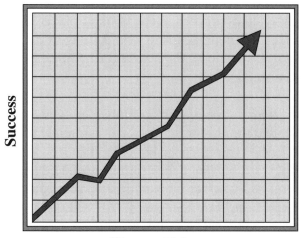

Human Values

Success (vertical axis label)

EPILOGUE

"Many people dream of success. To me success can be achieved only through repeated failure and introspection. In fact, success represents one percent of your work which results only from the ninety-nine percent that is called failure."

Soichiro Honda

All of the individuals profiled in this book displayed the need to achieve. In "Entrepreneurship and Management in the Years Ahead" in *Motives, Personality, and Society*, David McClelland observes:

> A particular type of human motivation which we called the need to achieve ... is essential for successful entrepreneurship. We had found that it was not what a man said he wanted that determined whether he would be a successful entrepreneur, but the extent to which his thoughts spontaneously turned to doing things better, improving his performance, and getting feedback on how well he was doing.... Further research demonstrated, however, that the desire to do things better, at lower cost, or with greater profit, suited people particularly to be successful small businessmen....[88]

All twenty-two of these individuals / teams worked to do things better, to improve their performance, and to obtain feedback on how they were doing. Some of them were unsuccessful, not because they weren't sufficiently motivated or lacked certain personal characteristics, but because strategic factors were against them.

We can learn from the twenty-two individuals profiled in this book, particularly about their personal characteristics and their human values. In displaying the drive and high level of motivation that contributed to their success, along with the persistence and the strong will that they demonstrated, they provide us with inspiring role models.

In today's environment, small businesses play a major role in the U. S. economy.

> ... small businesses, defined as companies with fewer than 500 workers, have been the

engine of U.S. economic growth in recent years. These firms have generated nearly all the new jobs, a role ... they will continue to play well into the next century. Current data shows that small companies account for:

- 52 percent of sales;
- 50 percent of private sector output;
- 54 percent of private sector employment;
- 99.7 percent of all employers.[89]

In the 1990s, many large corporations downsized, and many small and medium-sized businesses expanded. According to the Small Business Administration:

... corporate downsizing during the first half of the 1990s had a major impact on American society and the environment for small business and entrepreneurship, and that corporate downsizing would continue over the decade from 1995 to 2005, albeit at a slower pace.... The downsizing of larger corporations and the outsourcing of many of the functions previously performed internally offer new opportunities for small businesses ... Suddenly, the relative attractiveness of careers in large business versus the rewards associated with entrepreneurship and or working in the small business portion of the economy have been drastically changed.[90]

Despite the risk, increasing numbers of fledgling entrepreneurs are venturing out on their own. The Small Business Administration estimates that from 1994 to 2005, the number of self-employed men and women will increase from nine million to over eleven and a half million.

The future of entrepreneurship is bright. U.S. workers, who have become used to living with the uncertainty and the lack of security of working for large organizations, are evaluating alternatives in which they are more in control of their destinies. Starting a new venture and managing a small business are desirable alternatives to many of them.

NOTES

"Someone once said, 'Success is a journey, not a destination.' Happiness is to be found along the way, not at the end of the road, for then the journey is over and it is too late. Today, this hour, this minute is the day, the hour, the minute for each of us to sense the fact that life is good, with all of its trials and troubles, and perhaps more entertaining because of them."

Robert R. Updegraff

Prologue

1 Hisrich, Robert D., and Candida Brush. *The Woman Entrepreneur: Starting, Financing, and Managing a Successful New Business* (Lexington, MA: Lexington Books, 1985) 18.

2 Herbert, Robert F., and Albert H. Link. *The Entrepreneurs—Mainstream Views and Radical Critiques.* (New York: Praeger, 1982) 17.

3 Vesper, Karl. *New Venture Strategies* (Englewood Cliffs, NJ: Prentice-Hall, 1980) 2.

4 Drucker, Peter F. *Innovation and Entrepreneurship: Practice and Principles* (New York: Harper & Row, 1985) 2-3.

Chapter 1

5 Justin, Lawrence R. *Billy Durant: Creator of General Motors* (Grand Rapids: Eerdmans, 1973) 41.

6 Justin, Lawrence R. *Billy Durant: Creator of General Motors* (Grand Rapids: Eerdmans, 1973) 131.

7 Sloan, Alfred P. *Adventures of a White-Collar Man* (New York: Doubleday Doran, 1941) 202.

8 Justin, Lawrence R. *Billy Durant: Creator of General Motors* (Grand Rapids: Eerdmans, 1973) 261.

Chapter 2

9 Lacey, Robert. *Ford: The Men and The Machine* (Boston: Little, Brown, 1986) 100.

10 Harris, Jacqueline L. *Henry Ford* (New York: Franklin Watts, 1984) 39.

11 Ford, Henry, and Samuel Crowther. *My Life and Work.* (Garden City, NY: Doubleday, 1923) 83.

12 Lacey, Robert. *Ford: The Men and the Machine.* (Boston: Little, Brown, 1986) 122.

13 Harris, Jacqueline L. *Henry Ford* (New York: Franklin Watts, 1984) 103.

Chapter 3

14 Justin, Lawrence R. *Billy Durant: Creator of General Motors* (Grand Rapids: Eerdmans, 1973) 238.

15 Justin, Lawrence R. *Billy Durant: Creator of General Motors* (Grand Rapids: Eerdmans, 1973) 249.

Chapter 4

16 Boyd, Thomas. *Poor John Fitch: Inventor of the Steamboat* (New York: Putnam, 1935) 132.

17 Flexner, James Thomas. *Steamboats Come True: American Inventors in Action* (New York: Viking, 1944) 205.

Chapter 5

18 Philip, Cynthia Owen. *Robert Fulton: A Biography* (New York: Franklin Watts, 1985) vii.

19 Morgan, John S. *Robert Fulton.* (New York: Mason / Charter, 1977) 156.

20 Morgan, John S. *Robert Fulton.* (New York: Mason / Charter, 1977) 184.

21 Morgan, John S. *Robert Fulton.* (New York: Mason / Charter, 1977) 185.

Chapter 7

22 Thompson, Silvanus P. *Philipp Reis: Inventor of the Telephone* (London: Spon, 1883) 1.

23 Thompson, Silvanus P. *Philipp Reis: Inventor of the Telephone* (London: Spon, 1883) 5.

24 Thompson, Silvanus P. *Philipp Reis: Inventor of the Telephone* (London: Spon, 1883) 53.

25 Prescott, George B. *Bell's Electric Speaking Telephone: Its Invention, Construction, Application, Modification and History* (New York: Arno, 1972) 14.

26 Thompson, Silvanus P. *Philipp Reis: Inventor of the Telephone* (London: Spon, 1883) 41.

27 Thompson, Silvanus P. *Philipp Reis: Inventor of the Telephone* (London: Spon, 1883) 9.

Chapter 8

28 Mackensie, Catherine. *Alexander Graham Bell: The Man Who Contracted Space* (Boston: Houghton, Mifflin, 1928) 85.

29 Burlingame, Roger. *Out of Silence into Sound: The Life of Alexander Graham Bell* (New York: Macmillan, 1964) 65.

30 Burlingame, Roger. *Out of Silence into Sound: The Life of Alexander Graham Bell* (New York: Macmillan, 1964) 67.

31 Bruce, Robert V. *Bell: Alexander Graham Bell and the Conquest of Solitude* (Boston: Little, Brown, 1973) 181.

Chapter 10

32 Shurkin, Joel. *Engines of the Mind: A History of the Computer* (New York: W. W. Norton, 1984) 109.

Chapter 11

33 Rodgers, William. *Think: A Biography of the Watsons and IBM* (New York: Stein & Day, 1969) 21.

34 Rodgers, William. *Think: A Biography of the Watsons and IBM* (New York: Stein & Day, 1969) 21.

35 Belden, Thomas Graham, and Marva Robins Belden. *The Lengthening Shadow: The Life of Thomas J. Watson* (Boston: Little, Brown, 1962) 31.

36 Belden, Thomas Graham, and Marva Robins Belden. *The Lengthening Shadow: The Life of Thomas J. Watson* (Boston: Little, Brown, 1962) 118-19.

Chapter 13

37 Rifkin, Glenn, and George Harrar. *The Ultimate Entrepreneur: The Story of Ken Olsen and Digital Equipment Corporation* (Chicago: Contemporary Books, 1988) 92.

38 Rifkin, Glenn, and George Harrar. *The Ultimate Entrepreneur: The Story of Ken Olsen and Digital Equipment Corporation* (Chicago: Contemporary Books, 1988) 95.

39 Rifkin, Glenn, and George Harrar. *The Ultimate Entrepreneur: The Story of Ken Olsen and Digital Equipment Corporation* (Chicago: Contemporary Books, 1988) 96.

40 Rifkin, Glenn, and George Harrar. *The Ultimate Entrepreneur: The Story of Ken Olsen and Digital Equipment Corporation* (Chicago: Contemporary Books, 1988) 95.

41 Kidder, Tracy. *The Soul of a New Machine* (Boston: Little, Brown, 1981) 10.

Chapter 14

42 Rifkin, Glenn, and George Harrar. *The Ultimate Entrepreneur: The Story of Ken Olsen and Digital Equipment Corporation* (Chicago: Contemporary Books, 1988) 122.

43 Rifkin, Glenn, and George Harrar. *The Ultimate Entrepreneur: The Story of Ken Olsen and Digital Equipment Corporation* (Chicago: Contemporary Books, 1988) 312-13.

Chapter 15

44 Rifkin, Glenn, and George Harrar. *The Ultimate Entrepreneur: The Story of Ken Olsen and Digital Equipment Corporation* (Chicago: Contemporary Books, 1988) 99.

45 Rifkin, Glenn, and George Harrar. *The Ultimate*

Entrepreneur: The Story of Ken Olsen and Digital Equipment Corporation (Chicago: Contemporary Books, 1988) 184.

46 Seneker, Harold. "Data General—life in the fast lane." *Forbes.* 3 March 1980. 74.

Chapter 16

47 Smith, Douglas K., and Robert C. Alexander. *Fumbling the Future: How Xerox Invented, Then Ignored, the First Personal Computer* (New York: William Morrow, 1988) 66.

48 Smith, Douglas K., and Robert C. Alexander. *Fumbling the Future: How Xerox Invented, Then Ignored, the First Personal Computer* (New York: William Morrow, 1988) 241.

Chapter 17

49 Butcher, Lee. *Accidental Millionaire: The Rise and Fall of Steve Jobs at Apple Computer* (New York: Paragon House, 1988) 133.

Chapter 19

50 Richards, Norman. *Dreamers and Doers.* (New York: Atheneum, 1984) 48.

51 Babcock, Glenn D. "History of the United States Rubber Company: A Case Study in Corporation Management." Indiana Business Report No. 39 (Bloomington: Indiana UP, 1966) 16.

52 Manchester, Harland. *Trail Blazers of Technology: The Story of Nine Inventors* (New York: Scribner's, 1962) 56.

53 Hylander, C. J. *American Inventors* (New York: Macmillan, 1958) 104.

54 Woodruff, William. *The Rise of the British Rubber Industry During the Nineteenth Century* (Liverpool: Liverpool UP, 1958) 9.

Chapter 20

55 Hancock, Thomas. *Personal Narrative of the Origin and Progress of the Caoutchouc or India-Rubber Manufacture in England* (London: Longman, Brown, Green, Longmans, & Roberts, 1857) 89.

56 Hancock, Thomas. *Personal Narrative of the Origin and Progress of the Caoutchouc or India-Rubber Manufacture in England* (London: Longman, Brown, Green, Longmans, & Roberts, 1857) 91.

57 Woodruff, William. *The Rise of the British Rubber Industry During the Nineteenth Century* (Liverpool: Liverpool UP, 1958) 153.

58 Woodruff, William. *The Rise of the British Rubber Industry During the Nineteenth Century* (Liverpool: Liverpool UP, 1958) 13.

Chapter 22

59 Harris, Sherwood. *The First to Fly: Aviation's Pioneer Days* (Blue Ridge Summit, PA: Tab Aero, 1970) 8.

60 Harris, Sherwood. *The First to Fly: Aviation's Pioneer Days* (Blue Ridge Summit, PA: Tab Aero, 1970) 8.

61 Harris, Sherwood. *The First to Fly: Aviation's Pioneer Days* (Blue Ridge Summit, PA: Tab Aero, 1970) 10.

62 Breashear, John A. *The Autobiography of a Man Who Loved the Stars* New York: American Society of Mechanical Engineers, 1924) 131.

Chapter 23

63 Untermeyer, Louis. "Wilbur and Orville Wright." *Makers of the Modern World* (New York: Simon & Schuster, 1955) 365.

Chapter 26

64 Brandon, Ruth. *A Capitalist Romance: Singer and the Sewing Machine* (Philadelphia: Lippincott, 1977) 68.

65 Brandon, Ruth. *A Capitalist Romance: Singer and the*

Sewing Machine (Philadelphia: Lippincott, 1977) 85.

Chapter 28

66 Franz, Joe B. *Gail Borden: Dairyman to a Nation* (Norman: U of Oklahoma P, 1951) 189.

67 Franz, Joe B. *Gail Borden: Dairyman to a Nation* (Norman: U of Oklahoma P, 1951) 200.

68 Franz, Joe B. *Gail Borden: Dairyman to a Nation* (Norman: U of Oklahoma P, 1951) 211.

69 Franz, Joe B. *Gail Borden: Dairyman to a Nation* (Norman: U of Oklahoma P, 1951) 228.

70 Franz, Joe B. *Gail Borden: Dairyman to a Nation* (Norman: U of Oklahoma P, 1951) 239.

71 Baker, Nina Brown. *Texas Yankee: The Story of Gail Borden* (New York: Harcourt Brace, 1955) 59.

Chapter 29

72 Hendrickson, Robert. *The Grand Emporiums* (New York: Stein & Day, 1979) 63.

73 Hendrickson, Robert. *The Grand Emporiums* (New York: Stein & Day, 1979) 65.

Chapter 30

74 Scott, Sir Walter. *Tales of a Grandfather: History of Scotland* (Boston: Ticknor and Fields, 1861) 93-94.

75 Hendrickson, Robert. *The Grand Emporiums* (New York: Stein & Day, 1979) 68.

Chapter 31

76 Iacocca, Lee, and William Novak. *Iacocca: An Autobiography* (New York: Bantam, 1984) 127.

77 Iacocca, Lee, and William Novak. *Iacocca: An Autobiography* (New York: Bantam, 1984) 141.

78 Iacocca, Lee, and William Novak. *Iacocca: An Autobiography* (New York: Bantam, 1984) 149.

79 Wyden, Peter. *The Unknown Iacocca* (New York:

William Morrow, 1987) 134.

80 Iacocca, Lee, and William Novak. *Iacocca: An Autobiography* (New York: Bantam, 1984) 154.

81 Iacocca, Lee, and William Novak. *Iacocca: An Autobiography* (New York: Bantam, 1984) 150.

Chapter 32

82 Prichard, Peter. *The Making of McPaper: The Inside Story of USA Today* (Kansas City: Andrews, McMeel & Parker, 1987) 26.

83 Neuharth, Al. *Confessions of an S. O. B.* (New York: Doubleday, 1989) 166-167.

84 Prichard, Peter. *The Making of McPaper: The Inside Story of USA Today* (Kansas City: Andrews, McMeel & Parker, 1987) 334.

85 Neuharth, Al. *Confessions of an S. O. B.* (New York: Doubleday, 1989) 154.

86 Neuharth, Al. *Confessions of an S. O. B.* (New York: Doubleday, 1989) 119.

87 Prichard, Peter. *The Making of McPaper: The Inside Story of USA Today* (Kansas City: Andrews, McMeel & Parker, 1987) 378.

Epilogue

88 McClelland, David. "Entrepreneurship and Management in the Years Ahead." *Motives, Personality, and Society* (New York: Praeger, 1984) 310.

89 U.S. Small Business Administration. *The Third Millenium: Small Business and Entrepreneurship in the 21st Century.* (Washington, D.C.: Small Business Administration, 1995) 21-22.

90 U.S. Small Business Administration. *The Third Millenium: Small Business and Entrepreneurship in the 21st Century.* (Washington, D.C.: Small Business Administration, 1995) 5.

BIBLIOGRAPHY

Abbott, C. G. *The 1914 Tests of the Langley "Aerodrome."* Washington: Smithsonian Institution, 1942.

Adler, Cyrus. *I Have Considered the Days.* Philadelphia: Jewish Publication Society of America, 1941.

Abodaher, David. *Iacocca: A Biography.* New York: Bantam, 1984.

Aitken, William. *Who Invented the Telephone?* London: Blackie, 1939.

Baker, Nina Brown. *Texas Yankee: The Story of Gail Borden.* New York: Harcourt, Brace, 1955.

Bartlett, John. *Familiar Quotations.* Boston: Little, Brown, 1955.

Barker, P. W. *Charles Goodyear, Connecticut Yankee and Rubber Pioneer: A Biography.* Boston: Cabot, 1940.

Belden, Thomas Graham, and Marva Robins Belden. *The Lengthening Shadow: The Life of Thomas J. Watson.* Boston: Little, Brown, 1962.

Bilstein, Roger E. *Flight in America 1900-1983: From the Wrights to the Astronauts.* Baltimore: Johns Hopkins UP, 1984.

Boyd, Thomas. *Poor John Fitch: Inventor of the Steamboat.* New York: Putnam, 1935.

Brandon, Ruth. *A Capitalist Romance: Singer and the Sewing Machine.* Philadelphia: Lippincott, 1977.

Bruce, Robert V. *Bell: Alexander Graham Bell and the Conquest of Solitude.* Boston: Little, Brown, 1973.

Burlingame, Roger. *Henry Ford: A Great Life in Brief.* New York: Knopf, 1955.

—. *Out of Silence into Sound: The Life of Alexander Graham Bell.* New York: Macmillan, 1964.

Butcher, Lee. *Accidental Millionaire: The Rise and Fall of Steve Jobs at Apple Computer.* New York: Paragon House, 1988.

Byrne, John A. "Enterprise: How Entrepreneurs are Reshaping the Economy—and What Big Companies Can Learn." *Business Week.* Special 1993 Bonus Issue:

12-18.

Chrysler, Walter P., and Boyden Sparkes. *Life of an American Workman*. New York: Dodd, Mead, 1937.

Cortada, James W. *Before the Computer: IBM, NCR, Burroughs, and Remington Rand and the Industry They Created, 1865-1956*. Princeton: Princeton UP, 1993.

Comfort, Harold W. *Gail Borden and His Heritage since 1875*. New York: Newcomen Society in North America, 1953.

Cooper, Grace Rogers. *The Invention of the Sewing Machine*. Washington, D. C.: Smithsonian Institution, 1968.

Crabb, Richard. *Birth of a Giant*. Philadelphia: Chilton, 1969.

Crouch, Tom D. *The Bishop's Boys: A Life of Wilbur and Orville Wright*. New York: Norton, 1989.

Dessauer, John. *My Years with Xerox*. New York: Doubleday, 1971.

Drucker, Peter F. *Innovation and Entrepreneurship: Practice and Principles*. New York: Harper & Row, 1985.

Dyson, Esther. "The Perils of Success." *Forbes*. 4 February, 1991: 122.

Fadiman, Clifton, ed. *The Little, Brown Book of Anecdotes*. Boston: Little, Brown, 1985.

Ferris, J. T. *Romance of Forgotten Men*. New York: Harper, 1928.

Flexner, James Thomas. *Steamboats Come True: American Inventors in Action*. New York: Viking, 1944.

Forbes Magazine. *The Forbes Scrapbook of Thoughts of the Business of Life / Forbes Magazine*. New York: Forbes, 1976.

Ford, Henry, and Samuel Crowther. *My Life and Work*. Garden City, NY: Doubleday, 1923.

Frantz, Joe B. *Gail Borden: Dairyman to a Nation*. Norman: U of Oklahoma P, 1979.

Gelderman, Carol W. *Henry Ford: The Wayward Capitalist*. New York: Dial, 1981.

Gibbs-Smith, Charles H. *The Aeroplane: An Historical*

Survey of Its Origins and Development. London: Her Majesty's Stationery Office, 1960.

Goddard, Dwight. *Eminent Engineers.* New York: Derry-Collard, 1905.

Gordon, Maynard M. *The Iacocca Management Technique.* New York: Dodd, Mead, 1985.

Green, Constance M. *Eli Whitney and the Birth of American Technology.* Boston: Little, Brown, 1956.

Gustin, Lawrence R. *Billy Durant: Creator of General Motors.* Grand Rapids, MI: Eerdmans, 1973.

Hancock, Thomas. *Personal Narrative of the Origin and Progress of the Caoutchouc or India-Rubber Manufacture in England.* London: Longmans, 1857.

Harriman, Margaret Case. *And the Price Is Right.* Cleveland: World, 1958.

Harris, Jacqueline L. *Henry Ford.* New York: Franklin Watts, 1984.

Harris, Sherwood. *The First to Fly: Aviation's Pioneer Days.* Blue Ridge Summit, PA: Tab / Aero, 1970.

Helm, Leslie. "The New Data General Is Leaner—But Is It Meaner?" *Business Week.* 17 August, 1987: 86, 88.

Hendrickson, Robert. *The Grand Emporiums.* New York: Stein and Day, 1979.

Herbert, Robert F. and Albert H. Link. *The Entrepreneurs—Mainstream Views and Radical Critiques.* New York: Praeger, 1982.

Hisrich, Robert D., and Candida Brush. *The Woman Entrepreneur: Starting, Financing, and Managing a Successful New Business.* Lexington, MA: Lexington Books, 1985.

Hisrich, Robert D., and Michael P. Peters. *Entrepreneurship: Starting, Developing, and Managing a New Enterprise.* Boston: Irwin, 1992.

Hower, Ralph M. *History of Macy's of New York 1858-1919: Chapters in the Evolution of the Department Store.* Cambridge: Harvard UP, 1943.

Hubbard Elbert. *Elbert Hubbard's Scrapbook.* N.p., Wm. Wise &Co., 1923.

Hungerford, Edward. *The Romance of a Great Store.* New York: McBride, 1922.

Hylander, C. J. *American Inventors.* New York: Macmillan, 1958.

Iacocca, Lee, and Sonny Kleinfield. *Talking Straight.* Boston: G. K. Hall, 1988.

Iacocca, Lee, and William Nowak. *Iacocca: An Autobiography.* New York: Bantam, 1984.

Jakob, Peter L. *Visions of a Flying Machine: The Wright Brothers and the Process of Invention.* Washington: Smithsonian Institution, 1990.

Jennings, Walter Wilson. *A Dozen Captains of American Industry.* New York: Vantage Press, 1954.

Kelly, Fred C. *The Wright Brothers.* New York: Harcourt Brace, 1943.

Kidder, Tracy. *The Soul of a New Machine.* Boston: Little, Brown, 1981.

Lacey, Robert. *Ford: The Men and the Machine.* Boston: Little, Brown, 1986.

MacMeal, Harry. *The Story of Independent Telephony.* N.p.: Independent Pioneer Telephone Association, 1934.

Manchester, Harland. *Trail Blazers of Technology: The Story of Nine Inventors.* New York: Scribner's, 1962.

Maslow, Abraham H. *Motivation and Personality.* New York: Harper & Row, 1954.

Mackensie, Catherine. *Alexander Graham Bell: The Man Who Contracted Space.* Boston: Houghton Mifflin, 1928.

McClelland, David C. *Motives, Personality, and Society.* New York: Praeger, 1984.

Morgan, John S. *Robert Fulton.* New York: Mason / Charter, 1977.

Moritz, Michael, and Barrett Seaman. *Going for Broke: Lee Iacocca's Battle to Save Chrysler.* Garden City: Anchor / Doubleday, 1984.

Neuharth, Al. *Confessions of an S. O. B.* New York: Doubleday, 1989.

Nevins, Allan, and Frank Hill. *Ford: The Times, the Man, the Company.* New York: Scribners, 1954.

Olsen, Kenneth H. *Digital Equipment Corporation: The First Twenty-five Years.* New York: Newcomen Society, 1983.

Philip, Cynthia Owen. *Robert Fulton: A Biography.* New York: Franklin Watts, 1985.

Pound, Arthur. *The Turning Wheel: The Story of General Motors Through Twenty-five Years 1908-1933.* Garden City: Doubleday, 1934.

Prescott, George B. *Bell's Electric Speaking Telephone: Its Invention, Construction, Application, Modification and History.* New York: Appleton, 1884.

Prichard, Peter. *The Making of McPaper: The Inside Story of USA Today.* Kansas City: Andrews, McMeel & Parker, 1987.

Richards, Norman. *Dreamers and Doers.* New York: Atheneum, 1984.

Rifkin, Glenn, and George Harrar. *The Ultimate Entrepreneur: The Story of Ken Olsen and Digital Equipment Corporation.* Chicago: Contemporary Books, 1988.

Rodgers, William. *THINK: A Biography of the Watsons and IBM.* New York: Stein and Day, 1969.

Rosenberg, Jerry M. *The Computer Prophets.* New York: Macmillan, 1969.

Scaife, W. Lucien., ed. *John A. Brashear: The Autobiography of A Man Who Loved the Stars.* New York: American Society of Mechanical Engineers, 1924.

Senecker, Harold. "Data General—Life in the Fast Lane." *Forbes.* 3 March, 1980: 72,74.

Shurkin, Joel. *Engines of the Mind: A History of the Computer.* New York: Norton, 1984.

Slater, Robert. *Portraits in Silicon.* Cambridge: MIT Press, 1987.

Sloan, Alfred, Jr. *My Years With General Motors.* Garden City: Doubleday, 1964.

Smith, Douglas K., and Robert C. Alexander. *Fumbling the Future: How Xerox Invented, Then Ignored, the First Personal Computer.* New York: Morrow, 1988.

Sorensen, Charles, and Samuel T. Williamson. *My Forty Years with Ford.* New York: W. W. Norton, 1956.

Stolze, William J. *Start Up: An Entrepreneur's Guide to Launching and Managing a New Business.* Hawthorne, NJ: Career Press, 1992.

Solomon, Stephen. "The Walking Wounded of the Computer Wars." *Science Digest.* February 1983: 16, 18.

Thompson, Silvanus P. *Philipp Reis: Inventor of the Telephone.* London: Spon, 1883.

Uttal, Bro. "The Gentlemen and the Upstarts Meet in a Great Battle." *Fortune.* 23 April, 1979: 98-101, 105-106, 108.

Vesper, Karl. *New Venture Strategies.* Englewood Cliffs, NJ: Prentice-Hall, 1980.

Weisberger, Bernard A. *The Dream Maker: William C. Durant, Founder of General Motors.* Boston: Little, Brown, 1979.

Westcott, Thompson. *Life of John Fitch, Inventor of the Steamboat.* Philadelphia: Lippincott, 1857.

Wolf, Ralph F. *India Rubber Man: The Story of Charles Goodyear.* Caldwell, ID: Caxton, 1938.

Woodruff, William. *The Rise of the British Rubber Industry During the Nineteenth Century.* Liverpool: Liverpool UP, 1958.

Wulfrost, Harry. *Breakthrough to the Computer Age.* New York: Scribner's, 1982.

Wyden, Peter. *The Unknown Iacocca, An Unauthorized Biography.* New York: Morrow, 1987.

Young, Jeffrey S. *Steve Jobs: The Journey Is the Reward.* Glenview, IL: Scott, Foresman, 1988.

INDEX

ABOUT THE AUTHOR

Emerson Klees is an Adjunct Professor of Management in the College of Business at the Rochester Institute of Technology, where he teaches Entrepreneurship, Entrepreneurial Field Studies, and Introduction to Work Organizations. He has a B.S. in Electrical Engineering from Pennsylvania State University, a M.B.A. from New York University, and a M.A. in English Literature from the State University of New York—College at Brockport.

His experience in industry is with Eastman Kodak Company, Olin Corporation, IBM, and Douglas Aircraft Company. He served on active duty in the U.S. Navy at the New York Naval Shipyard, where he was Ship Superintendent for Electronics during the construction of the aircraft carriers USS *Independence* and USS *Constellation.*

Mr. Klees is the owner and editor / publisher of Friends of the Finger Lakes Publishing. He is also a partner in Friends of the Finger Lakes (www.fingerlakes.com), organized to promote the Finger Lakes Region of New York State via audio tour tapes, books, and videos. In addition, he is the vice president of the New York State Regional Publishers Association.

Mr. Klees has also written *One Plus One Equals Three— Pairing Man / Woman Strengths: Role Models of Teamwork*, the first book in the Role Models of Human Value Series, and eight books about the Finger Lakes Region. In 1994 and 1997, he was awarded First Place in the Elizabeth H. Corron National Historical Essay Contest.

He lives with his wife, Patricia, in Rochester, New York. They have three children. His hobbies include grapegrowing and winemaking.